# THE APPLICATION OF THE EUROPEAN CONVENTION ON HUMAN RIGHTS TO MILITARY OPERATIONS

The European Convention on Human Rights is being applied to military operations of every kind from internal operations in Russia and Turkey, to international armed conflicts in Iraq, Ukraine and elsewhere. This book exposes the challenge that this development presents to the integrity and universality of Convention rights. Can States realistically investigate all instances where life is lost during military operations? Can the Convention offer the same level of protection to soldiers in combat as it does its citizens at home? How can we reconcile the application of the Convention with other international law applicable to military operations? This book offers detailed analysis of how the Convention applies to military operations of all kinds. It highlights the creeping relativism of the standards applied by the European Court of Human Rights to military operations and offers guidance on how to interpret and apply the Convention to military operations.

Stuart Wallace is Lecturer in Law at Homerton College, University of Cambridge, where he teaches human rights law. He received an LLM in international human rights law from the Irish Centre for Human Rights and a PhD from the University of Nottingham. He has previously worked at the European Court of Human Rights, the International Criminal Court and the Human Rights Law Centre at the University of Nottingham.

# The Application of the European Convention on Human Rights to Military Operations

STUART WALLACE
University of Cambridge

CAMBRIDGE
UNIVERSITY PRESS

CAMBRIDGE
UNIVERSITY PRESS

Shaftesbury Road, Cambridge CB2 8EA, United Kingdom

One Liberty Plaza, 20th Floor, New York, NY 10006, USA

477 Williamstown Road, Port Melbourne, VIC 3207, Australia

314–321, 3rd Floor, Plot 3, Splendor Forum, Jasola District Centre, New Delhi – 110025, India

103 Penang Road, #05–06/07, Visioncrest Commercial, Singapore 238467

Cambridge University Press is part of Cambridge University Press & Assessment, a department of the University of Cambridge.

We share the University's mission to contribute to society through the pursuit of education, learning and research at the highest international levels of excellence.

www.cambridge.org
Information on this title: www.cambridge.org/9781108465915

DOI: 10.1017/9781108566469



First published 2019
First paperback edition 2026

*A catalogue record for this publication is available from the British Library*

ISBN 978-1-108-47518-1 Hardback
ISBN 978-1-108-46591-5 Paperback

*For Emma, co-author of my life*

# Contents

# Acknowledgements

This book started as a random thought, one that I have probably spent too much time thinking about. The thought first occurred to me while I was working as a trainee lawyer at the European Court of Human Rights almost a decade ago. I am immensely grateful to all of my former colleagues there whose hard work and dedication in extremely challenging circumstances was inspirational. I would like to thank Anna Austin and Guillem Cano Palomares, in particular, for their guidance and assistance during my time there.

The random thought eventually evolved into a PhD dissertation at the University of Nottingham. I would like to express my gratitude to the University of Nottingham for providing me with a scholarship to complete the dissertation that led to this book. I owe an immense debt to my supervisors, Marko Milanovic and Dominic McGoldrick, for their patience, guidance and support in completing my doctoral dissertation. I would also like to thank my examiners, Alistair Mowbray and Ed Bates, for their kindness and invaluable feedback.

The dissertation evolved over time and with plenty of assistance into a book. I am incredibly lucky to have crossed paths with some extremely talented and supportive friends and colleagues. Sarah Worthington provided sage advice and assistance with developing the book proposal. Hayley Hooper has been an indispensable consultant on all things book related and a valued friend. Conall Mallory has worked on several projects with me over the past few years with good humour and patience. I am immensely grateful for his input on earlier drafts and his help in refining my ideas. I am also grateful to the Shucksmith-Wesleys and Colm McGrath for their extensive moral and academic support over the past years. I should also thank the multifarious anonymous reviewers who have provided input on parts of this work over the years – it may well have been helpful.

At Cambridge University Press, I would like to thank Tom Randall, Priyaa Menon, Laura Blake and the project management staff at CUP who provided helpful guidance throughout the writing process. The comments of the anonymous reviewers for Cambridge University Press also enhanced the book immensely. Any remaining errors are my responsibility.

Finally, I would never have reached this stage without the support of my family, Kevin, Kathy, Elayne and my brother Jeff. I must thank my parents, in particular, for their support and understanding without necessarily understanding what I've been doing all this time. My nieces and nephews have given me perspective on what's really important – dinosaurs and bubbles. But most of all I must thank my eternally patient wife, Emma. Having married me, she understands the difficulties of speculative long-term projects more than most. So much more than just a loyal companion, she has proofread, encouraged, cajoled and consoled. She has restored my self-belief and determination when they waned and stood by my side along each step of this path. I could never have done this without her.

# Abbreviations

| | |
|---|---|
| AJIL | *American Journal of International Law* |
| BYIL | *British Yearbook of International Law* |
| ECtHR | European Court of Human Rights |
| EHRLR | *European Human Rights Law Review* |
| EHRR | European Human Rights Reports |
| EJIL | *European Journal of International Law* |
| GC | Grand Chamber of the European Court of Human Rights |
| HRLR | *Human Rights Law Review* |
| IAC | International Armed Conflict |
| IAComHR | Inter-American Commission on Human Rights |
| IACtHR | Inter-American Court of Human Rights |
| ICLQ | *International and Comparative Law Quarterly* |
| ICRC | International Committee of the Red Cross |
| IHL | International Humanitarian Law |
| HRL | International Human Rights Law |
| IRRC | *International Review of the Red Cross* |
| NIAC | Non-International Armed Conflict |
| NQHR | *Netherlands Quarterly of Human Rights* |
| UKHL | United Kingdom House of Lords |
| UKSC | United Kingdom Supreme Court |
| UNSCR | United Nations Security Council Resolution |

# Abbreviations

# Table of Cases

## A. EUROPEAN CASES

## B. INTER-AMERICAN CASES



## C. UNITED KINGDOM CASES

## D. OTHER JURISDICTIONS

# Table of International Agreements

# Introduction

International human rights law (HRL) was once conceived as a law for times of peace, an internal law, bound to the institutions of the State and its systems of governance.[1] This view has been supplanted as the application of HRL has shifted from the domestic sphere to the extra-territorial, and from peace to conflict. While traces of this shift have been evident for many years,[2] its full force is only now being felt. Recent years have seen truly profound developments at the European Court of Human Rights (the Court) with the European Convention on Human Rights (the Convention) applied to military operations of every kind throughout the world.[3]

The application of the Convention to military operations presents both benefits and challenges. A detailed body of law, international humanitarian law (IHL), already applies to many military operations. While both IHL and HRL are concerned with the protection of human life and share some basic rules,[4] fundamentally different assumptions underlie each body

1 Guglielmo Verdirame, 'Human Rights in Wartime: A Framework for Analysis' [2008] EHRLR 689, 689–90.

2 Cases on the extra-territorial application of the European Convention on Human Rights arise from the 1960s: X v. *Federal Republic of Germany* App no 1611/62 (EComHR, 25 September 1965). The crossover between human rights law and armed conflict begins in the 1950s – Cordula Droege, 'The Interplay between International Humanitarian Law and International Human Rights Law in Situations of Armed Conflict' (2007) 40 *Israel Law Review* 310, 312–17.

3 See, for example, *Al-Skeini and Others* v. *United Kingdom* (2011) 53 EHRR 18; *Medvedyev* v. *France* (2010) 51 EHRR 39; *Al-Jedda* v. *United Kingdom* (2011) 53 EHRR 23.

4 Claire Landais and Lea Bass, 'Reconciling the Rules of International Humanitarian Law with the Rules of European Human Rights Law' (2015) 97 IRRC 1295, 1300.

of law.[5] IHL is designed to function in a situation of widespread death and destruction, and a complete breakdown of law and order.[6] It presumes an environment in which killing and suffering are expected.[7] It tolerates preventive detention and incidental loss of life, where such practices are anathema to human rights law.[8] By contrast, HRL pre-supposes a functioning nation State with control over its territory and institutions at its disposal to guarantee human rights. Once these pre-conditions change, as they often do during military operations, realising human rights protection becomes more difficult. The State's limited control significantly reduces its capacity to guarantee human rights.[9]

Many violations of IHL go unpunished and it is an area of law characterised by weak enforcement.[10] When violations are addressed under IHL, the focus has been on punishing perpetrators with criminal sanctions rather than compensating victims.[11] The absence of forums in which to raise individual complaints concerning IHL violations has been a key driver behind individuals seeking redress through HRL at both domestic and

[5] Bill Bowring, 'Fragmentation, Lex Specialis and the Tensions in the Jurisprudence of the European Court of Human Rights' (2009) 14 *Journal of Conflict & Security Law* 485; Naz Modirzadeh, 'The Dark Sides of Convergence: A Pro-civilian Critique of the Extraterritorial Application of Human Rights Law in Armed Conflict' (2010) 86 *US Naval War College International Law Studies* 349. For an opposing view on how the similarities between the law should affect interpretation see Anthony Cassimatis, 'International Humanitarian Law, International Human Rights Law, and Fragmentation of International Law' (2007) 56 ICLQ 623.

[6] Audrey Benison, 'War Crimes: A Human Rights Approach to a Humanitarian Law Problem at the International Criminal Court' (2000) 88 *Georgetown Law Journal* 141, 152.

[7] David Kretzmer, 'Rethinking the Application of IHL in Non-International Armed Conflicts' (2009) 42 *Israel Law Review* 8, 21.

[8] Theodor Meron, 'The Humanization of Humanitarian Law' (2000) 94 AJIL 239, 240; Nancie Prud'homme, 'Lex Specialis: Oversimplifying a More Complex and Multifaceted Relationship?' (2007) 40 *Israel Law Review* 356, 361.

[9] Harmen van der Wilt and Sandra Lyngdorf, 'Procedural Obligations Under the European Convention on Human Rights: Useful Guidelines for the Assessment of 'Unwillingness' and 'Inability' in the Context of the Complementarity Principle' (2009) 9 *International Criminal Law Review* 39, 59.

[10] M. Cherif Bassiouni, 'Searching for Peace and Achieving Justice: The Need for Accountability' (1996) 59 *Law & Contemporary Problems* 9, 17–18.

[11] Jean-Marie Henckaerts, 'Concurrent Application of International Humanitarian Law and Human Rights Law: A Victim Perspective' in Noelle Quenivet and Roberta Arnold (eds), *International Humanitarian Law and Human Rights Law: Towards a New Merger in International Law* (Brill 2008) 249. The ICC aims to redress some of this bias by creating a permanent institution to prosecute international crimes occurring throughout the world. It also took some steps toward re-focusing on and offering reparations to victims of IHL, see Article 75, Rome Statute of the International Criminal Court (adopted 17 July 1998, entered into force 1 July 2002) 2187 UNTS 3 (hereinafter Rome Statute).

international levels.[12] The Convention system offers clear benefits to victims of violations of IHL. It has integrated domestic and supra-national forums to seek redress for human rights violations that are substantively similar to violations of IHL. It offers clear procedures, a developed jurisprudence and, perhaps crucially, a means of securing compensation for victims. The Convention's institutional and procedural architecture can complement the dearth of such elements in IHL.[13]

The benefits and challenges of this confluence of laws present a tantalising conundrum. These developments demand a fundamental re-evaluation of how law protects people during military operations of every kind. What happens when this human rights law is applied to military operations? How does it impact the way rules are interpreted and applied? What happens to IHL and is it possible to reconcile the application of these two bodies of law to the same military operation? These are some of the central questions addressed in this book. Before embarking on this discussion, this introductory chapter defines the parameters of this book. It provides a more detailed introduction to IHL and discusses the European Court of Human Rights' mandate to engage with IHL and apply the Convention to different types of military operation. It highlights the key differences between IHL and HRL, before outlining how these issues are addressed in the forthcoming chapters.

## THE EUROPEAN COURT OF HUMAN RIGHTS AND MILITARY OPERATIONS

The term 'military operations' is defined broadly for the purposes of this book and encompasses all actions whether they occur domestically or extra-territorially involving the armed forces of the State. The armed forces are defined as the State's entire organised armed forces, groups and units which are under a command responsible to the State for the conduct of its subordinates.[14] The definition is deliberately broad to encompass the breadth

[12] Noelle Quenivet, 'The Right to Life in International Humanitarian Law and Human Rights Law' in Roberta Arnold and Noelle Quenivet (eds), *International Humanitarian Law and Human Rights Law: Towards a New Merger in International Law* (Brill 2008) 9; Meron (n. 8) 247; Emiliano Buis, 'The Implementation of International Humanitarian Law by Human Rights Courts: The Example of the Inter-American Human Rights System' in Noelle Quenivet and Roberta Arnold (eds), *International Humanitarian Law and Human Rights Law: Towards a New Merger in International Law* (Brill 2008) 269–70.

[13] Meron (n. 8) 247; Kenneth Watkin, 'Controlling the Use of Force: A Role for Human Rights Norms in Contemporary Armed Conflict' (2004) 98 AJIL 1, 24.

[14] Louise Doswald-Beck and Jean-Marie Henckaerts (eds), *Customary International Humanitarian Law*. 2 vols. (Cambridge University Press 2004) vol I, 14.

of modern military deployments. The traditional paradigm, wherein military forces participated only in international armed conflicts (IACs) and non-international armed conflicts (NIACs), has been supplanted by one in which military forces occupy a variety of operational roles, including humanitarian support, security and even construction roles.[15]

This shift in practice has been accompanied by a broader sense that traditional IHL rules, applied to the military and designed to regulate IACs and belligerent occupations, are ill-suited to regulate modern military operations.[16] As faith in IHL has declined and the diversity of military operations increased, a debate has emerged over whether HRL, or a hybrid of both IHL and HRL, could replace it. The debate has ranged from whether this convergence is desirable in principle to whether it is achievable in practice.[17] This book aims firmly at the latter issue, examining the practicalities of applying the Convention to military operations. Before discussing those issues of convergence, it is necessary to lay a solid foundation for the application of HRL to military operations.

### *Applying the Convention to All Military Operations*

The Convention is designed to apply to functioning, democratic States in Europe. One need look no further than the text of the Convention to confirm this fact. Articles 9, 10 and 11 safeguard freedoms that are essential to the

15 Francisco Martin, 'Using International Human Rights Law for Establishing a Unified Use of Force Rule in the Law of Armed Conflict' (2001) 64 *Saskatchewan Law Review* 347, 352; Kenneth Watkin, 'Stability Operations: A Guiding Framework for "Small Wars" and Other Conflicts of the Twenty-First Century?' (2009) 85 *US Naval War College International Law Studies* 411, 412–15.

16 Fionnuala Ni Aolain, 'The No-Gaps Approach to Parallel Application in the Context of the War on Terror' (2007) 40 *Isarel Law Review* 563, 563–9; Nicolas Lamp, 'Conceptions of War and Paradigms of Compliance: The "New War" Challenge to International Humanitarian Law' (2011) 16 *Journal of Conflict & Security Law* 225; Gabor Rona, 'Interesting Times for International Humanitarian Law: Challenges from the "War on Terror"' (2003) 27 *Fletcher Forum of World Affairs* 55; Geoffrey Corn, 'Mixing Apples and Hand Grenades: The Logical Limits of Applying Human Rights Norms to Armed Conflict' (2010) 1 *International Humanitarian Legal Studies* 52, 64.

17 Roberta Arnold and Noelle Quenivet, *International Humanitarian Law and Human Rights Law: Towards a New Merger in International Law* (Brill 2008); Modirzadeh (n. 5); Aeyal Gross, 'Human Proportions: Are Human Rights the Emperor's New Clothes of the International Law of Occupation?' (2007) 18 EJIL 1; Christine Byron, 'A Blurring of the Boundaries: The Application of International Humanitarian Law by Human Rights Bodies' (2006–2007) 47 *Virginia Journal of International Law* 839; Barry Feinstein, 'The Applicability of the Regime of Human Rights in Times of Armed Conflict and Particularly to Occupied Territories: The Case of Israel's Security Barrier' (2005–2006) 4 *Northwestern University Journal of International Human Rights* 241.

correct functioning of democracy, such as freedom of religion, freedom of expression and freedom of assembly. Many articles pre-suppose the existence of a functioning judicial system, such as Articles 5(3) and 5(4), for example, which offer safeguards for people deprived of their liberty, pre-suppose the existence of courts and judges.[18] Article 13 on the provision of effective remedies pre-supposes the existence of public authorities capable of providing them.[19] As such, the Convention is State-centric and dependent on functioning administrative bodies in a democratic State. On what basis then has the Convention come to apply to military operations of all kinds, including those conducted by contracting States outside their own territory and far from the institutions of those States?

## The Convention Text

The text of the Convention clearly indicates that it is intended to continue to apply during military operations, including armed conflicts. There is no express reference to the Convention ceasing to apply as a matter of course during armed conflict and express provisions indicate it continues to apply. Article 2(2)(c), for example, permits the use of force 'in action lawfully taken for the purpose of quelling a riot or insurrection'. The latter term 'insurrection' refers to an organised attempt by a group of people to defeat and depose a government through violent means. This definition clearly overlaps with the definition of a NIAC under IHL,[20] which is defined as an armed conflict:

> which take[s] place in the territory of a High Contracting Party between its armed forces and dissident armed forces or other organized armed groups which, under responsible command, exercise such control over a part of its territory as to enable them to carry out sustained and concerted military operations.[21]

[18] Article 5(3) states that 'Everyone arrested or detained [...] shall be brought promptly before *a judge* or other officer authorised by law to exercise judicial power'. Article 5(4) states 'Everyone who is deprived of his liberty [...] shall be entitled to take proceedings by which the lawfulness of his detention shall be decided speedily by *a court*' emphasis added.

[19] Article 13 states 'Everyone whose rights and freedoms as set forth in this Convention are violated shall have an effective remedy *before a national authority*' emphasis added.

[20] Louise Doswald-Beck, *Human Rights in Times of Conflict and Terrorism* (Oxford University Press 2011) 193.

[21] Article 1, Protocol Additional to the Geneva Conventions of 12 August 1949, and relating to the Protection of Victims of Non-International Armed Conflicts (adopted 8 June 1977, entered into force 7 December 1978) 1125 UNTS 609 (hereinafter Additional Protocol 2).

Thus, Article 2 continues to apply to NIACs. Equally, Article 15 of the Convention states that there can be 'no derogation from Article 2, except in respect of deaths resulting from lawful acts of war'. The term 'war' naturally implies an IAC and there would be no need for this exception to exist if the Convention was not applicable to such a conflict in the first place.

The extension of the Convention extra-territorially is less straightforward; this is discussed extensively in Chapter 2. It suffices to note for now that the Convention does not expressly place a territorial limitation on its application, it simply states that: 'High Contracting Parties shall secure to everyone within their jurisdiction the rights and freedoms defined in Section I of this Convention.' The term 'jurisdiction' has been interpreted by the Court to encompass acts outside the normal territory of the contracting State.[22]

## International Practice

The application of human rights law to all military operations, including armed conflicts, is also endorsed by several international bodies, including the International Court of Justice (ICJ) and the Inter-American human rights bodies. The ICJ referred to the continued application of HRL during armed conflict in its Advisory Opinion on the *Legality of the Threat or Use of Nuclear Weapons* stating:

> the protection of the International Covenant for the Protection of Civil and Political Rights does not cease in times of war [...] In principle, the right not arbitrarily to be deprived of one's life applies also in hostilities.[23]

In a later Advisory Opinion on the *Legal Consequences of the Construction of a Wall in the Occupied Palestinian Territory*, the ICJ stated:

> the protection offered by human rights conventions does not cease in case of armed conflict, save through the effect of provisions for derogation.[24]

While the ICJ was referring to the application of the International Covenant on Civil and Political Rights (ICCPR) on both occasions, the same

[22] See, for example, *Al-Skeini and Others* v. *United Kingdom* (2011) 53 EHRR 18; *Cyprus* v. *Turkey* (1982) 4 EHRR 482; *Ocalan* v. *Turkey* (2003) 37 EHRR 10.

[23] *Legality of the Threat or Use of Nuclear Weapons*, Advisory Opinion, ICJ Reports 1996, p. 226 8 July 1996 at [25].

[24] *Legal Consequences of the Construction of a Wall in the Occupied Palestinian Territory*, Advisory Opinion, ICJ Reports 2004, p. 136 9 July 2004 at [106].

rationale applies equally to the Convention. The Inter-American human rights bodies have also applied HRL to armed conflict situations,[25] as has the UN Human Rights Committee.[26] Thus, there is a strong legal basis for the application of HRL to military operations of all kinds. The Court has applied the Convention to a variety of different types of military operations in its jurisprudence, including IACs,[27] foreign belligerent occupations,[28] peace-support operations,[29] domestic counter-insurgency operations,[30] and NIACs.[31] However, these military operations are often subject to the law of armed conflict or international humanitarian law, which begs the question, how do these different bodies of law compare to one another in their application to military operations?

## INTERNATIONAL HUMANITARIAN LAW

There are significant differences between IHL and the Convention, both in terms of their substantive content and their fundamental precepts. It is worth outlining the scope of IHL and exploring some of these differences to contextualise the discussion of how the Convention applies to military operations. IHL is a set of international rules, which seek to limit the effects of armed conflict. The primary aim of IHL is to protect non-participants in the armed conflict, e.g. civilians,[32] and those who have ceased to actively participate in the armed conflict, e.g. persons placed *hors de combat* by wounds or sickness[33] and prisoners of war.[34] It also seeks to place limits on the conduct of hostilities,

[25] See, for example, *Arturo Ribón Avilán* v. *Colombia* Report No 26/97 IAComHR 30 September 1997; *Juan Carlos Abella* v. *Argentina* Report No 55/97 IAComHR 18 November 1997; *Santo Domingo Massacre* v. *Colombia* Series No 259 IACtHR 30 November 2012; *Hugo Bustios Saavedra* v. *Peru* Report No 38/97 IAComHR 16 October 1997; *Las Palmeras* v. *Colombia* (Preliminary Objections) Series C No 67 IACtHR 4 February 2000.

[26] UN Human Rights Committee, General Comment No. 29, States of Emergency (Article 4), 31 August 2001, CCPR/C/21/Rev.1/Add.13 at [3].

[27] *Cyprus* v. *Turkey* (1982) 4 EHRR 482; *Georgia* v. *Russia (II)* (2012) 54 EHRR SE10.

[28] The occupation of Iraq in *Al-Skeini and Others* v. *United Kingdom* (2011) 53 EHRR 18.

[29] Kosovo in *Behrami* v. *France* (2007) 45 EHRR SE10.

[30] Counter-insurgency in South-East Turkey in *Ergi* v. *Turkey* (2001) 32 EHRR 18.

[31] Russian operations in Chechnya in *Isayeva* v. *Russia* (2005) 41 EHRR 38.

[32] Article 48 and Article 51(2), Protocol Additional to the Geneva Conventions of 12 August 1949, and relating to the Protection of Victims of International Armed Conflicts (adopted 8 June 1977, entered into force 7 December 1979) 1125 UNTS 3 (hereinafter Additional Protocol 1).

[33] See Article 3, Geneva Convention Relative to the Treatment of Prisoners of War (adopted 12 August 1949, entered into force 21 October 1950) 75 UNTS 135 (hereinafter Geneva Convention III). This article is the same in each of the Geneva Conventions 1949.

[34] See generally Geneva Convention III.

for example, by placing limitations on the types of weapons States can use and the circumstances in which they can be used.[35]

IHL only begins to apply once an armed conflict commences, this is generally understood to mean the resort to armed force.[36] IHL further distinguishes between different types of conflicts, IACs and NIACs, with some variations in the applicable rules depending on the nature of the conflict, although there is a body of customary international law applicable to both.[37] An IAC is an armed conflict in which at least two States are involved.[38] Such conflicts are regulated by several international treaties, perhaps most importantly the Geneva Conventions of 1949, the First Additional Protocol to the Geneva Conventions of 1977 and customary international law. Much of the law governing IACs also applies when territory is occupied by a hostile State (belligerent occupation).[39] A NIAC is an armed conflict restricted to a single State, involving either regular armed forces fighting groups of armed dissidents, or armed groups fighting each other.[40] These conflicts are regulated under a more limited and permissive legal regime in IHL, including Common Article 3 of the four Geneva Conventions, the Second Additional Protocol to the Geneva Conventions 1977 and customary international law. In contrast to the contextual limitations of IHL, the Convention applies at all times where the contracting State is exercising jurisdiction and provided the State has not derogated.

Many of the protections of IHL depend on the status that an individual holds, e.g. combatant, civilian, prisoner of war etc. If a person is classified as a civilian under IHL, for example, it is against the law to target them directly.[41] Whereas if a person is classified as a combatant, they may be made the object of an attack, but they are also immune from prosecution for lawful acts of war.[42] By contrast, the Convention confers protections on

[35] Some of the earliest international agreements in IHL relate to limitations on weapons, see for example, Declaration Renouncing the Use, in Time of War, of Explosive Projectiles Under 400 Grammes Weight (adopted 29 November 1868).

[36] ICTY, *The Prosecutor* v. *Dusko Tadic*, Decision on the Defence Motion for Interlocutory Appeal on Jurisdiction, IT-94-1-A, 2 October 1995 at [70].

[37] See Doswald-Beck and Henckaerts (n. 14).

[38] Article 2, Geneva Convention III – 'cases of declared war or of any other armed conflict which may arise between two or more of the High Contracting Parties'. This article is the same in each of the Geneva Conventions 1949.

[39] Article 2, Geneva Convention III – 'The Convention shall also apply to all cases of partial or total occupation of the territory of a High Contracting Party'. This article is the same in each of the Geneva Conventions 1949.

[40] Article 1(2), Additional Protocol 2 'all armed conflicts [...] which take place in the territory of a High Contracting Party between its armed forces and dissident armed forces or other organized armed groups'.

[41] Article 51(2), Additional Protocol 1.

[42] Article 43(2), Additional Protocol 1.

everyone once they fall within the jurisdiction of a contracting State and should not create distinctions based on status.

IHL as it pertains to IACs is specifically designed to govern the conduct of hostilities where control over territory between two States is contested, as such it is naturally extra-territorial. The application of Convention, by contrast, is specifically contingent on a jurisdictional link to a contracting State.

The differences are more acute when one considers the substantive content of the rules. Under IHL, for example, States are permitted to engage in security detention (internment) of various parties,[43] whereas Article 5(1) of the Convention places very strict limitations on the circumstances when persons can be deprived of their liberty. Similarly, IHL permits the targeting and killing of enemy combatants,[44] while Article 2(1) of the Convention places very strict limitations on the circumstances when persons can be deprived of their lives.

Thus, while both bodies of law are supposed to apply to military operations of various kinds, there are significant differences in their fundamental precepts and content. HRL has not been specifically designed for all military operations, whereas IHL has been specifically designed for armed conflicts. IHL will always be a body of law aiming to make the best of a bad situation, while HRL will always strive for the ideal. As a result, there are and perhaps will always be, unavoidable problems with applying HRL to military operations, a perfect solution is largely untenable. It is important to recognise the limits of the law and work around them as best we can.

### *The Court's Mandate and International Humanitarian Law*

This book argues that the Court should utilise IHL to guide and moderate its interpretation of the Convention where IHL is applicable. Before discussing the merits of this approach, we must address the issue of the Court's mandate to consider IHL. Many authors point out that the Court does not have an express mandate to interpret and apply IHL.[45] The Convention appears to limit the

43 See Article 21, Geneva Convention III; Article 42, Geneva Convention Relative to the Protection of Civilian Persons in Time of War (adopted 12 August 1949, entered into force 21 October 1950) 75 UNTS 287 (hereinafter Geneva Convention IV).

44 Doswald-Beck and Henckaerts (n. 14) 46.

45 Giulia Pinzauti, 'The European Court of Human Rights' Incidental Application of International Criminal Law and Humanitarian Law: A Critical Discussion of Kononov v. Latvia' (2008) 6 *Journal of International Criminal Justice* 1043, 1044; Michael O'Boyle and Jean Paul Costa, 'The ECtHR and IHL' in Christos Rozakis (ed), *The European Convention on Human Rights: A Living Instrument* (Bruylant Press 2011) 107. The Court itself has expressed some doubts about the scope of its mandate, see *Markovic* v. *Italy* (2007) 44 EHRR 52 at [108]–[109].

Court's subject matter jurisdiction to 'all matters concerning the interpretation and application of the Convention and the Protocols thereto'.[46] However, this article must be read in light of other provisions and international practice.

Firstly, other articles of the Convention seem to make it necessary for the Court to consider other bodies of law, including IHL. Article 15 demands that when States derogate from the Convention, those derogations must not be 'inconsistent with its other obligations under international law'. It is foreseeable that the Court could be called upon to determine whether a State's derogation is consistent with its obligations under IHL.[47] Article 15 also refers to the possibility of States derogating from Article 2 for 'lawful acts of war', meaning the legality of some acts in this context would need to be assessed by reference to IHL standards.[48] Article 7 also ensures that no one is held guilty of a criminal offence that does not constitute an offence under national 'or international law at the time when it was committed'. This may require the Court to assess whether an individual's conduct was contrary to IHL at the time they acted.[49] Thus, the argument that the Convention text constrains the Court's mandate solely to interpreting the Convention is unsustainable when one considers the wider requirements of the Convention text.

Secondly, as noted above, both the ICJ and the Inter-American human rights bodies have applied human rights law to armed conflict. In doing so, they have also interpreted human rights treaties in light of IHL norms. The ICJ set out its approach to interpretation where both IHL and HRL are applicable in its *Advisory Opinion on the Wall*:

> As regards the relationship between international humanitarian law and human rights law, there are thus three possible situations: some rights may be exclusively matters of international humanitarian law; others may be exclusively matters of human rights law; yet others may be matters of both these branches of international law. In order to answer the question put to it, the Court will have to take into consideration both these branches of international law, namely human rights law and, as lex specialis, international humanitarian law.[50]

[46] Article 32(1), European Convention on Human Rights 1950.

[47] Byron (n. 17) 839; Noam Lubell, 'Challenges in Applying Human Rights Law to Armed Conflict' (2005) 87 IRRC 737, 742–4.

[48] Doswald-Beck (n. 20) 192–3; O'Boyle and Costa (n. 45) 115.

[49] The Court has been called on to do this in practice. See, for example, *Korbely* v. *Hungary* (2010) 50 EHRR 48 and *Kononov* v. *Latvia (GC)* (2011) 52 EHRR 21. Pinzauti (n. 45) 1046–8.

[50] *Legal Consequences of the Construction of a Wall in the Occupied Palestinian Territory*, Advisory Opinion, ICJ Reports 2004, p. 136 9 July 2004 at [106].

In its *Nuclear Weapons Advisory Opinion*, the ICJ considered the concurrent application of the right to life in the ICCPR and provisions in IHL which permitted killing in certain circumstances. It concluded that IHL would not function to disapply the ICCPR norm. Instead the co-application of both bodies of law altered how 'arbitrary' deprivation of life was defined under the ICCPR.[51] The ICJ stated:

> The test of what is an arbitrary deprivation of life, however, falls to be determined by the applicable *lex specialis*, namely, the law applicable in armed conflict which is designed to regulate the conduct of hostilities. Thus whether a particular loss of life, through the use of a certain weapon in warfare, is to be considered an arbitrary deprivation of life contrary to Article 6 of the Covenant, can only be decided by reference to the law applicable in armed conflict and not deduced from the terms of the Covenant itself.[52]

Thus, both legal norms were applied by the ICJ, with the IHL norm conditioning the application of the human rights norm. The Court should aim to achieve similar outcomes as much as it can.

The Inter-American human rights bodies could serve as a model for how a regional court should approach the application of both IHL and human rights norms as its approach is very open.[53] In *Arturo Ribón Avilán* v. *Colombia*, for example, the Inter-American Commission on Human Rights (IAComHR) utilised IHL rules to determine whether people killed by the Columbian security forces were active combatants, and as a result legitimate objects of attack, or whether they were *hors de combat*, making attacks on them unlawful.[54] The Inter-American Court also invoked IHL in the case of *Santo Domingo Massacre* v. *Colombia*, when it examined an incident in which the Colombian air force dropped a cluster bomb as part of a counter-insurgency operation.

51 Iain Scobbie, 'Principle or Pragmatics? The Relationship between Human Rights Law and the Law of Armed Conflict' (2009) 14 *Journal of Conflict and Security Law* 449, 452–4.

52 *Legality of the Threat or Use of Nuclear Weapons*, Advisory Opinion, ICJ Reports 1996, p. 226 8 July 1996 at [25].

53 Laurence Burgorgue-Larsen and Amaya Úbeda de Torres, '"War" in the Jurisprudence of the Inter-American Court of Human Rights' (2011) 33 *Human Rights Quarterly* 148, 163; Buis, (n. 12) 286; Juan Pablo Perez-Leon Acevedo, 'The Role of the Inter-American Court of Human Rights in dealing with Armed Conflicts and Post-Conflict Reconstruction: Jurisprudential Analysis and Some Comparative Considerations' (2009) 7 *International Journal of Civil Society Law* 7, 9.

54 *Arturo Ribón Avilán* v. *Colombia* Report No 26/97 IAComHR 30 September 1997 at [133]–[134]; See also *Juan Carlos Abella* v. *Argentina* Report No 55/97 IAComHR 18 November 1997 at [161].

The bomb apparently missed its target and landed in a small village killing approximately 17 civilians. When considering the application of IHL, the Inter-American Court stated:

> since the events occurred in the context of a non-international armed conflict [...] the Court considers it useful and appropriate to interpret the scope of the treaty-based norms and obligations in a way that complements the norms of international humanitarian law.[55]

There is an important distinction to be drawn at this point between using IHL as a guide to interpret the Convention and the Court directly finding violations of IHL in its judgments. Some authors have argued in favour of using human rights courts to directly enforce substantive IHL norms.[56] The Inter-American Commission found violations of both the American Convention on Human Rights and IHL in some of its decisions.[57] However, the Inter-American Court decisively halted this practice in *Las Palmeras* v. *Colombia* when it held that the Inter-American bodies should stick solely to finding violations of the Inter-American treaties, although it could use IHL to aid its interpretation of this law where it was applicable.[58]

The European Court should follow the practice in *Las Palmeras* of solely finding violations of the European Convention on Human Rights and interpreting the Convention in light of IHL where both bodies of law are applicable. This is consistent with the Court's role and mandate. It is also consistent with Article 31(3)(c) of the Vienna Convention on the Law of Treaties, which demands that international treaties are interpreted in light of other applicable rules of international law.[59] The Convention does not apply 'in a vacuum',[60] nor is it the sole framework of reference for interpreting the rights within it.[61] It stands to reason

55 *Santo Domingo Massacre* v. *Colombia* Series No 259 IACtHR 30 November 2012 at [187].

56 Françoise Hampson, 'Using International Human Rights Machinery to Enforce the International Law of Armed Conflicts' (1992) 31 *Military Law and Law of War Review* 117; Liesbeth Zegveld, 'The Inter-American Commission on Human Rights and International Humanitarian Law: A Comment on the Tablada Case' (1998) 38 IRRC 505, 506.

57 *Arturo Ribón Avilán* v. *Colombia* at [134]; The Inter-American Commission found a violation of common Article 3 of the Geneva Conventions in *Hugo Bustios Saavedra* v. *Peru* Report No 38/97 IAComHR 16 October 1997 at [88].

58 *Las Palmeras* v. *Colombia* Series C No 90 IACtHR 6 December 2001 at [33]–[34].

59 Article 31(3)(c), Vienna Convention on the Law of Treaties (adopted 23 May 1969, entered into force 27 January 1980) 1155 UNTS 331. See also *Varnava and Others* v. *Turkey* App no 16064/90 (ECtHR, 18 September 2009) at [185].

60 See, for example, *Ocalan* v. *Turkey* (2005) 41 EHRR 45 at [163]; *Al-Adsani* v. *United Kingdom* (2002) 34 EHRR 11 at [55]; *Hassan* v. *United Kingdom* App no 29750/09 (ECtHR, 16 September 2014) at [77].

61 *Demir and Baykara* v. *Turkey* (2009) 48 EHRR 54 at [67].

that where IHL is relevant, it must be taken into account when interpreting the Convention and the Court has itself acknowledged this fact.[62]

## CENTRAL ARGUMENTS

The foregoing analysis clearly shows that both IHL and HRL have a role to play in regulating military operations, as not all military operations occur in the context of an armed conflict and even when they do, HRL continues to apply. There is a legal imperative to ensure both bodies of law apply. Even without it, the Rubicon has already been crossed; HRL is already being applied to military operations by the Court. This book will show that, for the most part, the Court could do a much better job of applying the Convention to military operations. Adapting human rights law to 'fit' military operations presents several problems for the Court and poses a potential threat to the content of human rights law itself.[63]

Two central hypotheses are examined in this book. First, human rights law could impose standards upon States that are difficult, if not impossible, to achieve during some military operations. Second, applying human rights law to military operations could compromise the integrity and strength of human rights norms. This book identifies inconsistency in the way the Convention is applied to military operations and uncovers a creeping relativism in the standards accepted by the Court. It is argued that key aspects of the Convention will be extremely difficult, if not impossible, to apply during all military operations, which places the Court in a difficult position. If it tries to maintain standards, it risks imposing obligations that are impossible to achieve. If it attenuates standards, it risks compromising its broader jurisprudence.

The book posits two potential solutions to these problems. Firstly, the Court needs to openly and transparently engage with IHL and interpret the Convention in light of it whenever both bodies of law are applicable. Secondly, States need to consider their capacity to uphold Convention obligations during military operations and derogate from the Convention where they are unable to uphold those obligations and the Convention permits derogation. It is argued that although derogation and concurrent application of IHL and HRL are not a panacea, they will go some way toward ensuring impossible standards are not imposed and that the broader jurisprudence of the Court is not compromised.

62 *Varnava and Others* v. *Turkey* App no 16064/90 (ECtHR, 18 September 2009) at [185]; *Georgia* v. *Russia (II)* (2012) 54 EHRR SE10 at [72].

63 Watkin, 'Controlling the Use of Force' (n. 13) 22.

A number of inconsistencies in the Court's application of Convention standards to military operations are identified throughout this book. It argues that these inconsistencies arise, in part, from the Court's failure to openly and transparently engage with IHL where it is applicable. The Court seldom directly refers to IHL when it applies the Convention to military operations and provisions of IHL are also applicable.[64] At times the implicit influence of IHL in the Court's judgments is clear and the correlation between IHL standards and those applied by the Court is startlingly obvious.[65] At other times, the Court appears to be cultivating a new 'human rights law of armed conflict' applying the Convention to conflicts, not referring to IHL and reaching outcomes at odds with it.[66] The Court's inconsistent practice presents the risk that implicit applications of IHL will compromise Convention standards, as the content of IHL rules drifts into the mainstream of human rights jurisprudence.

The exact reason behind the Court's reluctance to engage with IHL is unclear. This book postulates that it may be motivated by the Court's general aversion to subordinating Convention norms to any other body of law.[67] It may be that the judges and staff lack sufficient knowledge and awareness of IHL.[68] Whatever the reason, the Court cannot ignore the applicability of IHL to situations it is adjudicating. If the issue is one of awareness and familiarity, the Court should directly address this by making greater use of its research facilities and raising awareness of IHL among staff and judges. When both bodies of law are applicable, the Court should follow the ICJ's approach. It should openly and transparently engage with IHL and interpret the Convention in light of IHL. This does not mean that IHL should automatically take precedence over the Convention. The Court should

[64] Quenivet (n. 12) 332; Eriko Tamura, 'The Isayeva Cases of the European Court of Human Rights: The Application of International Humanitarian Law and Human Rights Law in Non-International Armed Conflicts' (2011) 10 *Chinese Journal of International Law* 129, 137; Magdalena Forowicz, *The Reception of International Law in the European Court of Human Rights* (Oxford University Press 2010) 331; Alexander Orakhelashvili, 'The Interaction between Human Rights and Humanitarian Law: Fragmentation, Conflict, Parallelism, or Convergence?' (2008) 19 EJIL 161, 174.

[65] See, for example, *Ergi* v. *Turkey* (2001) 32 EHRR 18 at [79]. Discussed further in Chapter 3.

[66] Abresch argues that this is happening in practice at the Court – William Abresch, 'A Human Rights Law of Internal Armed Conflict: the European Court of Human Rights in Chechnya' (2005) 16 EJIL 741. See also Karima Bennoune, 'Towards a Human Rights Approach to Armed Conflict: Iraq 2003' (2004) 11 *UC Davis Journal of International Law and Policy* 171.

[67] See Chapter 5.

[68] See Chapter 6.

instead seek to reconcile the concurrent application of each body whenever possible. The Court has taken a positive step in this direction in the case of *Hassan* v. *United Kingdom*.[69] In that case, the Court expressly interpreted Article 5 in light of IHL to permit States to intern civilians and detain prisoners of war notwithstanding the exhaustive list of permitted reasons for detention outlined in the text of Article 5.[70] It remains to be seen whether this becomes the consistent practice of the Court.

Alongside concurrent application, it is argued that States should derogate from the Convention during domestic and extra-territorial military operations. Derogations are specifically designed to alter the State's obligations when their capacity to uphold them is reduced by war or other public emergencies. It makes sense for States to utilise this provision to avoid having impossible burdens placed on their military forces by the Convention. It is argued that a derogation could sensibly limit the scope of the State's obligations in respect of the right to life and offer a sounder basis for certain types of detention during military operations. While states of emergency can be abused by States and there is a risk that human rights abuses may occur when a State has derogated,[71] this risk will be curtailed if the Court strictly polices the safeguards in the derogation system. An irreducible core of non-derogable rights would remain in place.[72] Any derogation made by the State is required to be consistent with the State's other obligations under international law, meaning the State must still abide by IHL and other international law measures. While the States do have a degree of discretion over the measures they adopt in derogation from their obligations, their capacity to derogate is limited. It is subject to the Court's supervision and States may only derogate from their obligations to the extent 'strictly required by the exigencies of the situation'.[73] Having set out the over-arching argument, the following sections address the discrete issues and content addressed in each chapter.

[69] *Hassan* v. *United Kingdom* App no 29750/09 (ECtHR, 16 September 2014).

[70] Ibid at [96]–[107], esp. [104].

[71] Scott Sheeran, 'Reconceptualizing States of Emergency under International Human Rights Law: Theory, Legal Doctrine, and Politics' (2012–2013) 34 *Michigan Journal of International Law* 491, 492–4; Christina Cerna, 'The History of the Inter-American System's Jurisprudence as Regards Situations of Armed Conflict' (2011) 2 *International Humanitarian Legal Studies* 3, 15.

[72] Article 15(2), European Convention on Human Rights 1950.

[73] Article 15(1), European Convention on Human Rights 1950.

## Territorial Bias

The opening chapters of this book address the relationship between territory and the application of the Convention. The applicability of IHL depends on the existence of an armed conflict,[74] its field of application mirrors the conflict, which may transcend geographical borders, and it can be naturally extra-territorial. The application of the Convention mirrors the State's jurisdiction, which is 'primarily territorial'.[75] This distinction causes issues that simply do not exist for IHL, as shifting authority and control over territory can make it extremely difficult to establish which State bears the duty for protecting rights. Chapter 1 considers what happens when a State loses control over its territory during the course of a military operation and whether the State still has to guarantee the human rights of those within its lost territory.

The territorial bias of the Convention gives rise to different problems when the State acts extra-territorially, a subject considered extensively in Chapter 2. If one considers the classic case of *Bankovic et al.* v. *Belgium et al.*, the differences between IHL and HRL become apparent.[76] That case involved the aerial bombardment of a television and radio station in Belgrade by NATO aircraft in 1999, which resulted in civilian casualties. From the standpoint of IHL, the States ordering those aircraft to attack had to take into consideration the principles of military necessity, proportionality and minimise the risk of civilian casualties as best they could etc. At the Court, this case is refracted through the territorial lens of the Convention, prompting questions of whether such an extra-territorial act triggers the application of the Convention, whether the norms of IHL displace and take precedence over the Convention and whether the acts undertaken in the name of NATO are attributable to the States ordering the aircraft. Thus, while IHL immediately cuts to the substance of the issue, whether the attack was legal, HRL entertains a host of preliminary issues before it even reaches that stage. As a result, the issue of jurisdiction has been a central focus of many cases relating to military operations before the Court and that focus is reflected in the opening chapters.[77]

As the Convention has been applied to domestic and extra-territorial military operations with greater frequency, some have called for a shift in focus

74 Article 2, Geneva Convention III. This article is the same in each of the Geneva Conventions 1949.

75 *Bankovic and Others* v. *Belgium and Others* (2007) 44 EHRR SE5 at [59].

76 *Bankovic and Others* v. *Belgium and Others* (2007) 44 EHRR SE5.

77 See, for example, *Medvedyev* v. *France* (2010) 51 EHRR 39; *Al-Skeini and Others* v. *United Kingdom* (2011) 53 EHRR 18; *Al-Jedda* v. *United Kingdom* (2011) 53 EHRR 23.

away from preliminary issues like jurisdiction and toward considering the practicalities of applying the substance of human rights law to military operations.[78] In the words of one academic, it is time to 'stop debating the theory and start defining the pragmatic'.[79] Yet, in the jurisprudence of the Court these issues are not sealed off from one another. The question of jurisdiction and the application of the substantive obligations in the Convention are so closely intertwined that one cannot discuss one without the other. These opening chapters show that the Court's rulings on jurisdiction also have a huge bearing on the scope and content of the obligations the State is held to under the Convention.

### *Operationalising Human Rights Protection*

The question of how to give effect to the protections of the Convention during military operations is a running theme in this book. Under the Convention, for example, when a State knows, or ought to have known, of a real and immediate risk to the life of an individual, it must take measures within the scope of its powers that judged reasonably might have been expected to avoid that risk.[80] This is the positive obligation to protect people under Article 2. Yet how can a State put such an obligation into practice for its own soldiers when being placed in life threatening situations is part of their job? This obligation could raise expectations of protection and impose standards upon States that are impossible to achieve during active hostilities.[81] Chapter 3 examines the problems States may encounter when attempting to operationalise this obligation and how States can potentially mitigate its impact.

The State is also obliged to investigate any death or life-threatening injury inflicted on a person within its jurisdiction.[82] This obligation typically requires significant administrative support to discharge, such as police, pathologists

[78] Modirzadeh (n. 5) 368; Scobbie (n. 51); Daniel Bethlehem, 'The Relationship between International Humanitarian Law and International Human Rights Law in Situations of Armed Conflict' (2013) 2 *Cambridge Journal of International and Comparative Law* 180.

[79] Corn (n. 16) 90.

[80] *Osman* v. *United Kingdom* (2000) 29 EHRR 245 at [115]; The Inter-American Court has inferred a similar obligation holding that a State can be held responsible where it did not take the necessary steps in order to prevent the particular violation from taking place – *Velásquez-Rodríguez* v. *Honduras* Series C No 4 IACtHR 29 July 1988 at [30]–[31].

[81] Meron (n. 8) 240–1; Modirzadeh (n. 5) 351; Verdirame (n. 1) 693; Francoise Hampson, 'Direct Participation in Hostilities and the Interoperability of the Law of Armed Conflict and Human Rights Law' (2011) 87 *US Naval War College International Law Studies* 187, 192.

[82] *Ergi* v. *Turkey* (2001) 32 EHRR 18 at [82].

and judges, which may not be available during a military operation.[83] At the same time, the widespread violence and death that may occur during a military operation can increase the scale of the burden on the State. Such an obligation could prove operationally debilitating and difficult to uphold in practice.[84] The question of how this procedural obligation applies during military operations is of increasing concern to many contracting States,[85] it forms the primary focus of Chapter 4.

### *Substantive Content*

As noted above, there are differences between the substantive content of IHL and the Convention, particularly the rules governing the use of force and detention. The disparate content of the rules is considered throughout this book, but the book focuses on the inherent risk that applying the Convention to all military operations will compromise the integrity and universality of human rights protections. Watkin observes that 'the attempt to apply human rights standards to a situation of armed conflict could have an adverse impact on the integrity and strength of peacetime norms'.[86] This book demonstrates that it is having such an effect. The application of the right to life in Article 2 of the Convention to military operations, for example, is resulting in weaker standards of protection as Chapter 3 clearly shows. The temptation for the Court has been to adapt the standards to fit military operations, to divide and tailor the rules and to only apply the sections 'relevant to the situation'.[87] The problem is not simply the lack of consistency in the standards themselves, but also the casuistic and haphazard way in which the standards have been modified by the Court. Any changes to the Convention's standards need to be justified and clearly contained in order to avoid them exercising a deleterious influence on the standard norms of the Convention. This is why derogation from the Convention and clear, transparent interpretation of the Convention in light of IHL are advocated in Chapters 5 and 7, as these can provide a contextual barrier to any changes of the standards and a clear justification for divergent interpretations.

83 *Edwards* v. *United Kingdom* (2002) 35 EHRR 19 at [71].

84 Corn (n. 16) 83.

85 See *Jaloud* v. *Netherlands* (2015) 60 EHRR 29 and *Al-Skeini and Others* v. *United Kingdom* (2011) 53 EHRR 18.

86 Watkin, 'Controlling the Use of Force' (n. 13) 22.

87 *Al-Skeini and Others* v. *United Kingdom* (2011) 53 EHRR 18 at [137].

### *Relationship between the Convention and IHL*

The relationship between the Convention and IHL is another central theme of this book. It has been argued that taking these two branches of international law as a coherent and complete whole appears to be the only satisfactory solution for dealing with the issues raised by their concurrent application.[88] However, conflicts are bound to arise between each of these bodies of law. Chapter 5 considers how the Court approaches norm conflicts and the prospects for harmonious interpretation of both IHL and the Convention after the *Hassan* v. *United Kingdom* judgment.

While the Court has a legal imperative to apply the Convention to military operations and interpret the Convention in light of IHL, this does not mean that the Court is well suited to the tasks. Concerns have been expressed about the Court's expertise in IHL.[89] Chapter 6 considers the Court's capacity to interpret and apply IHL by looking at its approach to Article 7 of the Convention. This Article prevents States from punishing people where their actions are not specifically proscribed by law and it compels the Court to evaluate external sources of law, including IHL and international criminal law. Analysing how the Court utilises IHL in Article 7 provides a unique opportunity to assess the Court's proficiency in the interpretation and application of IHL, as it has a free rein to apply it here. It is argued that the Court has made some errors in its interpretation of IHL in its Article 7 jurisprudence. This should militate against implicit applications of IHL under other Articles of the Convention, because when the Court is acting outside its main field of expertise, it should open itself to proper scrutiny. There may be a broader correlation between the absence of expertise in this field and the failure to transparently engage with IHL elsewhere.

Finally, Chapter 7 looks at Article 15, which is designed to offer States a means of derogating from certain human rights provisions when emergencies arise. Article 15 could offer a ready-made solution within the Convention to give States greater flexibility to adjust their obligations for military operations. This chapter explores the potential benefits that derogation offers States in respect of military operations while also examining some of the problems presented by derogations and how they can be addressed in practice.

The challenges posed by applying the Convention to military operations are very real. Applying the Convention to military operations will impose

[88] Landais and Bass (n. 4) 1301.

[89] Byron (n. 17) 881–2; Meron (n. 8) 247.

obligations on States that are extremely difficult, if not impossible, to achieve. Evidence is presented throughout this book that the application of Convention norms to military operations is having an adverse impact on the integrity and strength of Convention norms. If we wish to avoid these issues, a co-ordinated response will be required. The Court must improve its institutional competence to deal with IHL and it must be transparent, holistic and consistent in its interpretation of the Convention. At the same time, the onus is on States to assume responsibility for derogating when they cannot meet the obligations imposed by the Convention.

# 1

# Jurisdiction over Domestic Military Operations

## 1.1 INTRODUCTION

The first two chapters of this book deal with jurisdiction. The first addresses how the Court's rulings on jurisdiction apply to military operations in the State's normal domestic territory. The second chapter addresses how the Court's rulings on jurisdiction apply to extra-territorial military operations. Article 1 of the Convention states that: 'The High Contracting Parties shall secure to everyone within their jurisdiction the rights and freedoms defined in Section I of this Convention.' The application of the Convention is contingent upon the State exercising jurisdiction over an applicant. The State's jurisdiction is therefore a threshold criterion, which must be overcome before the treaty obligations begin to apply.[1] States regularly attempt to deny their responsibility for human rights violations during military operations by claiming that they were not exercising jurisdiction under the Convention. Such denials have served to stifle contributions from governments to the debate on the relationship between IHL and HRL.[2] As jurisdiction is repeatedly challenged in this context, determining when the State is exercising its jurisdiction represents a fundamental practical issue, which must be addressed before discussing how the substantive obligations apply. In fact, the question of jurisdiction and the application of the substantive obligations in the Convention are so closely intertwined that one cannot discuss one without the other. The following

[1] *Ilascu and Others* v. *Moldova and Russia* (2005) 40 EHRR 46 at [312]; Marko Milanovic, 'From Compromise to Principle: Clarifying the Concept of State Jurisdiction in Human Rights Treaties' (2008) 8 HRLR 411, 415.

[2] Daniel Bethlehem, 'The Relationship between International Humanitarian Law and International Human Rights Law in Situations of Armed Conflict' (2013) 2 *Cambridge Journal of International and Comparative Law* 180, 188.

chapters clearly demonstrate that the Court's rulings on jurisdiction have a huge bearing on the scope and content of the obligations the State is held to under the Convention.

The following two chapters show that recent developments in the Court's jurisprudence have expanded the circumstances in which State jurisdiction arises, both domestically and extra-territorially. These developments have made it more difficult for States to deny that they are exercising jurisdiction. As outright denials of jurisdiction have become increasingly untenable, it is argued that the need to consider the practicalities of applying the Convention to military operations, both domestically and extra-territorially, becomes more urgent. There is a significant disparity between the obligations the Court expects the State to uphold when it has lost de facto control over its territory and what is realistically achievable. The following chapters also identify and analyse some of the remaining practical issues arising from the Court's Article 1 jurisprudence.

## 1.2 DEFINING JURISDICTION

The term jurisdiction can describe many different things. Jurisdiction can, for example, refer to geographical boundaries or to the limits of a court's authority.[3] The term 'jurisdiction' in Article 1 refers to the jurisdiction of a contracting State.[4] The Convention only applies, according to Article 1, where a contracting State has jurisdiction over an applicant.[5] So what defines State jurisdiction under Article 1?

The Court regularly refers to the jurisdiction of contracting States as being 'primarily territorial'.[6] Statehood is defined partly by the possession of a stable,

[3] Peter Malanczuk, *Akehurst's Modern Introduction to International Law* (7th edn, Routledge 1997) 109.

[4] Milanovic (n. 1) 415.

[5] Michael O'Boyle, 'The European Convention on Human Rights and Extraterritorial Jurisdiction: A Comment on "Life After Bankovic"' in Fons Coomans and Menno Kamminga (eds), *Extraterritorial Application of Human Rights Treaties* (Intersentia 2004) 125; Marko Milanovic and Tatjana Papic, 'As bad as it gets: The European Court of Human Rights's Behrami and Saramati Decision and General International Law' (2009) 58 ICLQ 267, 272; Ralph Wilde, 'Legal "Black Hole"? Extraterritorial State Action and International Treaty Law on Civil and Political Rights' (2005) 26 *Michigan Journal of International Law* 739, 797–8.

[6] See *inter alia Al-Skeini and Others* v. *United Kingdom* (2011) 53 EHRR 18 at [131]; *Soering* v. *United Kingdom* (1989) 11 EHRR 439 at [86]; *Bankovic and Others* v. *Belgium and Others* (2007) 44 EHRR SE5 at [59].

physically delimited territory.[7] States exercise sovereignty, supreme or exclusive authority, over this territory,[8] thus there is a strong link between a State's jurisdiction and sovereignty. When one refers to a State's jurisdiction under general international law, one is referring to a manifestation of its sovereignty. A State manifests its sovereignty over territory by exercising legislative, judicial and executive jurisdiction,[9] although this is different from the type of jurisdiction contemplated in Article 1. Many of the terms used thus far, sovereignty, jurisdiction, authority are synonymous with control and control is the key factor. Territory can be viewed as the medium, the spatial realm, in which the State exercises its control. When the Court speaks of jurisdiction under Article 1 as being primarily territorial,[10] we should understand that possession of territory is a natural condition of Statehood and territory is the spatial realm in which the State's jurisdiction/control is manifested.

The Court also regularly opines that 'jurisdiction is presumed to be exercised normally throughout the State's territory'.[11] Notwithstanding a few limited exceptions,[12] Cassese notes: 'no territory exists that is not subject to a sovereign Power [...] there consequently exists an absolute nexus between territory and sovereignty'.[13] These notions are underpinned by principles of international law such as the principle that a State may not perform any governmental act in the territory of another State without the latter's consent (principle of territorial sovereignty) and that a State may not intervene in the internal affairs of another State (principle of non-intervention).[14] This is because the exercise of

[7] The Montevideo Convention on Rights and Duties of States 1933 declares: 'The State as a person of international law should possess the following qualifications: (a) a permanent population (b) a defined territory (c) government; and (d) capacity to enter relations with the other State' – Montevideo Convention on Rights and Duties of States 1933 (adopted 26 December 1933, entered into force 26 December 1934) 165 LNTS 19; Ian Brownlie, *Principles of Public International Law* (Cambridge University Press 2008) 105; Malcolm Shaw, *International Law* (Cambridge University Press 2008) 198; Antonio Cassese, *International Law* (Oxford University Press 2005) 73.

[8] Brownlie (n. 7) 488; Lassa Oppenheim, Robert Jennings and Arthur Desmond Watts, *Oppenheim's International Law Vol. 1, pt. 2–4, Peace* (Longman 1992) 122.

[9] Oppenheim, Jennings and Watts (n. 8) 458; Brownlie (n. 7) 299; Cassese (n. 7) 50; For a full explanation of what each type of jurisdiction entails see Shaw (n. 7) 649–51.

[10] *Bankovic and Others* v. *Belgium and Others* (2007) 44 EHRR SE5 at [59].

[11] *Assanidze* v. *Georgia* (2004) 39 EHRR 32 at [139]; *Al-Skeini and Others* v. *United Kingdom* at [131]. A similar presumption arises under the American Convention on Human Rights as the Inter-American Commission noted in *Saldaño* v. *Argentina* Report No 38/99 IAComHR 11 March 1999 at [16].

[12] There are certain places over which no country may exercise sovereignty as a result of treaty regimes, e.g. Antarctica, international protectorates and de-militarised zones.

[13] Cassese (n. 7) 82–3.

[14] Malanczuk (n. 3) 109; Cassese (n. 7) 53–5; Article 55(1), Vienna Convention on Consular Relations (adopted 24 April 1963, entered into force 19 March 1967) 596 UNTS 261.

jurisdiction by a State outside its own territory may impinge upon the exercise of sovereignty by another State over its territory.

General international law seeks to mediate the disputes over sovereignty that arise when States exercise jurisdiction extra-territorially. As a result, discussions of State jurisdiction under general international law are primarily concerned with establishing legal bases upon which States can seek to exercise their jurisdiction in circumstances where the territorial State is presumed to have jurisdiction.[15] In criminal law, for example, a State could seek to exercise its jurisdiction where one of its nationals is the victim of a crime in another State.[16] The State's ability to enforce this jurisdiction is, however, limited by the sovereignty of the other State.[17] Thus, State jurisdiction under general international law is primarily concerned with the sovereign legal rights of States to act in a given situation,[18] and determining the circumstances in which a State may legally exercise its jurisdiction, e.g. enforce its national laws, outside its own territory.[19]

The concept of State jurisdiction under the Convention must be distinguished from that under general international law.[20] Jurisdiction under Article 1 is not about extending the State's municipal legal order to the territory of another State or claiming a legal basis to exercise jurisdiction elsewhere. Jurisdiction under Article 1 is concerned with establishing whether a contracting State has de facto control over space/territory or people, such that it triggers the application of the Convention's obligations,[21] whether this is at home or abroad. The pivotal factor is the extent of the factual control exercised by the State and not the State's legal capacity to act.[22] This chapter focuses on jurisdiction within a State's de jure territory, the next chapter looks at how the State's jurisdiction is determined extra-territorially, outside its normal borders.

15 Samantha Besson, 'The Extraterritoriality of the European Convention on Human Rights: Why Human Rights Depend on Jurisdiction and What Jurisdiction Amounts to' (2012) 25 *Leiden Journal of International Law* 857, 869.

16 Shaw (n. 7) 659–66.

17 Oppenheim, Jennings and Watts (n. 8) 463.

18 Conall Mallory, 'European Court of Human Rights Al-Skeini and Others v. United Kingdom (Application No 55721/07) Judgment of 7 July 2011' (2012) 61 ICLQ 301, 309.

19 Milanovic (n. 1) 420–2.

20 Milanovic (n. 1) 419; Mallory (n. 18) 309; Besson (n. 15) 869.

21 Milanovic (n. 1) 417.

22 See *Al-Skeini and Others* v. *United Kingdom* at [136]; Michael Duttwiler, 'Authority, Control and Jurisdiction in the Extraterritorial Application of the European Convention on Human Rights' (2012) 30 NQHR 137, 139–41.

The final distinction that should be drawn when introducing Article 1 jurisdiction is between State jurisdiction and State responsibility.[23] The distinction can easily be seen in the Articles on State Responsibility drafted by the International Law Commission, which determine the legal consequences of a failure to fulfil international obligations, e.g. treaty obligations. For State responsibility to arise, two criteria must be met. The conduct consisting of an action or omission must be (a) attributable to the State under international law and (b) it must constitute a breach of the State's international obligations.[24] Before a State can breach an obligation, the obligation must first be owed.[25] In the context of the Convention, this means that the applicant must, generally speaking, be within the State's jurisdiction before attribution is determined and State responsibility held to arise.[26] Thus, State responsibility may not arise for every act/omission that occurs within a State's jurisdiction. The State may not be held responsible for the acts of private actors, because those acts may not be attributable to it.[27] Equally, acts that are attributable to the State may not give rise to State responsibility where it does not owe obligations to the victims under international law, which may be contingent on the exercise of jurisdiction.

In summary, the jurisdiction the Court refers to when discussing Article 1 is a State's jurisdiction. The State's jurisdiction is linked to its territory, because the State is presumed to exercise jurisdiction within its own territory. Article 1 jurisdiction is primarily about determining whether the State has de facto control over space/territory or people and as such must be distinguished from the conception of State jurisdiction under general international law. Finally, we must distinguish between State jurisdiction and State responsibility, the latter of which often depends on the existence of the former.

23 *Catan and Others* v. *Moldova and Russia* App no 43370/04 (ECtHR, 19 October 2012) at [115].

24 James Crawford, 'Draft Articles on Responsibility of States for Internationally Wrongful Acts, with commentaries' (2001) 2 *Yearbook of the International Law Commission*, 34.

25 Besson (n. 15) 867; O'Boyle (n. 5) 130.

26 Crawford (n. 24) 35; Milanovic (n. 1) 437. Occasionally the Court may be required to determine whether the acts of particular soldiers are attributable to the State first before considering the issue of control: see Milanovic and Papic (n. 5) 273.

27 James Crawford and Simon Olleson, 'The Nature and Forms of International Responsibility' in Malcolm Evans (ed), *International Law* (3rd edn, Oxford University Press 2010) 454. However, it should be noted that the Court has at times conflated jurisdiction and State responsibility in its judgments, see Stefan Talmon, 'The Responsibility of Outside Powers for Acts of Secessionist Entities' (2009) 58 ICLQ 493, 508–9 and *Isaak and Others* v. *Turkey* App no 44587/98 (ECtHR, 28 September 2006).

## 1.3 JURISDICTION OVER DOMESTIC TERRITORY

Jurisdiction under the Convention is contingent on a State having de facto control over people or territory. States are presumed to have such control over their own territory.[28] The ingrained territorial bias of human rights law is clear.[29] However, States can lose de facto control over their territory and this presumption is rebuttable.[30] A State will typically resort to military operations before losing control by, for example, attempting to repel a foreign aggressor, or trying to suppress an insurrection. Military operations are closely related to losing de facto control. As jurisdiction under the Convention is contingent on de facto control, it is important to consider what effect a loss of control over the State's home territory can have on the State's Convention obligations.

When a State loses de facto control over its territory, the jurisprudence shows that uncertainty arises over the obligations the State owes. In *Ilascu and Others* v. *Moldova and Russia*,[31] the Court examined a situation where a State had lost de facto control over its de jure territory. Moldova was part of the Union of Soviet Socialist Republics (USSR) until it collapsed in the 1990s. Moldova declared independence in 1991 and claimed Transdniestria as part of its territory. Transdniestria was part of the Moldavian Soviet Socialist Republic, which was succeeded by Moldova. After the Soviet Union collapsed, the USSR's fourteenth army remained in Transdniestria and it declared independence as the 'Moldavian Republic of Transdniestria' (MRT) in 1991. The MRT has not been internationally recognised as an independent State.[32] Moldova continues to claim Transdniestria, although it has been unable to exercise de facto control there for decades. Similar situations where a State claiming de jure title to territory fails to exercise de facto control are evident elsewhere and have been

[28] *Ilascu and Others* v. *Moldova and Russia* (2005) 40 EHRR 46 at [312]; *Assanidze* v. *Georgia* (2004) 39 EHRR 32 at [139] Anthony Cullen and Steven Wheatley, 'The Human Rights of Individuals in De Facto Regimes under the European Convention on Human Rights' (2013) 13 HRLR 691, 702.

[29] This begins to manifest itself in the Court's jurisprudence in *Soering* v. *United Kingdom* (1989) 11 EHRR 439 at [86] and *Bankovic and Others* v. *Belgium and Others* (2007) 44 EHRR SE5 at [59].

[30] Kjetil Mujezinovic Larsen, 'Territorial Non-Application of the European Convention on Human Rights' (2009) 78 *Nordic Journal of International Law* 73, 79; Ralph Wilde, 'The Extraterritorial Application of International Human Rights Law on Civil and Political Rights' in Scott Sheeran and Nigel Rodley (eds), *Routledge Handbook of International Human Rights Law* (Routledge 2013) 647–8.

[31] *Ilascu and Others* v. *Moldova and Russia* (2005) 40 EHRR 46.

[32] Ibid at [28]–[41].

dealt with by the Court.[33] The facts in *Ilascu* are not particularly important in this context and a brief summary will suffice.

The four applicants were arrested in the MRT in 1992 and charged with various offences, including murder and 'anti-Soviet activities'. They were tried and sentenced by the Supreme Court of the MRT and detained for several years. The applicants alleged that numerous violations of the Convention had arisen from their trial and detention. They sought to hold Russia and Moldova responsible for these alleged violations. They claimed that Moldova should have interceded on their behalf with the MRT to stop the Convention violations arising from their detention. They alleged that Russia was exercising jurisdiction in the MRT because it exercised de facto control there and should therefore be held responsible for the Convention violations.

The focus here is on Moldova's jurisdiction over the MRT. The Court ruled that the Moldovan Government was the only legitimate government of the Republic of Moldova under international law, but that it did not exercise authority over the MRT.[34] However, the lack of control over this territory was not a barrier to Moldova exercising jurisdiction for the purposes of Article 1, the Court stated:

> where a Contracting State is prevented from exercising its authority over the whole of its territory by a constraining de facto situation [...] it does not thereby cease to have jurisdiction within the meaning of Art. 1 of the Convention over that part of its territory [...] such a factual situation reduces the scope of that jurisdiction in that the undertaking given by the State under Article 1 must be considered by the Court only in the light of the Contracting State's positive obligations towards persons within its territory. The State in question must endeavour, with all the legal and diplomatic means available to it vis-à-vis foreign States and international organisations, to continue to guarantee the enjoyment of the rights and freedoms defined in the Convention.[35]

This is a clear example of jurisdiction influencing the scope of the substantive obligations the State is held to. Once the precept of the State's administrative control is removed, the scope, content and even the very application of the Convention is cast in doubt. The scope of Moldova's jurisdiction was reduced

33 Cypriot control over the Turkish Republic of Northern Cyprus in *Cyprus* v. *Turkey* (1982) 4 EHRR 482; Georgian control over South Ossetia and Abkhazia in *Georgia* v. *Russia (II)* (2012) 54 EHRR SE10; Azerbaijani and Armenian control over different parts of Nagorno-Karabakh in *Sargsyan* v. *Azerbaijan* App no 40167/06 (ECtHR, 14 December 2011) and *Chiragov and Others* v. *Armenia* App no 13216/05 (ECtHR, 14 December 2011). More recently Ukrainian control over Crimea.

34 *Ilascu and Others* v. *Moldova and Russia* at [330].

35 Ibid at [333].

so that it was only obliged to uphold its positive obligations. The exact positive obligations it had to uphold are extremely unclear. The positive obligations in the Convention would typically include things like the obligation to investigate suspicious deaths[36] and the obligation to take preventive measures to protect people from the imminent criminal acts of third parties where such a risk is known to the authorities.[37] A thorough discussion of the problems arising from applying positive obligations in the context of military operations is given in the subsequent chapters, but for the purposes of this chapter, it suffices to note that the very idea that States can owe positive obligations when they are not exercising de facto control is questionable.[38] According to the Court, the State must 'take the diplomatic, economic, judicial or other measures that it is in its power to take and are in accordance with international law to secure to the applicants the rights guaranteed by the Convention'.[39] It later stated:

> Although it is not for the Court to indicate which measures the authorities should take in order to comply with their obligations most effectively, it must verify that the measures actually taken were appropriate and sufficient in the present case. When faced with a partial or total failure to act, the Court's task is to determine to what extent a minimum effort was nevertheless possible and whether it should have been made.[40]

The Court ruled that Moldova had positive obligations to re-establish control over its territory and to take measures to ensure the applicants' rights.[41] While Moldova had made efforts to regain control, it had not made sufficient efforts to secure the applicants' release. The Court concluded that after one applicant had been released, Ilie Ilascu, Moldova had not made sufficient efforts to secure the others' release, because it had not raised the issue during negotiations with Russia over the MRT.[42]

36 *Armani da Silva* v. *United Kingdom* (2016) 63 EHRR 12 at [229]–[239].

37 *Osman* v. *United Kingdom* (2000) 29 EHRR 245 at [116].

38 Michal Gondek, 'Extraterritorial Application of the European Convention on Human Rights: Territorial Focus in the Age of Globalization?' (2005) 52 *Netherlands International Law Review* 349, 368; Hampson argues that certain positive obligations require the kind of control a State only has over its own territory before they can be fulfilled – Francoise Hampson, 'Direct Participation in Hostilities and the Interoperability of the Law of Armed Conflict and Human Rights Law' (2011) 87 *US Naval War College International Law Studies* 187, 189.

39 *Ilascu and Others* v. *Moldova and Russia* at [331].

40 Ibid at [334].

41 Ibid at [339]. Interestingly, the Ukraine has submitted an inter-State application to the European Court of Human Rights alleging that Russia has violated a number Convention rights in Crimea, Donetsk and Luhansk while it has exercised effective control over the areas or separatists within them – *Ukraine* v. *Russia (IV)* App no 42410/15).

42 *Ilascu and Others* v. *Moldova and Russia* at [349].

The standard introduced in *Ilascu* has been applied in other cases.[43] The loss of de facto control should have made it more difficult for applicants to take cases, because it created the possibility for States to deny that they were exercising jurisdiction over the lost territory.[44] However, *Ilascu* actually broadens the scope of the State's jurisdiction, making it more difficult for States to deny that they are exercising jurisdiction. *Ilascu* also compromises the integrity of the Convention standards as States are only held to unspecified and uncertain positive obligations. It represents a halfway house between protection of the Convention and no protection. Securing these obligations will be difficult, if not impossible, for States when they have lost control over their territory.

## 1.4 LOSING CONTROL

Control is the lynchpin of jurisdiction. However, despite losing de facto control over the MRT in *Ilascu*, Moldova was still found to be exercising some jurisdiction under Article 1 and was obliged to uphold positive obligations toward the inhabitants of that territory. This ruling was confirmed in numerous subsequent judgments.[45] This is due, in part, to the fact that there is a presumption that a State exercises jurisdiction over its own territory in Article 1 and while this presumption is rebuttable, it is difficult to rebut it in practice.[46] In this section, the Court's approach toward this presumption is evaluated to illustrate the uncertain consequences that a loss of de facto control actually has on jurisdiction and the rights the State is obliged to uphold.

In *Assanidze* v. *Georgia*, the Court addressed the presumption of jurisdiction. The case concerned a politician who was detained in the Ajarian Autonomous Republic, which is part of Georgia's territory. The Georgian Supreme Court ordered his release, but the Ajarian authorities refused to release him. The politician took a case against Georgia claiming *inter alia*

[43] See *Ivantoc and Others* v. *Moldova and Russia* App no 23687/05 (ECtHR, 15 November 2011); *Catan and Others* v. *Moldova and Russia* App no 43370/04 (ECtHR, 19 October 2012); *Sandu and Others* v. *Moldova and Russia* App no 21034/05 (ECtHR, 17 July 2018).

[44] See, for example, *Azemi* v. *Serbia* App no 11209/09 (ECtHR, 5 November 2013).

[45] *Ivantoc and Others* v. *Moldova and Russia* App no 23687/05 (ECtHR, 15 November 2011); *Catan and Others* v. *Moldova and Russia* App no 43370/04 (ECtHR, 19 October 2012); *Mozer* v. *Moldova and Russia* App no 11138/10 (ECtHR, 23 February 2016).

[46] This is in part down to the international legal principle of territorial integrity see Marcelo G. Kohen, *Secession: International Law Perspectives* (Cambridge University Press 2006) 369 and Enrico Milano, *Unlawful Territorial Situations in International Law – Reconciling Effectiveness, Legality and Legitimacy* (Martinus Nijhoff 2006) 123–5.

that his right to liberty under Article 5 was being infringed. The Court began its analysis of jurisdiction stating:

> The Ajarian Autonomous Republic is indisputably an integral part of the territory of Georgia and subject to its competence and control. In other words, there is a presumption of competence. The Court must now determine whether there is valid evidence to rebut that presumption.[47]

The Court acknowledges Georgia's de jure jurisdiction over the territory, which prompted the presumption that it exercised de facto control and jurisdiction for the purposes of Article 1. However, neither the applicant, nor the State disputed Georgia's claim to the territory under international law and the presumption that Georgia exercised jurisdiction over the territory was not questioned by the parties. The Court examined whether the presumption had been rebutted of its own volition. A number of elements were considered: the fact that Georgia had extended the Convention to the entire territory, it had not issued any reservations to the Convention, and the territory had no separatist aspirations and was not subject to the effective overall control of another State.[48] The Court concluded that based on these elements, the presumption was not rebutted.

The Court carried out a similar inquiry into Moldova's control over the MRT in the *Ilascu* case, examining whether reservations had been issued in relation to the MRT and considering whether secessionist entities were acting within the territory.[49] *Assanidze* could therefore be viewed as establishing a principle that where there is a question mark over the State's de facto control over its de jure territory, for example when the State is engaged in a NIAC with a secessionist entity, the Court should conduct a detailed examination of legal and factual elements to determine whether the conflict has rebutted the presumption of jurisdiction. However, the Court's practice has been far from consistent on this issue.

In *Isayeva* v. *Russia*,[50] there were serious doubts over Russia's de facto control over its de jure territory in Chechnya. In that case, it was alleged that the Russian armed forces had bombed a route leading from the besieged city of Grozny. The route had been established as a safe exit route from the city. The applicant's life and that of her family members had been put at risk by the

47 *Assanidze* v. *Georgia* at [139]. The Court here uses the term competence interchangeably with jurisdiction see ibid at [137].

48 Ibid at [140]–[142].

49 *Ilascu and Others* v. *Moldova and Russia* at [324]–[325].

50 *Isayeva* v. *Russia* App no 57950/00 (ECtHR, 24 February 2005).

bombing. At the time, Russian control over Chechnya was challenged by an entrenched insurgency and in October 1999, Grozny was under the control of Chechen insurgents who launched attacks on the Russian armed forces.[51] Russia had clearly lost de facto control over Grozny and laid siege to the city to regain control. The Court itself implicitly acknowledged that Russia had lost control over the area stating '[t]he situation in Chechnya had called for exceptional measures on behalf of the State in order to *regain control* over the Republic and to suppress the illegal armed insurgency' (emphasis added).[52] It is worth noting that the Court had previously envisioned that such a situation could rebut the presumption of control in *Ilascu* stating that:

> jurisdiction is presumed to be exercised normally throughout the State's territory. This presumption may be limited in exceptional circumstances, particularly where a State is prevented from exercising its authority in part of its territory. That may be as a result of military occupation by the armed forces of another State which effectively controls the territory concerned, *acts of war or rebellion*, or the acts of a foreign State supporting the installation of a separatist State within the territory of the State concerned.[53] (emphasis added)

The Court has accepted that control had been lost noting the need to 'regain control'. It had also previously noted that the presumption of control could be rebutted where a State is prevented from exercising its authority by 'acts of rebellion'. The logical consequence of this would be for the Court to assess whether the presumption was rebutted and modify the obligations owed pursuant to the precedent set by *Ilascu*. The Court instead treated this as a normal case, declining to address the presumption of jurisdiction or modify the State's obligations, ultimately finding multiple violations of Article 2.

Contrasting *Ilascu* and *Assanidze* with *Isayeva*, it seems that the Court is not holding States to the same standards or consistently assessing whether the presumption of jurisdiction is rebutted of its own volition. There are numerous possible reasons for this. First, in many cases where a State actively denies that it is exercising jurisdiction, the Court holds the State to a corresponding lower level of obligations.[54] In *Isayeva* no such denial was made. There is a pattern here, many contracting States have conducted

[51] William Abresch, 'A Human Rights Law of Internal Armed Conflict: The European Court of Human Rights in Chechnya' (2005) 16 EJIL 741, 754.

[52] *Isayeva* v. *Russia* App no 57950/00 (ECtHR, 24 February 2005) at [178].

[53] *Ilascu and Others* v. *Moldova and Russia* at [312].

[54] *Ilascu and Others* v. *Moldova and Russia*; *Catan and Others* v. *Moldova and Russia* App no 43370/04 (ECtHR, 19 October 2012); *Azemi* v. *Serbia* App no 11209/09 (ECtHR, 5 November 2013); *Jularic* v. *Croatia* App no 20106/06 (ECtHR, 20 January 2011).

military operations against insurgent groups within their territory, including the UK in Northern Ireland, Turkey in the South-East of Turkey and Russia in Chechnya. A unifying characteristic of these engagements is the States' denial that a NIAC was occurring in their territory,[55] even though in some cases, most notably the conflict in Chechnya, academics have convincingly argued there was such a conflict.[56] There is a reluctance on the part of the State to acknowledge any corresponding loss of control, which arguably leads the Court to play along with the fiction. Secondly, it has been argued that where a secessionist entity lacks the support of another State, it cannot rebut the presumption of jurisdiction.[57] This distinction between the natures of secessionist entities is crucial to understanding the underlying motive for the Court's refusal to consider whether the presumption of jurisdiction has been rebutted. If the Court had concluded that Russia did not owe full human rights obligations to the people of Grozny in *Isayeva*, it would have resulted in a lacuna in the Convention's protection.[58] As States are the primary guarantors of human rights protection, unless a secessionist entity is supported by another State there is no other party available to assume the duty to guarantee human rights within the territory in place of the State.[59] As such, ruling that the de jure State is no longer exercising jurisdiction is likely to result in poorer protection of victims.

This interpretation of the law was expressly confirmed in *Sargsyan* v. *Azerbaijan*.[60] That case revolved around the village of Gulistan, which was situated on the line of contact between Azerbaijan and Armenia in their protracted dispute over the Nagorno-Karabakh region. A number of villagers were displaced from their homes in Gulistan by the conflict and sought compensation for their loss of property as the village was effectively in no man's land between the two armies. Azerbaijan claims the village is part of its de jure territory and its armed forces occupied the village, but they have

55 Abresch (n. 51) 756.

56 Françoise Hampson, 'The Relationship between International Humanitarian Law and Human Rights Law from the Perspective of a Human Rights Treaty Body' (2008) 90 IRRC 549, 563; Philip Leach, 'The Chechen Conflict: Analysing the Oversight of the European Court of Human Rights' [2008] EHRLR 732, 733; Abresch (n. 51) 754.

57 Larsen (n. 30) 82–3.

58 Note the Court's desire to avoid any such gaps in protection in other cases such as *Bankovic and Others* v. *Belgium and Others* at [80]; *Al-Skeini and Others* v. *United Kingdom* at [142]; *Bijelic* v. *Montenegro and Serbia* App no 11890/05 (ECtHR, 28 April 2009) at [67]–[70].

59 For a thorough discussion of the human rights obligations of de facto entities see Cullen and Wheatley (n. 28).

60 *Sargsyan* v. *Azerbaijan* App no 40167/06 (ECtHR, 16 June 2015) at [94].

been surrounded by Armenian troops in a strategically superior position for many years and the area is surrounded by mines. Azerbaijan argued that they should not be obliged to uphold full human rights obligations in the Convention in disputed zones or 'areas which are rendered inaccessible by the circumstances'.[61] While the Court accepted that Azerbaijan 'may encounter difficulties at a practical level in exercising their authority in the area of Gulistan',[62] this did not alter their human rights obligations there. Gulistan remained subject to the de facto control of the Azerbaijani government and as a result the presumption that it exercised jurisdiction there was not displaced. It noted that the State's responsibility has only been limited in previous cases when another State or separatist regime exercises effective control over the territory.[63] The Court expressly referred to the 'need to avoid a vacuum in Convention protection',[64] which could be caused by creating an exception like that suggested by Azerbaijan. It therefore ruled that Azerbaijan continued to exercise jurisdiction there for the purposes of the Convention, even though Azerbaijan had such limited control over the territory.

The foregoing issues are further complicated by the case of *Azemi* v. *Serbia*, where the Court examined how Kosovo's independence impacted upon Serbia's Convention obligations there. The applicant's employment was terminated in 1990 and he took legal action challenging the legality of the termination, but the case was never examined. In January 2002, a municipal court in Kosovo ruled that the termination of his employment was unlawful and ordered his reinstatement. The applicant eventually took a case against Serbia under Article 6, because the authorities in Kosovo failed to enforce the judgment. Serbia claims de jure title over Kosovo territory, despite having lost de facto control over the territory in 1999 and Kosovo declaring independence from Serbia in 2008, which has been recognised by over 100 States. In this situation, Serbia was in a comparable position to Moldova *vis-à-vis* the MRT or Cyprus and the Turkish Republic of Northern Cyprus (TRNC), although admittedly Kosovo's independence is much more broadly recognised than those entities. Serbia claimed it lacked de facto control over the territory and that the responsibility to guarantee the applicant's rights rested with the UN-sponsored international administrators of Kosovo.

61 Ibid at [146].
62 Ibid at [150].
63 Ibid at [140].
64 Ibid at [148].

The Court began with the presumption that Serbia exercised jurisdiction over this territory noting that:

> the Court must examine all the objective facts capable of limiting the effective exercise of a State's authority over its territory as well as the State's positive obligations under the Convention to take all the appropriate measures which are still within its power to take to ensure respect for the Convention's rights and freedoms within its territory.[65]

The Court begins by treating the case as one of a territorial State (Serbia) losing de facto control over its de jure territory (Kosovo). One would expect the Court to examine factors rebutting the presumption of jurisdiction, as it had in *Assanidze*. Instead the Court inverted its jurisdiction test by applying its 'effective overall control' test to Serbia, the territorial State. This test is not normally applied to the State which has lost de facto control over its de jure territory, but is instead applied to a State in adverse possession of territory to determine whether it is exercising sufficient control to have to guarantee human rights obligations there. In *Ilascu*, for example, the Court applied this test to Russia in respect of the MRT to determine whether it was exercising sufficient control over the MRT to generate a jurisdictional link between Russia and the region.[66] In *Azemi*, the Court considered Serbia's lack of control over the UN-sponsored international administrators of Kosovo and the institutions it had established in Kosovo and decided that Serbia had not supported Kosovo's institutions 'militarily, economically, financially or politically'.[67] It concluded that Serbia lacked jurisdiction for the purposes of Article 1 and that it 'cannot point to any positive obligations that the respondent State had towards the applicant'.[68]

The Court's jurisprudence is obviously inconsistent. The consequences of losing de facto control on the presumption of jurisdiction remain uncertain. The Court has engaged in unpredictable assessments of the loss of de facto control. When it has examined the issue, the Court has applied different tests, as can be seen if one compares the cases of *Assanidze* and *Azemi*. The cases of *Ilascu, Assanidze* and *Azemi* suggest that the Court will inquire into whether the presumption of jurisdiction was rebutted and modify the State's

[65] *Azemi* v. *Serbia* at [42].

[66] *Ilascu and Others* v. *Moldova and Russia* at [315]–[319] and [379]–[385]; The Court also applied this test to Turkey in the TRNC in *Loizidou* v. *Turkey (Merits)* (1997) 23 EHRR 513 at [56]; See also Talmon (n. 27) 508–17.

[67] *Azemi* v. *Serbia* at [45] – the Court expressly referred to the test applied to determine Russia's responsibility, not Moldova's, in *Ilascu and Others* v. *Moldova and Russia* at [392].

[68] *Azemi* v. *Serbia* at [47].

obligations. While *Isayeva* and *Sargsyan*, by contrast, suggest that even where the loss of de facto control is recognised by the Court, it may not always modify the State's obligations. The Court is clearly holding States in similar situations to different standards and it needs to offer consistent evaluations of whether the presumption of jurisdiction is rebutted by a loss of de facto control and once a loss of de facto control has been established, the State should not be obliged to uphold Convention obligations.

## 1.5 POSITIVE OBLIGATIONS

The consequences of losing control for jurisdiction are unclear, but a deeper level of uncertainty pervades. In this section, the nature of the obligations the State is obliged to uphold once it has lost de facto control of an area are explored further.

One of the key problems arising from the *Ilascu* case is the lack of clarity surrounding the State's positive obligations when it has lost de facto control over part of its territory. In *Ilascu*, the Court said the 'scope' of the State's jurisdiction is 'reduced' when it loses de facto control, but it does not elaborate on what it is reduced to. The judgment suggests that the test is functional, as noted above the State must take the diplomatic, economic, judicial or other measures that are within its power to take. In other words, the State should intervene to the extent that it is able to. Some academics advocate using this functional test to determine jurisdiction domestically and extraterritorially.[69] There are many problems with a functional approach. First, it naturally undermines the clarity of the law. When the scope of the obligation is contingent on capacity, the obligation itself becomes variable. Second, the State's capacity to act is also difficult to assess and will vary widely depending on the circumstances. Third, the State's capacity to act may also be greater than it realises or is willing to pursue for policy reasons.

The Court contends that it will not enforce an impossible or disproportionate burden on the State.[70] Yet, it refuses to specify the measures, or even the

[69] See, for example, Monica Hakimi, 'State Bystander Responsibility' (2010) 21 EJIL 341, 374–6; Rick Lawson, 'Really Out of Sight? Issues of Jurisdiction and Control in Situations of Armed Conflict under the ECHR' in Antoine Buyse (ed), *Margins of Conflict: The ECHR and Transitions to and from Armed Conflict* (Intersentia 2011) 74–5; Yuval Shany, 'Taking Universality Seriously: A Functional Approach to Extraterritoriality in International Human Rights Law' (2013) 7 *The Law & Ethics of Human Rights* 47; Moor and Simpson advocate it in the domestic territorial context in Louise Moor and Brian Simpson, 'Ghosts of Colonialism in the European Convention on Human Rights' (2005) 76 BYIL 121, 125.

[70] *Ilascu and Others* v. *Moldova and Russia* at [332].

type of measures, the State must take in advance, advocating assessment on a case-by-case basis.[71] One could argue this is necessitated by the functional approach, but without indications of the type of actions the State must undertake, the approach becomes extremely erratic. The Court may hold the State responsible for failing to satisfy obligations which it has not specified. The State is left guessing what it must do. In *Ilascu*, for example, the State was obliged to raise the issue of the applicants' detention during diplomatic negotiations and attempt to regain control over its territory. One could argue that the measures the State had to take and its obligations could be inferred from the surrounding circumstances. However, the second obligation, to regain control over its territory, was not self-evident from the Convention, no article of the Convention specifically demands it. This position can be clearly contrasted with the case of *Jularic* v. *Croatia*.[72] There, the applicant's husband was allegedly killed by Serbian paramilitaries in October 1991 in a Croatian town near the Serbian border. These paramilitaries and Yugoslav forces entered the area in August 1991 and eventually gained complete control over the region in November 1991. The applicant complained that the Croatian authorities had not upheld their positive obligation to investigate her husband's death, but instead of holding that Croatia had to guarantee this positive obligation to investigate within its de jure territory, even though it had lost de facto control, the Court decided it would:

> examine only the part of the inquiry that took place after January 1998 since before then the Croatian authorities had had no real authority in the town of Vukovar.[73]

If we compare the outcomes of these two cases the confusion is quite blatant. In *Ilascu*, the State is held responsible for not upholding a positive obligation that did not obviously arise from the Convention, e.g. regain control over territory. In *Jularic*, the Court refuses to hold Croatia responsible for failing to guarantee positive obligations that were clear in the Convention, e.g. the positive obligation to investigate suspicious deaths. In the wake of *Ilascu* it remains unclear what positive obligations are owed by the State within their lost territory and what actions they must undertake to discharge their Convention obligations. This serves as a clear example of how the application of the Convention to military operations has undermined the unity and coherency of the Convention's obligations.

71 Cullen and Wheatley (n. 28) 703–4; Moor and Simpson (n. 69) 125.

72 *Jularic* v. *Croatia* App no 20106/06 (ECtHR, 20 January 2011).

73 Ibid at [46].

## 1.6 DISCHARGING POSITIVE OBLIGATIONS

The obvious counter-argument is that positive obligations are inherently variable.[74] Therefore determining their scope is inherently variable. While that is certainly true, the variability in the positive obligations where a State loses de facto control over its territory runs much deeper than the variation generally incumbent with positive obligations. When the State acts within its own territory, its obligations are relatively static and clear: guarantee all the rights in the Convention. When the State has lost de facto control, it may be required to guarantee some or all of the Convention rights. The uncertainty goes much deeper than mere uncertainty over the scope or content of a given positive obligation to whether the positive obligation is even owed. Such uncertainty is extremely unwelcome in the context of military operations where States need to communicate coherent and easily understandable rules to their armed forces.

Even assuming we accept the functional test advanced in *Ilascu* as valid, the test itself is undermined by a later statement in the judgment. The Court states that when it is faced with 'a partial or total failure to act' on the part of the State, 'the Court's task is to determine to what extent a minimum effort was nevertheless possible and whether it should have been made'.[75] This is clearly a much lower burden for the State to discharge and arguably rewards States for their inaction. If the State fails to act, or does not do enough, the Court holds it to a lower standard, e.g. a minimum effort.

This 'minimum effort' approach seems to find support elsewhere in the Court's jurisprudence. In *Boumediene* v. *Bosnia and Herzegovina*, Bosnian citizens were transferred from Bosnia to a US detention facility in Guantanamo Bay. The domestic Human Rights Chamber in Bosnia demanded that the Bosnian authorities 'take all possible steps' to prevent the detainees from being subjected to the death penalty and secure their release. The Bosnian authorities visited the detention centre and the Prime Minister openly requested their return. The domestic courts considered that the authorities had failed to take all the possible steps to secure the applicants' human rights.[76] Yet, when the

[74] Dimitris Xenos, *The Positive Obligations of the State under the European Convention of Human Rights* (Routledge 2012) 4; Alastair Mowbray, *The Development of Positive Obligations under the European Convention on Human Rights by the European Court of Human Rights* (Hart 2004).

[75] *Ilascu and Others* v. *Moldova and Russia* at [334]; The disparity between these two tests was pointed out by the High Court of England and Wales in *R. (Al-Skeini)* v. *Secretary of State for Defence* [2004] EWHC 2911 (Admin) at [341].

[76] *Boumediene and Others* v. *Bosnia and Herzegovina* App no 38703/06 (ECtHR, 18 November 2008) at [46] and [59].

Court examined the case, it praised the State authorities' repeated interventions, specifically noting the visit to the site and attempts to secure diplomatic assurances on treatment and release. The Court considered that the authorities were taking 'all possible steps to the present date to protect the basic rights of the applicants'.[77] With conflicting approaches like this in the jurisprudence, it remains unclear whether the State must take measures within their power or simply expend the minimum effort in resolving the issue. Where the State has multiple options available to protect the rights within the territory, the obligation is much more difficult to infer and the Court does not offer any real guidance over which option should be preferred or any basis upon which the contracting State could choose.

In *Ilascu*, the Court effectively held Moldova liable for failing to raise the applicants' detention during negotiations with Russia and the MRT. In a later case, *Ivantoc and Others* v. *Moldova and Russia*,[78] some of the applicants from *Ilascu*, who had remained in detention until 2007 despite the Court's ruling to release them in 2004, took a further case challenging their detention. They sought to hold Moldova responsible for not doing all they could to secure their Convention rights. However, this time the Court held that Moldova had discharged its positive obligations, because after the *Ilascu* judgment they had 'constantly raised the issue of the applicants' fate in their bilateral relations with the Russian Federation' and continually sought assistance from international organisations and other States.[79] Moldova had altered their diplomatic activity *vis-à-vis* the applicants' case and this change meant the State had satisfied its positive obligation to the applicants.

Both *Ilascu* and *Ivantoc* draw the Court into the uncertain territory of potentially dictating the foreign policy of States. Both the Court and the Inter-American bodies have oscillated between demanding action and refusing to compel action on the foreign policy front. The Inter-American Court has, for example, demanded that States engage in diplomatic activity to seek the extradition of perpetrators of human rights violations, even former heads of State, who have fled to other States.[80] The Inter-American Court considered this to be part of the State's duty to investigate and punish human rights violations.[81] By contrast, the Inter-American Commission has not obliged States to take certain legal steps, for example, pursuing inter-State litigation before the

77 Ibid at [67].

78 *Ivantoc and Others* v. *Moldova and Russia* App no 23687/05 (ECtHR, 15 November 2011).

79 Ibid at [109].

80 *Goiburú and Others* v. *Paraguay* Series C No 153 IACtHR 22 September 2006 at [5] operative.

81 *La Cantuta* v. *Peru* Series C No 162 IACtHR 29 November 2006 at [159].

Inter-American bodies to raise claims of human rights abuses by other States.[82] The European bodies have a similarly mixed record. Early cases from the European Commission uphold the view that the Convention does not impose any obligations on States to intervene with the authorities of another State on behalf of an applicant.[83] In *Palic* v. *Bosnia and Herzegovina*, the Court was hesitant to impose obligations on the State to carry out diplomatic actions. The Court refused to address whether Bosnia had a positive obligation to demand that Serbia investigate alleged violations of IHL as the applicant could have requested a Serbian investigation herself.[84] By contrast, the Court regularly demands that States seek diplomatic assurances when expelling people to countries where they face a risk of human rights abuses.[85]

Foreign policy remains an area in which courts have historically exercised a high degree of judicial restraint,[86] which the Court has itself tacitly endorsed.[87] While judicial intervention in foreign policy is growing, and this has been driven in part by human rights law,[88] the rationales motivating judicial restraint remain relevant. Courts cannot be held democratically accountable for the conduct of foreign policy in the same way as the executive or legislature.[89] Equally, courts do not have the tools to evaluate foreign policy,[90] and there is a lack of 'judicial or manageable standards' by which to judge foreign policy decisions.[91]

[82] *Saldaño* v. *Argentina* Report No 38/99 IAComHR 11 March 1999 at [30].

[83] *Bertrand Russell Peace Foundation* v. *United Kingdom* App no 7597/76 (EComHR, 2 May 1978); *Dobberstein* v. *Germany* App no 25045/94 (EComHR, 12 April 1996).

[84] *Palic* v. *Bosnia and Herzegovina* App no 4704/04 (ECtHR, 15 February 2011) at [65].

[85] *Saadi* v. *Italy* (2009) 49 EHRR 30 at [147]–[149].

[86] *R. (Abbasi)* v. *Secretary of State for Foreign and Commonwealth Affairs* [2002] EWCA Civ 1598. Courts at the supra-national level apply similar rules, e.g. Article 275, Treaty on the Functioning of the European Union.

[87] In *Markovic* v. *Italy* (2007) 44 EHRR 52, an Italian court decided that a case challenging the use of Italian bases to launch NATO attacks on the former Yugoslavia was not justiciable, the Court held that this finding of non-justiciability was not a violation of the applicant's rights under Articles 6 and 13.

[88] Dominic McGoldrick, 'The Boundaries of Justiciability' (2010) 59 ICLQ 981; Rabinder Singh, 'Justiciability in the Areas of Foreign Relations and Defence' in Phil Shiner and Andrew Williams (eds), *The Iraq War and International Law* (Hart Publishing 2008). For a practical example see *Rahmatullah* v. *Secretary of State for Foreign and Commonwealth Affairs* [2011] EWHC 2008 (Admin).

[89] In *Secretary of State for the Home Department* v. *Rehman* [2003] 1 AC 153 at [62] the courts referred to this rationale in the context of judicial review of national security, but the rationale applies equally to foreign policy.

[90] *R. (Al-Rawi)* v. *Secretary of State for Foreign and Commonwealth Affairs* [2006] EWHC 972 (Admin) at [92].

[91] *Buttes Gas & Oil Co* v. *Hammer (No.3)* [1982] AC 888 at 938.

The Court's intervention may lead to unintended consequences or impair the State's ability to engage in diplomacy.[92] The Court needs to consider the broader implications of its rulings in *Ilascu* and *Ivantoc* in light of these issues.[93] It is possible that positive obligations demanded by the Court, such as for example regaining control over territory and securing the release of a given person, could be better achieved independently of each other. It may be better to avoid a thorny issue, such as prisoner release, if it leads to more productive negotiations elsewhere and brings the State closer to regaining control over its territory. This would in turn put the State in a better position to secure the prisoner and other peoples' rights sooner. The Court is clearly not in the best position to assess this and as a result should probably steer clear of it.

The Court has, unfortunately, not taken a consistent approach. In the case of *Catan and Others* v. *Moldova and Russia*,[94] the Court appeared cognisant of the problems arising from dictating the foreign policy activities of a contracting State. In that case, the MRT had imposed a language policy, which banned the use of Latin script in schools and forced them to only use Cyrillic script. This meant pupils and teachers were forcibly evicted from their schools and moved to 'Latin script' schools. The applicants complained that Moldova had not satisfied its positive obligations to protect their right to education and should have raised the issue in diplomatic negotiations with the Russian and MRT authorities.[95] One would assume, based on the *Ilascu* and *Ivantoc* judgments, that Moldova had an obligation to raise the issue diplomatically. However, the Court did not hold that Moldova was obliged to raise the issue with the Russian and MRT authorities. It held that Moldova had satisfied its positive obligations by refurbishing the Latin script schools, paying their rent and covering other costs of running them.[96] Thus offering material support alone was sufficient to satisfy Moldova's positive obligations.

In the more recent case of *Mozer* v. *Moldova and Russia*,[97] the applicant, a German national, had been detained by the MRT and complained *inter alia*

[92] *R. (Abbasi)* v. *Secretary of State for Foreign and Commonwealth Affairs* at [107]; *Kuwait Airways Corporation* v. *Iraqi Airways Corporation* [2002] 2 AC 883 at [319]. Judge Nicolas Bratza expressed his discomfort with the Court assuming such a role in his partly dissenting opinion in *Ilascu and Others* v. *Moldova and Russia* at [8].

[93] McGoldrick (n. 88) 985; Jide Nzelibe, 'The Uniqueness of Foreign Affairs' (2004) 89 *Iowa Law Review* 941.

[94] *Catan and Others* v. *Moldova and Russia* App no 43370/04 (ECtHR, 19 October 2012).

[95] Ibid at [129].

[96] Ibid at [147]–[148].

[97] *Mozer* v. *Moldova and Russia* App no 11138/10 (ECtHR, 23 February 2016).

that his detention was unlawful. The Court reverted to its test in *Ilascu* stating that Moldova had to 'use all the legal and diplomatic means available to it to continue to guarantee the enjoyment of the rights and freedoms defined in the Convention to those living [in the MRT]'.[98] The Court eventually concluded that Moldova had satisfied its positive obligations because it had appealed to intergovernmental organisations and other countries, including Russia, to assist in securing the applicant's rights,[99] in essence it had altered its foreign relations activities in response to the case.

The situations in each of these cases, *Ilascu*, *Ivantoc*, *Catan* and *Mozer* are comparable. Each case involved people suffering human rights violations on territory that belonged to Moldova de jure but was outside its de facto control. Yet the court's approach to each case was different. Can we conclude that the duty to raise issues politically and diplomatically is only applicable to some rights and not others? Does this amount to relativism in the standards applied by the Court, with possible violations of the prohibition on torture, inhuman and degrading treatment or punishment in *Ivantoc* and *Ilascu* or the right to liberty and security in *Mozer* demanding diplomatic action, while other violations such as the right to education in *Catan* do not require such interventions on the part of the State? Is there any rational basis for such a distinction? The distinction appears arbitrary and the Court's approach to it variable.

## 1.7 CONCLUSION

This chapter has provided a potent illustration of how dependent human rights law is on having a functioning nation State for its proper operation. The ingrained territorial bias of human rights law is fully evident and once the precept of the functioning State is removed, the scope, content and even the very application of the law becomes extremely fluid. The application of the Convention to this context has clearly undermined the coherency of the Convention's obligations.

An intractable judicial policy decision lies at the heart of the jurisdiction issue examined in this chapter. The inability to hold non-State actors responsible for human rights violations in places like the MRT is clearly a driving force behind the Court imposing these vestigial positive obligations on contracting States. It is also understandable that a court seeking to protect victims of human rights violations would adopt such an approach to protect

98 Ibid at [100].
99 Ibid at [153]–[155].

vulnerable people and avoid impunity. However, even if one accepts the logic that the State should retain some positive obligations in this situation, which is a dubious proposition on its own, one cannot overlook the absence of clarity concerning these obligations. The law is currently in a lamentable state. There are glaring inconsistencies in the jurisprudence. There is confusion over the circumstances in which control is lost and States do not have sufficient information about what positive obligations they must uphold or how they must go about discharging those obligations. If the Court is going to persist in demanding that States uphold positive obligations in these situations, it must provide greater clarity on the nature of those obligations and how States must discharge them. The next chapter reveals that a very similar situation persists with respect to extra-territorial jurisdiction.

# 2

# Jurisdiction over Extra-Territorial Military Operations

## 2.1 INTRODUCTION

This chapter builds on the previous chapter's discussion of jurisdiction. Jurisdiction remains a significant threshold issue in military operations cases. Generally speaking, the Court's jurisprudence has broadened the circumstances in which States are held to exercise jurisdiction extra-territorially. This has made it more difficult for States to deny that they are exercising jurisdiction during extra-territorial military operations and emphasises the need to move beyond the question of whether human rights law should apply to military operations on to discussing the practicalities of applying it. However, as this chapter and the previous chapter show, the question of jurisdiction has a direct bearing on the scope and content of the obligations to which States are being held. The circumstances in which jurisdiction is held to arise and the scope of the obligations States must uphold have become increasingly unclear.

The chapter begins with a primer on extra-territorial jurisdiction, introducing the central concepts of personal or State agent authority jurisdiction and spatial or effective control of an area jurisdiction. The analysis then moves on to consider the seminal judgments of *Bankovic and Others* v. *Belgium and Others* and *Al-Skeini* v. *United Kingdom* with an extended critique of those judgments. The chapter focuses on three central issues. Firstly, the circumstances in which individual extra-territorial acts, such as bombings or shootings, give rise to jurisdiction under the Convention. Secondly, the jurisdictional consequences of belligerent occupation and the uncertain scope of the State's extra-territorial obligations in this context. Thirdly, the consistency of the Court's approach to testing extra-territorial jurisdiction.

## 2.2 EXTRA-TERRITORIAL JURISDICTION: A PRIMER

This section introduces the two main types of extra-territorial jurisdiction, personal jurisdiction and spatial jurisdiction. A substantial disclaimer is required. The simple division described here between personal and spatial jurisdiction, while appropriate for a general introduction and functional at the level of principle, belies the complexity of the Court's jurisprudence. This chapter clearly demonstrates that these models of jurisdiction are not always applied consistently, the result has been a gradual blurring of the boundaries between these two main types. It is argued later that the Court has created an intermediate category of jurisdiction in *Al-Skeini and Others* v. *United Kingdom*.

### 2.2.1 *Personal Jurisdiction*

The earliest cases dealing with extra-territorial jurisdiction in the European Convention's system relate to what is commonly referred to as personal jurisdiction or State agent authority jurisdiction.[1] This type of jurisdiction arises where the State agents of a contracting State exercise authority and control over an individual abroad. The first examples of this form of jurisdiction arise, unsurprisingly, in the context of diplomacy. The 1965 Commission decision of X v. *Federal Republic of Germany* offers an example of this type of jurisdiction. The facts of the case are unimportant, but the principle established is. The Commission stated:

> in certain respects the nationals of a contracting state are within its 'jurisdiction' even when domiciled or resident abroad [...] in particular the diplomatic and consular representatives of their country of origin perform certain duties with regard to them which may in certain circumstances make that country liable in respect of the convention.[2]

The Commission's approach is followed in the later case of X v. *United Kingdom* and *WM* v. *Denmark*.[3]

[1] This approach to jurisdiction is mirrored within the Inter-American system of human rights protection where personal jurisdiction predominates, see *Coard et al.* v. *United States* Report No 109/99 IAComHR 29 September 1999 at [37]; Oona A. Hathaway and others, 'Human Rights Abroad: When Do Human Rights Treaty Obligations Apply Extraterritorially?' (2011) 43 *Arizona State Law Journal* 389, 414; Sarah H. Cleveland, 'Embedded International Law and the Constitution Abroad' (2010) 110 *Columbia Law Review* 225, 251.

[2] X v. *Federal Republic of Germany* App no 1611/62 (EComHR, 25 September 1965).

[3] X v. *United Kingdom* App no 7547/76 (EComHR, 15 December 1977); *W.M.* v. *Denmark* (1993) 15 EHRR CD28; see also Sarah Miller, 'Revisiting Extraterritorial Jurisdiction: A Territorial Justification for Extraterritorial Jurisdiction under the European Convention' (2009) 20 EJIL 1223, 1238–40.

A strong line of case law applying this principle also develops from extra-judicial transfers of suspected criminals. In these cases, State agents from contracting States travel to another State, which is not party to the Convention, to capture and return an individual to face trial in the contracting State. One of the earliest examples, from 1980, is the arrest of Franco Freda in Costa Rica. In that case the applicant was taken into custody by local police before being handed over to Italian authorities. The Commission stated that the applicant was:

> from the time of being handed over in fact under the authority of the Italian State and thus within the 'jurisdiction' of that country, even if this authority was in the circumstances exercised abroad.[4]

The Commission used virtually identical language in a 1989 decision concerning the extra-judicial transfer of Luc Reinette from Saint Vincent to France,[5] and in the 1994 decision concerning the transfer of Ilich Sanchez Ramirez from Sudan to France.[6] The creation of jurisdictional links through such acts was settled case law by the time the former Kurdistan Workers Party (PKK) leader Abdullah Ocalan was arrested by members of the Turkish security forces inside a Turkish aircraft in the international zone of Nairobi Airport. The Grand Chamber endorses the Commission's earlier decisions noting:

> It is common ground that, directly after being handed over to the Turkish officials by the Kenyan officials, the applicant was under effective Turkish authority and therefore within the 'jurisdiction' of that State for the purposes of Article 1 of the Convention, even though in this instance Turkey exercised its authority outside its territory.[7]

The pivotal factor in these cases is the extent of the factual control exercised by the State and not the State's legal capacity to act.[8] In each of the extra-judicial transfer cases, for example, the applicants challenged the legality of State agents' actions, either contending that the correct extradition procedure

4 *Freda* v. *Italy* App no 8916/80 (EComHR, 7 October 1980).

5 *Reinette* v. *France* App no 14009/88 (EComHR, 2 October 1989).

6 *Sanchez Ramirez* v. *France* App no 28780/95 (EComHR, 24 June 1996).

7 *Ocalan* v. *Turkey (Merits)* (2005) 41 EHRR 45 at [91].

8 See *Al-Skeini and Others* v. *United Kingdom* (2011) 53 EHRR 18 at [136]; Michael Duttwiler, 'Authority, Control and Jurisdiction in the Extraterritorial Application of the European Convention on Human Rights' (2012) 30 NQHR 137, 139–41; Nehal Bhuta, 'Conflicting International Obligations and the Risk of Torture and Unfair Trial: Critical Comments on R. (Al-Saadoon and Mufdhi) v. Secretary of State for Defence and Al-Saadoon and Mufdhi v. United Kingdom' (2009) 7 *Journal of International Criminal Justice* 1133, 1138; Mirja Trilsch and Alexandra Ruth, '*Bankovic* v. *Belgium*' (2003) 97 AJIL 168, 171.

was not followed,[9] or that they were unlawfully detained.[10] The response of the Court and the Commission was to focus on factual control, repeatedly using the term 'in fact under the authority' of the contracting State, the legality of the State's actions was not considered relevant.

### 2.2.2 *Personal Jurisdiction and Military Personnel*

The personal jurisdiction approach is applied directly to military personnel during a military operation in the case of *Cyprus* v. *Turkey*. In that case, Cyprus brought two applications to the Commission and the Court concerning the Turkish invasion of Cyprus on 20 July 1974. The applications alleged that Turkish soldiers had committed a series of human rights violations during the invasion and subsequent occupation of Northern Cyprus. While analysing Turkish responsibility for the acts of the soldiers in Cyprus, the Commission declared:

> authorised agents of a State, including diplomatic or consular agents bring other persons or property within the jurisdiction of that State to the extent that they exercise authority over such persons or property.[11]

As the Turkish State did not dispute that the Turkish soldiers were under its control, the Commission made a very clear statement in its report on the case concerning the Turkey's liability for their actions:

> It follows that these armed forces are authorised agents of Turkey and that they bring any other persons or property in Cyprus 'within the jurisdiction' of Turkey, in the sense of Article 1 of the Convention, to the extent that they exercise control over such persons or property. Therefore, in so far as these armed forces, by their acts or omissions, affect such persons' rights or freedoms under the Convention, the responsibility of Turkey is engaged.[12]

From these relatively straightforward origins we see a range of complexities arise in subsequent cases – how is control over persons or property defined? Must the State guarantee all the rights in the Convention in this context? Are instantaneous acts, such as the firing of a weapon or missile, sufficient to trigger a State's jurisdiction? These issues will be explored further below,

[9] *Reinette* v. *France* App no 14009/88 (EComHR, 2 October 1989); *Sanchez Ramirez* v. *France* App no 28780/95 (EComHR, 24 June 1996).

[10] *Freda* v. *Italy* App no 8916/80 (EComHR, 7 October 1980); *Ocalan* v. *Turkey (Merits)* (2005) 41 EHRR 45.

[11] *Cyprus* v. *Turkey* (1982) 4 EHRR 482 at [83].

[12] *Cyprus* v. *Turkey* (1975) 31 DR 125, 137.

but first the Court's other main approach to extra-territorial jurisdiction, spatial jurisdiction, will be introduced.

### 2.2.3 *Spatial Jurisdiction*

The second main type of extra-territorial jurisdiction is commonly referred to as spatial jurisdiction or jurisdiction arising from effective control over an area.[13] This form of jurisdiction developed as a direct response to the circumstances of Northern Cyprus and is first mentioned by the Court in the case of *Loizidou* v. *Turkey*.[14] In that case, the applicant owned property in Northern Cyprus and was prevented from accessing it following the Turkish invasion of Cyprus and the de facto partition of the island. She alleged that Turkey was responsible for denying her peaceful enjoyment of her property. The Court had to decide whether territory in Northern Cyprus, which was occupied by Turkey since the 1970s, came within the jurisdiction of Turkey for the purposes of Article 1. Turkey argued that it was not exercising jurisdiction because the acts in question were not committed by Turkish State agents, they were attributable to an autonomous local administration installed in 1983, the Turkish Republic of Northern Cyprus (TRNC).[15] The Court could potentially have viewed the TRNC agents as acting on behalf of Turkey as de facto State agents, thereby triggering a personal jurisdictional link to the State.[16] The Court instead opted to develop another approach to extra-territorial jurisdiction stating:

> the responsibility of a Contracting Party may also arise when as a consequence of military action – whether lawful or unlawful – it exercises effective control of an area outside its national territory. The obligation to secure, in such an area, the rights and freedoms set out in the Convention, derives from the fact of such control whether it be exercised directly, through its armed forces, or through a subordinate local administration.[17]

The jurisdictional link arises because the State is controlling an area or piece of territory rather than individual people. It is worth emphasising that the focus is on de facto control, as it was in personal jurisdiction, the jurisdictional

[13] See, for example, Marko Milanovic, 'Al-Skeini and Al-Jedda in Strasbourg' (2012) 23 EJIL 121, 122; Ralph Wilde, 'The Extraterritorial Application of International Human Rights Law on Civil and Political Rights' in S Sheeran and N Rodley, *Routledge Handbook of International Human Rights Law* (Routledge 2013) 641; Lea Raible, 'The Extraterritoriality of the ECHR: Why Jaloud and Pisari Should be Read as Game Changers' [2016] EHRLR 161, 163.

[14] *Loizidou* v. *Turkey (Preliminary Objections)* (1995) 20 EHRR 99.

[15] Ibid at [47].

[16] *Stocke* v. *Germany* (1991) 13 EHRR CD126 at [168].

[17] *Loizidou* v. *Turkey (Preliminary Objections)* (1995) 20 EHRR 99 at [62].

link derives 'from the fact of such control'. The legality, 'whether lawful or unlawful', is irrelevant to the Court.[18] The Court also refers to the rights and freedoms in general, implying that the State must guarantee all the rights and freedoms in the Convention.[19] The Court later confirms this in the case of *Cyprus* v. *Turkey* stating:

> Having effective overall control over northern Cyprus [...] Turkey's 'jurisdiction' must be considered to extend to securing the entire range of substantive rights set out in the Convention and those additional Protocols which she has ratified.[20]

The Court refers directly to substantive rights without mentioning procedural rights, although it has since applied the procedural rights in Article 2, to investigate suspicious deaths, extra-territorially.[21] It is reasonable to assume that they must also be guaranteed.

Both spatial and personal jurisdiction models established relatively straightforward rules concerning extra-territorial jurisdiction. However, as time progressed, the Court's approach to extra-territorial jurisdiction became increasingly inconsistent.[22] The overarching trend has been to apply the Convention to extra-territorial military operations, but the basis for the State's liability and the scope of their obligations have become increasingly uncertain and much of this uncertainty stems from a single case – *Bankovic* v. *Belgium and Others*.[23]

## 2.3 BANKOVIC

The *Bankovic* case concerned the bombing of a television and radio headquarters in Belgrade by NATO aircraft in 1999. Five of the applicants were relatives of people killed in the bombing, while the sixth applicant was injured in the bombing. They took a case against the contracting States who were NATO members participating in the joint military operation against Serbia. The applicants

[18] Matthew Happold, 'Bankovic v. Belgium and the Territorial Scope of the European Convention on Human Rights' (2003) 3 HRLR 77, 86–7.

[19] Noam Lubell, 'Human Rights Obligations in Military Occupation' (2012) 94 IRRC 317, 320.

[20] *Cyprus* v. *Turkey* (2002) 35 EHRR 30 at [77].

[21] *Al-Skeini and Others* v. *United Kingdom* (2011) 53 EHRR 18; *Jaloud* v. *Netherlands* (2015) 60 EHRR 29.

[22] This inconsistency has drawn scathing criticism from the British judiciary and even from some judges at European Court of Human Rights itself. See *R (Al-Skeini)* v. *Secretary of State for Defence* [2005] EWCA Civ 1609 at [193]; *R (Al-Skeini)* v. *Secretary of State for Defence* [2007] UKHL 26 at [67]; concurring opinion of Judge Bonello *Al-Skeini* v. *United Kingdom* (2011) 53 EHRR 18.

[23] *Bankovic and Others* v. *Belgium and Others* (2007) 44 EHRR SE5.

alleged multiple violations of the Convention, including Article 2, the right to life. The case marked a significant departure from the Court's early jurisprudence on extra-territorial jurisdiction and is a significant source of inconsistency. Some of the inconsistencies were cleared up in the subsequent seminal judgment of *Al-Skeini and Others* v. *United Kingdom*,[24] though that case gave rise to inconsistencies of its own and issues arising from *Bankovic* still linger in the jurisprudence as the rest of this chapter will demonstrate. It is worth briefly outlining the findings in *Bankovic* before delving deeper into them.

Firstly, *Bankovic* reflected a shift in interpretation of the term 'jurisdiction' away from the Court's earlier jurisprudence and toward the understanding of that term in general international law. Secondly, a shift in mindset occurred whereby extra-territorial jurisdiction was no longer seen as a natural consequence of the actions of State agents abroad and was instead viewed as exceptional and requiring special justification. Thirdly, the Court advanced an idea that the Convention could only be applicable in the legal space or 'espace juridique' of the Contracting States. Finally, the central issue in the case, the Court ruled that instantaneous acts of a contracting States' armed forces overseas would not trigger that State's jurisdiction and its responsibility for violations of the Convention arising from the acts would not be engaged.

### 2.3.1 *The Court's Understanding of Jurisdiction*

The first significant shift is in the Court's approach to interpreting the word 'jurisdiction'. In the cases before *Bankovic*, the Court focused on de facto control as the basis for jurisdiction. In *Bankovic*, the Court interpreted extra-territorial jurisdiction under the Convention by reference to legal bases for the exercise of extra-territorial jurisdiction under general international law:

> While international law does not exclude a state's exercise of jurisdiction extra-territorially, the suggested bases of such jurisdiction (including nationality, flag, diplomatic and consular relations, effect, protection, passive personality and universality) are, as a general rule, defined and limited by the sovereign territorial rights of the other relevant states.[25]

The types of extra-territorial jurisdiction mentioned in the quote describe the circumstances in which States are *legally* permitted to extend the application

[24] *Al-Skeini* v. *United Kingdom* (2011) 53 EHRR 18.

[25] *Bankovic and Others* v. *Belgium and Others* (2007) 44 EHRR SE5 at [57]; for a classical statement of these bases of jurisdiction see Draft Convention on Jurisdiction with Respect to Crime (1935) 29 AJIL Supp 439.

of their domestic law in the face of other States' territorial jurisdiction.[26] As noted in the previous chapter, this is not the same as extra-territorial jurisdiction under Article 1 of the Convention, which is derived from factual control and does not depend on any legal authority to act. As Orakhelashvili describes it, jurisdiction under Article 1 is a tool for identifying whether alleged violations of the Convention may be imputable to one or another contracting State.[27] This clearly illustrates some uncertainty concerning the theoretical basis for extra-territorial jurisdiction at the Court, which manifests itself in many forms in the jurisprudence as the following sections illustrate.

### 2.3.2 *Exceptional Jurisdiction*

The pre-*Bankovic* cases illustrated that jurisdiction arose as a natural consequence of the activities of State agents abroad. The position is clearly illustrated in the Commission's decision in *Cyprus* v. *Turkey*:

> In Art. 1 of the Convention, the High Contracting Parties undertake to secure the rights and freedoms defined in Section 1 to everyone 'within their jurisdiction' (in the French text: 'relevant de leur juridiction'). The Commission finds that this term is not, as submitted by the respondent Government, equivalent to or limited to the national territory of the High Contracting Party concerned. It is clear from the language, in particular of the French text, and the object of this Article, and from the purpose of the Convention as a whole, that the High Contracting Parties are bound to secure the said rights and freedoms to all persons under their actual authority and responsibility, whether that authority is exercised within their own territory or abroad.[28]

The *Bankovic* case represents a departure from that precedent and a change in mindset. In *Bankovic*, the Court views extra-territorial jurisdiction as exceptional and requiring special justification:

> Article 1 of the Convention must be considered to reflect this ordinary and essentially territorial notion of jurisdiction, other bases of jurisdiction being exceptional and requiring special justification.[29]

[26] See Chapter 1 – Section 1.2. For a comprehensive analysis of this issue see Alexander Orakhelashvili, 'Restrictive Interpretation of Human Rights Treaties in the Recent Jurisprudence of the European Court of Human Rights' (2003) 14 EJIL 529, 539–42; Marko Milanovic, 'From Compromise to Principle: Clarifying the Concept of State Jurisdiction in Human Rights Treaties' (2008) 8 HRLR 411, 420–2; Happold (n. 18) 87; Kerem Altiparmak, '*Bankovic*: An Obstacle to the Application of the European Convention on Human Rights in Iraq?' (2004) 9 *Journal of Conflict & Security Law* 213, 223–4.

[27] Orakhelashvili (n. 26) 540.

[28] *Cyprus* v. *Turkey* App no 6780/74 & 6950/75) (1975) 31 DR 125, 136.

[29] *Bankovic and Others* v. *Belgium and Others* (2007) 44 EHRR SE5 at [59].

There is a clear shift from the territorial agnosticism of jurisdiction in the earlier jurisprudence to this focus on territory. This change in mindset leads the Court both to limit the application of the Convention to the *espace juridique* of the contracting States and to refuse to apply it to instantaneous acts. There are a few points to unpick here. The Court is right that extra-territorial jurisdiction is exceptional, but only in the sense that the majority of the State's activities regulated by the Convention will take place within its territory. We need to be careful not to draw further conclusions from this factual description by demanding special justifications for this type of jurisdiction. Just because jurisdiction is 'primarily territorial',[30] does not mean that it cannot also be exercised in one form or another outside a State's territory,[31] or that jurisdiction should not flow as a natural consequence from the activities of State agents abroad.

### 2.3.3 *Espace Juridique*

The focus on territory leads the Court to curtail the application of the Convention to the *espace juridique* of the contracting States, noting:

> the Convention is a multi-lateral treaty operating [...] in an essentially regional context and notably in the legal space (*espace juridique*) of the Contracting States. The [Federal Republic of Yugoslavia] clearly does not fall within this legal space. The Convention was not designed to be applied throughout the world, even in respect of the conduct of Contracting States.[32]

In the previous chapter, there was evident confusion over the circumstances in which obligations would be owed to people in territory over which contracting States had lost control. This uncertainty is mirrored here with the *espace juridique* comment running counter to both the Convention wording and States' expectations. The idea that the State in which an extra-territorial act occurs and the State responsible for the act must both be contracting parties to the Convention before the Convention can regulate the activities of the acting State is obviously at odds with the previous jurisprudence on extra-territorial jurisdiction, under which jurisdiction arose wherever State agents were acting. Even on a technical level, the Convention was clearly intended to have the *potential* to apply throughout the world, otherwise the drafters

[30] Ibid at [57].

[31] Loukis Loucaides, 'Determining the Extra-Territorial Effect of the European Convention: Facts, Jurisprudence and the Bankovic case' [2006] EHRLR 391, 395.

[32] *Bankovic and Others* v. *Belgium and Others* (2007) 44 EHRR SE5 at [78].

would not have included an express provision in Article 56 permitting it to apply to the overseas territories of contracting States.[33] The comment prompted extensive academic commentary.[34] The Court's approach drew criticism for apparently permitting States to adopt different, lower standards abroad than they applied 'at home'.[35] It was also relied upon in at least one domestic case to deny the existence of extra-territorial jurisdiction.[36]

The Court resiled from the *espace juridique* approach quickly. In the context of personal jurisdiction, the *espace juridique* restriction was not even considered in *Ocalan* v. *Turkey*, where the Convention was held to apply to extra-territorial acts of Turkish agents in Kenya.[37] It was then expressly disavowed in the case of *Pad* v. *Turkey*.[38] In that case, Turkish military forces were patrolling the border between Turkey and Iran when two Turkish helicopters opened fire on some suspected smugglers, killing them. It was unclear whether the smugglers were within Turkish or Iranian territory at the time, but Turkey did not dispute that they came within Turkish jurisdiction. We will return to discuss this case in relation to instantaneous acts below, but at this point the Court's statement on the *espace juridique* point is instructive:

> a State may be held accountable for violations of the Convention rights and freedoms of persons who are in the territory of another State which does not necessarily fall within the legal space of the Contracting States, but who are found to be under the former State's authority and control through its agents operating – whether lawfully or unlawfully – in the latter State.[39]

The Court implicitly disavowed the *espace juridique* restriction in the context of spatial jurisdiction in the case of *Issa* v. *Turkey*.[40] In that case, the applicants

33 Loucaides (n. 31) 398–9.

34 Rick Lawson, 'Really Out of Sight? Issues of Jurisdiction and Control in Situations of Armed Conflict under the ECHR' in Antoine Buyse (ed), *Margins of Conflict: The ECHR and Transitions to and from Armed Conflict* (Hart 2011) 75; Guglielmo Verdirame, 'Human Rights in Wartime: A Framework for Analysis' [2008] EHRLR 689, 696; Efthymios Papastavradis, 'European Court of Human Rights: Medvedyev et al. v. France (Grand Chamber, application no.3394/03) judgment of 29 March 2010' (2010) 59 ICLQ 867, 870; Nuala Mole, 'Issa v. Turkey: Delineating the Extra Territorial Effect of the European Convention on Human Rights?' [2005] EHRLR 86, 89–90.

35 Happold (n. 18) 88; Philip Leach, 'The British Military in Iraq – The Applicability of the Espace Juridique Doctrine under the European Convention on Human Rights' [2005] *Public Law* 448, 450–1.

36 *R. (Al Skeini)* v. *Secretary of State for Defence* [2004] EWHC 2911 (Admin) at [274]–[277].

37 *Ocalan* v. *Turkey* (2003) 37 EHRR 10.

38 *Pad* v. *Turkey* App no 60167/00 (ECtHR, 28 June 2007).

39 Ibid at [53].

40 *Issa* v. *Turkey* (2005) 41 EHRR 27.

alleged that Turkish military forces had crossed the border into Northern Iraq and detained their relatives. The applicants alleged that their relatives were ill-treated and killed by Turkish military forces after their detention. The Court considered whether the applicant's relatives fell within Turkey's jurisdiction stating that it:

> does not exclude the possibility that, as a consequence of this military action, the respondent State could be considered to have exercised, temporarily, effective overall control of a particular portion of the territory of northern Iraq. Accordingly, if there is a sufficient factual basis for holding that, at the relevant time, the victims were within that specific area, it would follow logically that they were within the jurisdiction of Turkey (and not that of Iraq, which is not a Contracting State and clearly does not fall within the legal space of the Contracting States.[41]

While the Court ultimately determined that there was insufficient evidence to conclude that Turkey had conducted military operations in that area at the time, it was prepared to accept that spatial jurisdiction could arise in Northern Iraq, which is outside the *espace juridique*.[42] The Court conclusively discarded the *espace juridique* limitation in the case of *Al-Skeini* v. *United Kingdom*.[43]

### 2.3.4 *Instantaneous Acts*

At its heart, *Bankovic* was a case about collateral damage, incidental damage to non-combatants resulting from combat action against a legitimate military objective.[44] In the Convention system, this issue was transmuted into a question of whether an instantaneous act of a contracting State's armed forces outside its territory, such as bombing a television and radio station

[41] Ibid at [74].

[42] Barbara Miltner, 'Broadening the Scope of Extraterritorial Application of the European Convention on Human Rights?' [2007] EHRLR 172, 176–7; Mole, (n. 34) 90–1.

[43] *Al-Skeini and Others* v. *United Kingdom* (2011) 53 EHRR 18 at [142]. The Court here endorses explanations for the *espace juridique* comment provided by O'Boyle, 'The European Convention on Human Rights and Extraterritorial Jurisdiction: A Comment on "Life After Bankovic"' in Kamminga & Coomans, *Extraterritorial Application of Human Rights Treaties* (Intersentia 2004) 137; See also Ralph Wilde, 'The "Legal Space" or "Espace Juridique" of the European Convention on Human Rights: Is it Relevant to Extraterritorial State Action?' [2005] EHRLR 115, 118.

[44] The validity of the action must be assessed under various fundamental principles of IHL, particularly the principles of distinction (Art. 48, 51(2) and 52(2), proportionality (Art. 51(5)(b) and 57) and precaution in attack (Art. 57(1) Protocol Additional to the Geneva Conventions of 12 August 1949, and relating to the Protection of Victims of International Armed Conflicts (adopted 8 June 1977, entered into force 7 December 1979) 1125 UNTS 3.

in Belgrade, could create a jurisdictional link to that contracting State and lead to its responsibility for violations of the Convention arising from that act. The personal jurisdiction model should support such a jurisdictional link. The Inter-American Commission, for example, relied on the personal jurisdiction model to establish a jurisdictional link when a Cuban military aircraft shot down a civilian aircraft in international airspace in the case of *Alejandre* v. *Cuba*,[45] which was decided before *Bankovic*. However, the Court in *Bankovic* clearly denied that such jurisdictional links could be established under the Convention stating:

> the applicants' submission is tantamount to arguing that anyone adversely affected by an act imputable to a Contracting State, wherever in the world that act may have been committed or its consequences felt, is thereby brought within the jurisdiction of that State for the purpose of Article 1 of the Convention. The Court is inclined to agree with the Governments' submission that the text of Article 1 does not accommodate such an approach to 'jurisdiction'.[46]

While some voiced support for the logic of the Court's approach,[47] the decision drew significant criticism from others. It has been argued that whether the State kills a person with a missile or detains them, it is still exercising power and control over them and drawing distinctions between the two is arbitrary.[48] One former Court judge described the Court's ruling on instantaneous acts as a 'ludicrous result',[49] while others argued it created a perverse incentive for States to shoot people, rather than attempting to capture and arrest them, in

45 In this case the act of firing on the aircraft was considered to amount to an exercise of authority for the purposes of personal jurisdiction – *Alejandre* v. *Cuba* Report No 86/99 IAComHR 29 September 1999 at [25]; Cerna argues the Inter-American Commission took a similar approach in *Salas and Others* v. *United States* Report No 31/93 IAComHR 14 October 1993 at [6] – Christina Cerna, 'Out of Bounds? The Approach of the Inter-American System for the Promotion and Protection of Human Rights to the Extraterritorial Application of Human Rights Law' [2006] 6/2006 Center for Human Rights and Global Justice Working Papers 1, 14. Cerone has criticised the decision arguing that the threshold for responsibility is too low in *Alejandre* and any intentional infringement by a State of an individuals' rights anywhere would be sufficient to bring those individuals within the State's jurisdiction – John Cerone, 'Jurisdiction and Power: The Intersection of Human Rights Law and the Law of Non-International Armed Conflict in an Extraterritorial Context' (2007) 40 *Israel Law Review* 396, 425–6.

46 *Bankovic and Others* v. *Belgium and Others* (2007) 44 EHRR SE5 at [73].

47 Raible (n. 13) 166.

48 Milanovic, 'Al-Skeini and Al-Jedda in Strasbourg' (n. 13) 129; *R. (Al-Saadoon)* v. *Secretary of State for Defence* [2015] EWHC 715 (Admin) at [95]–[98].

49 Loucaides (n. 31) 400.

order to avoid a jurisdictional link.[50] Such a distinction is anathema to the objectives of human rights law.

The jurisprudence on instantaneous acts post-*Bankovic* has, perhaps unsurprisingly, been extremely inconsistent. In the case of *Pad*, mentioned above, when the helicopters opened fire on the suspected smugglers it was unclear which side of the Iran-Turkey border the suspected smugglers were on when they were killed, but Turkey did not dispute that they came within Turkish jurisdiction. The Court held that it was unnecessary to determine the exact location, as Turkey had already admitted that the fire discharged from the helicopters had caused the deaths of the applicants' relatives.[51] In the Court's eyes the fact that the helicopters had fired and caused death created a jurisdictional link to the State. It is hard to see a qualitative difference between a weapon fired from a helicopter over Iran and a missile fired from a plane over Serbia, yet in one case the Court found the location of the helicopter was irrelevant and in the other the plane's location was decisive.

In *Andreou* v. *Turkey*, the applicant was shot while attending a funeral near the UN-patrolled 'buffer zone' between the Turkish-controlled TRNC and the Cypriot southern part of the island. The shot was fired from the North across the buffer zone and hit the applicant on the southern side. Turkey claimed it did not have jurisdiction because the applicant was not on Turkish territory when the alleged violation occurred. The Court noted that the applicant's injuries were caused by Turkish or Turkish-Cypriot uniformed personnel who opened fire and stated that:

> In these circumstances, even though the applicant sustained her injuries in territory over which Turkey exercised no control, the opening of fire on the crowd from close range, which was the direct and immediate cause of those injuries, was such that the applicant must be regarded as 'within [the] jurisdiction' of Turkey within the meaning of Article 1 and that the responsibility of the respondent State under the Convention is in consequence engaged.[52]

The act itself was sufficient to bring the victim within Turkey's jurisdiction. As Lawson notes, it is difficult to maintain that these decisions are faithful to *Bankovic*.[53] These cases were decided by Chambers of the Court, while

50 Dominic McGoldrick, 'Extraterritorial Application of the International Covenant on Civil and Political Rights' in Fons Coomans and Menno Kamminga (eds), *Extraterritorial Application of Human Rights Treaties* (Intersentia 2004), 72; Marko Milanovic, *Extraterritorial Application of Human Rights Treaties: Law, Principles, and Policy* (Oxford University Press 2011) 191.

51 *Pad* v. *Turkey* App no 60167/00 (ECtHR, 28 June 2007) at [54].

52 *Andreou* v. *Turkey* App no 45653/99 (ECtHR, 27 October 2009).

53 Lawson, 'Really Out of Sight?' (n. 34) 70.

*Bankovic* was a decision of the Grand Chamber, which carries more authority in the Strasbourg system. The Grand Chamber continued to hold true to *Bankovic* in *Medvedyev* v. *France*, which concerned a military operation in which French naval forces boarded a Cambodian registered ship suspected of drug smuggling on the high seas and detained the crew. In that case the Grand Chamber referred to instantaneous acts as an 'excluded situation' noting that Article 1 did not admit of a 'cause and effect' notion of 'jurisdiction'.[54] Thus, the *Bankovic* judgment gave rise to serious inconsistencies regarding the extra-territorial application of the Convention.

## 2.4 AL-SKEINI

The later Grand Chamber case of *Al-Skeini and Others* v. *United Kingdom* was intended to clarify the law on extra-territorial jurisdiction after the uncertainty caused by *Bankovic*.[55] In that case, six Iraqi civilians took cases against the UK. They were all relatives of people who had died in Iraq between May 2003 and November 2003 when the UK was in belligerent occupation of Basrah and its environs in South-Eastern Iraq. The UK's soldiers were involved to varying degrees in the deaths of these civilians and their relatives claimed that the UK had an obligation to investigate the deaths of each of their relatives. When an individual has been killed as a result of the use of force by a State agent, the Convention demands some form of effective official investigation.[56] The UK denied that the Convention applied to the occupied territory and this dispute over jurisdiction went to the Grand Chamber of the Court.

In its judgment the Court recapitulated the bases for extra-territorial jurisdiction. Under the heading 'State agent authority and control' (personal jurisdiction), the Court stated that extra-territorial jurisdiction arises in three circumstances. The first is uncontroversial and arises when diplomatic or consular agents of the State exert authority and control over others.[57] The second and third bases are more complex and require further analysis.[58] The next circumstance creating personal jurisdiction arose from the use of force by

54 *Medvedyev* v. *France* (2010) 51 EHRR 39 at [64].

55 *Al-Skeini and Others* v. *United Kingdom* (2011) 53 EHRR 18.

56 *McCann and Others* v. *United Kingdom* (1996) 21 EHRR 97 at [161]; See discussion in Chapter 4.

57 *Al-Skeini and Others* v. *United Kingdom* at [134].

58 The order in which these bases are discussed in this chapter differs from the order the Court uses in the judgment for narrative purposes.

a State's agents operating outside its territory, for example, when the agents apprehend someone abroad.[59] The Court stated:

> the Court's case-law demonstrates that, in certain circumstances, the use of force by a State's agents operating outside its territory may bring the individual thereby brought under the control of the State's authorities into the State's Article 1 jurisdiction. This principle has been applied where an individual is taken into the custody of State agents abroad.[60]

It then cited cases in which people were apprehended and detained extra-territorially.[61] The reference to the 'use of force' here is unusual.[62] The term is normally used to describe the resort to military force by States,[63] or at the individual level, the use of lethal and other forms of force by State agents in a human rights context.[64] In this quote, the Court uses it to describe arrest and detention. Does this mean the use of deadly force by a plane bombing a target is implicitly excluded from this category? The Court also says the use of force 'may bring' a person within the State's jurisdiction, not 'will bring'. This implies that the Court retains some latent discretion over whether or not the person falls within the State's jurisdiction even if State agents use force extra-territorially. There is a huge amount of hedging and conditionality here making it extremely unclear when jurisdiction will arise from such a 'use of force'.

The statement also makes it unclear whether the jurisdictional link arises from the continuous act of holding the person in custody, or the instantaneous act of arresting them. The term 'thereby brought under the control of the State's authorities' could be interpreted to support either conclusion. The distinction may seem trifling, but if the instantaneous act of arrest is the point at which jurisdiction arises, jurisdiction could equally arise from the instantaneous act of firing a missile. If the continuous act of detaining the person

59 *Al-Skeini and Others* v. *United Kingdom* at [136].

60 Ibid at [136].

61 The Court cited *Ocalan* v. *Turkey (Merits)*; *Issa* v. *Turkey* (2005) 41 EHRR 27; *Al-Saadoon and Mufdhi* v. *United Kingdom (Admissibility)* (2009) 49 EHRR SE11 and *Medvedyev* v. *France* (2010) 51 EHRR 39.

62 The Inter-American Commission takes the approach that jurisdiction can arise for a State party to the American Declaration: 'Where it is asserted that a use of military force has resulted in noncombatant deaths, personal injury, and property loss, the human rights of the noncombatants are implicated' – *Salas and Others* v. *United States* at [6].

63 Article 2(4), Charter of the United Nations (adopted 26 June 1945, entered into force 24 October 1945) 1 UNTS 16 (UN Charter).

64 Article 2(1), European Convention on Human Rights 1950 and further discussion in Chapter 3.

creates the jurisdictional link, the opposite conclusion is reached. King argues that the instantaneous act of taking custody triggers the jurisdictional link.[65] The Inter-American Commission has also interpreted this section of *Al-Skeini* to mean that the instantaneous act of apprehension was decisive in creating the jurisdictional link.[66]

The Court referred to another circumstance where jurisdiction could arise, stating that jurisdiction arises when a contracting State 'exercises all or some of the public powers normally to be exercised [by the government of the State]',[67] and within that context, its agents exercise authority and control over a person. The Court then applied this model, which will be referred to as 'personal plus jurisdiction', to the case at hand and held that instantaneous acts of UK soldiers, such as shootings, automatically created a jurisdictional link to the State:

> the United Kingdom [...] assumed in Iraq the exercise of some of the public powers normally to be exercised by a sovereign government. In particular, the United Kingdom assumed authority and responsibility for the maintenance of security in South-East Iraq. In these exceptional circumstances, the Court considers that the United Kingdom, through its soldiers engaged in security operations in Basrah during the period in question, *exercised authority and control over individuals* killed in the course of such security operations, so as to establish a jurisdictional link between the deceased and the United Kingdom for the purposes of Art. 1 of the Convention.[68] (emphasis added)

The key difference between this model and standard personal jurisdiction is that where the State is exercising some public powers overseas, the Court treats the power to kill and the instantaneous act of doing so as 'authority and control' over the individual,[69] which would not meet the test for standard personal jurisdiction if *Bankovic* is good law. This personal plus jurisdiction lies somewhere between spatial jurisdiction, which relies on the exercise of public powers and effective control over areas, and personal jurisdiction, which relies on authority and control over individuals. Lubell has described the Court's approach here as 'a badly mixed cocktail,

[65] Hugh King, 'The Extraterritorial Human Rights Obligations of States' (2009) 9 HRLR 521, 534.
[66] *Ameziane* v. *United States* Report No 17/12 IAComHR 20 March 2012 at [31].
[67] *Al-Skeini and Others* v. *United Kingdom* at [135].
[68] Ibid at [149].
[69] Mads Andenas and Eirik Bjorge, 'Human Rights and Acts by Troops Abroad: Rights and Jurisdictional Restrictions' (2012) 18 *European Public Law* 473, 480.

unsuccessfully attempting to fuse concepts of control over the territory with the question of state agent authority'.[70]

Many commentators viewed *Al-Skeini* as endorsing the *Bankovic* approach to instantaneous acts. Ryngaert argues that *Al-Skeini* re-introduced *Bankovic* through the back door, by demanding an element of effective control over territory before finding jurisdiction.[71] Cowan also argued that it was unlikely that the Court would come to a different result deciding *Bankovic* now.[72] We should perhaps be more cautious in our appraisal. The Court did not have to decide a *Bankovic*-type scenario in *Al-Skeini* and it is unclear what influence previous cases like *Pad* and *Andreou* would have on the outcome of a future *Bankovic*-type case.[73] The Court's approach in *Bankovic* has also been the subject of extensive academic criticism, which the Court may address in a future *Bankovic*-type case.

### 2.4.1 *Instantaneous Acts after Al-Skeini*

There is considerable doubt in the jurisprudence of the Court over the circumstances in which instantaneous acts give rise to State jurisdiction following *Al-Skeini* and other cases. The cases of *Pisari* v. *Russia and Moldova* and *Jaloud* v. *the Netherlands* are further illustrations of jurisdiction apparently arising from instantaneous acts.[74] Both cases involved checkpoints manned by foreign troops and remarkably similar fact patterns.

In *Pisari*, the applicant's son drove through a checkpoint on the Dniester river in Moldova without stopping. The checkpoint was manned by a combination of Russian, Moldovan and MRT soldiers. A Russian soldier opened fire on the vehicle as it drove away, hitting the applicant's son, who later died in hospital. The Russian authorities accepted that the applicant's son fell within their jurisdiction for the purposes of the Convention. The Court determined that the extra-territorial use of force by State agents may bring an individual within a State's jurisdiction, which 'may include the exercise of extra-territorial jurisdiction by a Contracting State when, in accordance with custom, treaty or other agreement, its authorities carry out executive functions

[70] Lubell (n. 19) 321.

[71] Cedric Ryngaert, 'Clarifying the Extraterritorial Application of the European Convention on Human Rights' (2012) 28 *Utrecht Journal of International and European Law* 57, 59.

[72] Anna Cowan, 'A New Watershed? Re-evaluating Bankovic in light of Al-Skeini' (2012) 1 *Cambridge Journal of International and Comparative Law* 213, 225.

[73] Milanovic, 'Al-Skeini and Al-Jedda in Strasbourg' (n. 13) 131–2.

[74] *Jaloud* v. *Netherlands* (2015) 60 EHRR 29; *Pisari* v. *Moldova and Russia* App no 42139/12 (ECtHR, 21 April 2015).

on the territory of another State'.[75] The fact that the checkpoint was manned and commanded by Russian soldiers in the context of enforcing a peace agreement seems to have been decisive for the Court.

The case seems to be applying personal plus jurisdiction from *Al-Skeini*, there is an instantaneous use of force, opening fire, coupled with the exercise of some public powers, e.g. maintaining peace and security in the context of a peace agreement. The fact that the Court is once again referring to a legally valid basis for acting, the peace treaty, is problematic. This echoes the uncertainty over the theoretical basis for jurisdiction identified above in *Bankovic*.[76] The Court is again looking for a discrete legal basis for the State's actions rather than examining the issue of de facto control. In *Pisari*, the Court leaves the door open to other bases for jurisdiction by utilising the words 'may include', implying that there are other potential circumstances in which an extra-territorial use of force may give rise to a jurisdictional link. The Court also refers to 'other agreements' serving as a source of power to carry out executive functions on the territory of another State, which could clearly include a UN Security Council Resolution (UNSCR). UNSCRs are arguably more powerful than the international agreement grounding Russia's presence in Moldova given that they have the power to override treaties.[77] If a UNSCR authorised the creation of a no-fly zone within the territory of a non-contracting State (e.g. Libya),[78] this could in principle result in instantaneous acts of bombing generating jurisdictional links to the contracting State.

In the case of *Jaloud* v. *Netherlands*, the applicant's son was shot at a checkpoint in South-Eastern Iraq in April 2004. The car he was in approached a checkpoint manned by Dutch and Iraqi soldiers at high speed. The soldiers opened fire on the car, killing the applicant's son. While the Netherlands troops were not occupying powers in Iraq at the time the incident occurred, the Court concluded that 'the Netherlands assumed responsibility for providing security in that area, to the exclusion of other participating States, and retained full command over its contingent there'.[79] The Court concluded that *Jaloud* was:

> fired upon while passing through a checkpoint manned by personnel under the command and direct supervision of a Netherlands Royal Army officer [...] the respondent Party exercised its 'jurisdiction' within the

[75] *Pisari* v. *Moldova and Russia* App no 42139/12 (ECtHR, 21 April 2015) at [33].

[76] See Section 2.3.1 above.

[77] Article 103, UN Charter 1945.

[78] See, for example, UNSC Res 1973 (17 March 2011) UN Doc S/RES/1973.

[79] *Jaloud* v. *Netherlands* (2015) 60 EHRR 29 at [149].

limits of its [Stabilization Force in Iraq] mission and for the purpose of asserting authority and control over persons passing through the checkpoint.[80]

The exact basis on which the Court establishes jurisdiction here (personal, spatial, personal plus) is not entirely clear,[81] and the Court itself was reticent on the issue. Raible is dismissive of the idea that *Jaloud* can be understood as grounded in spatial jurisdiction, because a checkpoint is too small of an area to count as a form of territory and it can also quite easily be moved around.[82] Ryngaert and Haijer argue that by embracing 'checkpoint jurisdiction' the Court has abandoned its opposition to instantaneous act jurisdiction in all but name.[83] Yet the Court's judgment still falls short of jurisdiction arising purely from instantaneous acts as an element of territorial control, e.g. control over the checkpoint, still seems to be required in conjunction with the instantaneous act.[84] This may be a further example of personal plus jurisdiction as the Court deliberately downplays the significance of belligerent occupation as the basis for jurisdiction here,[85] while emphasising that the Netherlands assumed responsibility for providing security in the area, placing the Netherlands in a position analogous to belligerent occupiers responsible for ensuring public order and safety in *Al-Skeini*.[86] By downplaying the significance of belligerent occupation, the Court is again leaving the door open for jurisdiction to arise outside of that exact context, potentially where a State establishes a no-fly zone.

In concluding our analysis of the relationship between instantaneous acts and jurisdiction, the trend is clear with the Court increasingly applying the Convention to extra-territorial military actions. However, the exact circumstances in which jurisdiction will arise and the basis on which this jurisdiction is grounded remain mysterious and problematic. The Court has been understandably reluctant to fully endorse the consequences of the *Bankovic* ruling. This is evident in the prevarication between the *Andreou*,

80 Ibid at [152].

81 Friederycke Haijer and Cedric Ryngaert, 'Reflections on Jaloud v. the Netherlands' (2015) 19 *Journal of International Peacekeeping* 174, 179–82; Aurel Sari, 'Untangling Extra-Territorial Jurisdiction from International Responsibility in Jaloud v. Netherlands: Old Problem, New Solutions?' (2014) 53 *Military Law and Law of War Review* 287, 301.

82 Raible (n. 13) 164.

83 Haijer and Ryngaert (n. 81) 180.

84 Haijer and Ryngaert (n. 81) 181; Sari, (n. 81) 298.

85 *Jaloud* v. *Netherlands* (2015) 60 EHRR 29 at [142].

86 Although Sari is critical of the Court's findings here, noting the magnitude of the powers assumed by the Netherlands was lower than that attributed to it by the Court, see Sari (n. 81) 299.

*Pad* and *Medvedyev* judgments. However, the *Al-Skeini* judgment, which was expected to bring some clarity to this issue, has not succeeded in clarifying the law. In the subsequent judgments of *Pisari* and *Jaloud*, the Court has been non-committal on the exact source of the jurisdictional link to the contracting State and the law continues to be characterised by a high degree of conditionality, with States not having a clear idea of when an extra-territorial act will give rise to a jurisdictional link for the purposes of the Convention.

### 2.4.2 *Integrity of Convention Obligations*

One of the over-arching themes of this book is that the application of the Convention to military operations has undermined the unity and coherency of the Convention's obligations. The *Bankovic* judgment made a noble attempt to maintain consistency stating:

> the wording of Article 1 does not provide any support for the applicants' suggestion that the positive obligation in Article 1 to secure 'the rights and freedoms defined in Section I of this Convention' can be divided and tailored in accordance with the particular circumstances of the extra-territorial act in question.[87]

However, this approach was later undermined by *Al-Skeini* where the Court made comments concerning the scope of the obligations arising under the personal jurisdiction model. The Court stated:

> It is clear that, whenever the State through its agents exercises control and authority over an individual, and thus jurisdiction, the State is under an obligation under Article 1 to secure to that individual the rights and freedoms under Section 1 of the Convention that are relevant to the situation of that individual. In this sense, therefore, the Convention rights can be 'divided and tailored'.[88]

The Court also looked at the difficulties that the UK faced in upholding their procedural obligations to investigate the deaths of the applicants' relatives, noting the shortages of local pathologists and facilities for autopsies. The Court then stated that 'in circumstances such as these the procedural duty under Article 2 must be applied realistically, to take account of specific problems faced by investigators'.[89] There is a remarkable parallel between this ruling and the *Ilascu* judgment discussed in the previous chapter. Just as the *Ilascu*

87 *Bankovic and Others* v. *Belgium and Others* at [73].
88 *Al-Skeini and Others* v. *United Kingdom* at [137].
89 Ibid at [168].

case created uncertainty over the positive obligations the State owes when it loses de facto control over its *de jure* territory,[90] *Al-Skeini* created uncertainty over the scope of the positive obligation to investigate extra-territorially. The Court in *Ilascu* also stressed that it would not impose an impossible or disproportionate burden on the State in this circumstance,[91] just as the Court indicates that it will apply the law 'realistically' in *Al-Skeini*.

These conclusions introduce a great deal of uncertainty into the law, creating scope for States to argue that they did not consider that a right being claimed was relevant to the applicant's situation or that it was unrealistic to expect the State to uphold the right in the circumstances. The parallels between *Al-Skeini* and the Court's approach to the cases of *Mozer, Ilascu* and *Ivantoc* are obvious.[92] Following *Al-Skeini*, the State cannot be certain how the Convention's obligations will be 'divided and tailored' to its extra-territorial military operation or how exactly the State should discharge its Convention obligations. There are no clear indications from the Court what accommodations will be made here. This subject will be discussed extensively in the following chapters.[93] At this point it is sufficient to note that the State was found to have breached its procedural obligations in *Al-Skeini* and *Jaloud*, suggesting the adjustments for the unique context of those cases may be limited.

### 2.4.3 *Early Occupation*

The previous sections reviewed the impact of *Al-Skeini* on personal jurisdiction examining both instantaneous acts and the dividing and tailoring of obligations, this section considers the impact *Al-Skeini* has had on spatial jurisdiction.

Following the judgment in *Al-Skeini*, States will have difficulty determining the exact scope of their obligations under the Convention as this will depend on the type of jurisdiction the State is considered to be exercising – personal, personal plus or spatial jurisdiction. The most onerous burden arises from spatial jurisdiction, under which the State has:

> the responsibility under Article 1 to secure, within the area under its control, the entire range of substantive rights set out in the Convention and those additional Protocols which it has ratified.[94]

90 See Chapter 1 – Section 1.4 and *Ilascu and Others* v. *Moldova and Russia* at [333].

91 *Ilascu and Others* v. *Moldova and Russia* at [332].

92 See Chapter 1 – Section 1.6.

93 See Chapters 3 and 4.

94 *Al-Skeini and Others* v. *United Kingdom* at [138].

Where personal jurisdiction is engaged, the State is only obliged to secure the rights that are relevant to the situation.[95] As noted above, these rights may be divided and tailored, must be applied realistically by the Court and may exclude instantaneous acts involving the use of force. Where personal plus jurisdiction is engaged, the State can be held responsible for both violations of rights relevant to the applicant's situation and instantaneous acts occurring within the territory that violate the applicant's rights. Determining the exact type of jurisdiction that the State is exercising may be difficult, especially where the State may be exercising spatial jurisdiction. In the early stages of occupation, for example, the State may be exercising spatial, personal or personal plus jurisdiction with the obligations varying depending on the type of jurisdiction. This problem is exacerbated by many things. The first issue is that the tests for each type of jurisdiction overlap. The second issue is that the Court does not consistently apply the test for spatial jurisdiction.

## 2.5 SPATIAL JURISDICTION TESTS

When determining the existence of spatial jurisdiction, the Court considers two elements: whether the contracting State exercised all or some of the public powers normally exercised by the territory's government[96] and whether the State is exercising effective overall control over the territory.[97]

### 2.5.1 *Public Powers*

The relevance of public powers to jurisdiction is first mentioned in *Bankovic*.[98] Public powers are mentioned in passing in a few cases citing *Bankovic*, but the term itself is not defined or directly applied in those cases.[99] The Court

95 Ibid at [137]–[138]; Max Schaefer, 'Al-Skeini and the Elusive Parameters of Extraterritorial Jurisdiction' [2011] EHRLR 566, 578; Barbara Miltner, 'Revisiting Extraterritoriality after Al-Skeini: The ECHR and its Lessons' (2012) 33 *Michigan Journal of International Law* 693, 697.

96 *Bankovic and Others* v. *Belgium and Others* at [69].

97 *Loizidou* v. *Turkey (Merits)* at [56].

98 Rick Lawson, 'Life after Bankovic: On the Extraterritorial Application of the European Convention on Human Rights' in Fons Coomans and Menno Kamminga (eds), *Extraterritorial Application of Human Rights Treaties* (Intersentia 2004) 111; Ralph Wilde, 'Legal "Black Hole"? Extraterritorial State Action and International Treaty Law on Civil and Political Rights' (2005) 26 *Michigan Journal of International Law* 739, 801; Milanovic, 'From Compromise to Principle' (n. 26) 419.

99 *Treska* v. *Albania and Italy* App no 26937/04 (ECtHR, 29 June 2006); *Kalogeropoulou and Others* v. *Greece and Germany* App no 59021/00 (ECtHR, 12 December 2002).

refers to public powers in *Behrami and Saramati* v. *France and Others* where the Court attempted to establish whether individual contracting States, which had contributed forces to the UN-led international administration of Kosovo, were responsible for the removal of mines and security detention there. The Court noted that military control as well as legislative, executive and judicial powers had been vested in international organisations in Kosovo, but not the individual contracting States. It specifically referred to *Bankovic* stating that:

> Kosovo was [...] under the effective control of the international presences which exercised the public powers normally exercised by the Government of the [Former Yugoslav Republic].[100]

The Court was not applying the standard spatial jurisdiction test here,[101] but the definition of public powers as including legislative, executive and judicial powers is sensible.

The exercise of public powers is a factor in determining whether spatial jurisdiction exists and whether personal plus jurisdiction exists.[102] This is problematic because where the State is exercising public powers, it could potentially be found to exercise either form of jurisdiction, the State may not know which and its obligations would differ depending on the type of jurisdiction. In *Al-Skeini*, for example, the Court determined that a jurisdictional link arose partly because of the public powers the UK was exercising namely authority and responsibility for the maintenance of security in Iraq.[103] The Court found this generated personal plus jurisdiction even though it could just as easily have been evidence of spatial jurisdiction. The Court never considered whether spatial jurisdiction was being exercised in *Al-Skeini*.

### 2.5.2 *Effective Control over Territory*

The Court expressly refers to spatial jurisdiction arising where a contracting State exercises effective control of an area outside its national territory as a result of lawful or unlawful military action.[104] One would expect

100 *Behrami* v. *France* (2007) 45 EHRR SE10 at [70].

101 Some have argued that the Court was applying a distinct 'ultimate authority and control' test – Kjetil Mujezinovic Larsen, 'Attribution of Conduct in Peace Operations: The "Ultimate Authority and Control" Test' (2008) 19 EJIL 509, 520–2; Marko Milanovic and Tatjana Papic, 'As bad as It Gets: The European Court of Human Rights's Behrami and Saramati Decision and General International Law' (2009) 58 ICLQ 267, 285–6.

102 *Al-Skeini and Others* v. *United Kingdom* at [149].

103 Ibid.

104 Ibid at [138].

that belligerent occupation should give rise to spatial jurisdiction, indeed a complete overlap should exist between the establishment of a belligerent occupation and spatial jurisdiction. Under IHL, territory is considered occupied when it is placed under the authority of the hostile army and this extends only to the territory where its authority has been established and can be exercised.[105] Both the tests for spatial jurisdiction and whether a State is in belligerent occupation of territory are based on de facto authority and control. As Milanovic notes, 'a belligerent occupation without effective control … is simply no longer an occupation'.[106] Yet in practice belligerent occupations do not seem to automatically trigger spatial jurisdiction and the Court is not testing for spatial jurisdiction consistently. Just as in the previous chapter where the jurisdictional consequences of losing control of territory were unclear between *Assanidze* and *Isayeva*, the jurisdictional consequences of acquiring control over territory outside the contracting State are equally uncertain.

Before *Al-Skeini* went to Strasbourg, the Court of Appeal in England considered whether the UK was exercising spatial jurisdiction in Basrah. The judgment was important because it had a significant bearing on the future hearings,[107] such that by the time the case got to Strasbourg, the European Court did not even consider whether spatial jurisdiction was being exercised. At the time of the events in *Al-Skeini*, the UK and US were recognised as belligerent occupiers of Iraq in a UN Security Council Resolution.[108] As occupation is determined by factual control, which changes over time, the UNSCR could not be determinative of the issue, but the Court of Appeal itself repeatedly acknowledged the UK's status as a belligerent occupier in its judgment.[109] However, the Court of Appeal expressly denied that holding the status of belligerent occupier automatically equated to effective control stating that 'it is a feature of Strasbourg jurisprudence that the court will

[105] Article 42, Hague Convention (IV) Respecting the Laws and Customs of War on Land and Its Annex: Regulations concerning the Laws and Customs of War on Land (adopted 18 October 1907, entered into force 26 January 1910) 205 CTS 277. *Armed Activities on the Territory of the Congo (Democratic Republic of the Congo* v. *Uganda)*, Judgment, ICJ Reports 2005, p. 168 at [173], [176]–[180].

[106] Milanovic, *Extraterritorial Application of Human Rights Treaties: Law, Principles, and Policy* (n. 50) 146.

[107] The Court of Appeal's conclusion that the Convention did not apply to the occupied territory was later upheld by the House of Lords – *R. (Al-Skeini)* v. *Secretary of State for Defence* [2007] UKHL 26 at [83].

[108] UNSC Res. 1483 (May 22, 2003) U.N. Doc. S/RES/1483.

[109] *R. (Al-Skeini)* v. *Secretary of State for Defence* [2005] EWCA Civ 1609 at [12] and [124].

examine the facts of each particular case to see if the requisite control is in fact exercised'.[110] In the past the European Court has referred to a number of indicators of effective control: the strength of the contracting State's military presence on the territory;[111] whether it had a large number of troops there on active duty;[112] whether it patrolled the territory and had checkpoints on main lines of communication;[113] whether the troops had been deployed for a long time;[114] and whether or not the State created and supported a subordinate local administration in the territory.[115] The Court of Appeal applied these elements in its consideration.

The Court of Appeal contrasted the UK's presence in Basrah with Turkish control over Northern Cyprus. It considered the number of troops deployed in each circumstance noting that Turkey had deployed sufficient troops to ensure effective control, but the UK had not deployed enough troops to secure effective control.[116] This seems to be a denial that the UK were in belligerent occupation of Basrah, which is plausible given the insurgency in Iraq at the time and small number of troops deployed. However, it clearly contradicts the Court of Appeal's earlier acceptance that the UK was a belligerent occupier, if the UK was unable to secure effective control, it could not be a belligerent occupier.

The Court of Appeal also considered that Turkey intended to exercise control over the Northern Cyprus on a long-term basis, while the UK intended to transfer responsibility to Iraqi authorities as soon as possible.[117] All belligerent occupations should be transient,[118] this conclusion seems to imply that belligerent occupation alone cannot trigger spatial jurisdiction and that only prolonged occupations/de facto annexations will trigger spatial jurisdiction. The European Court has never expressly stated this must be the case. It also prompts questions concerning the duration of occupation required to trigger spatial jurisdiction.

110 Ibid at [128]; There are echoes of this approach in the more recent Court of Appeal judgment of *R. (Al-Saadoon)* v. *Secretary of State for Defence* [2016] EWCA Civ 811 at [54].
111 *Al-Skeini and Others* v. *United Kingdom* at [139].
112 *Loizidou* v. *Turkey (Merits)* at [56].
113 Ibid at [16].
114 *Issa* v. *Turkey* at [75]; for an opposing view see Leach (n. 35) 454.
115 *Ilascu and Others* v. *Moldova and Russia* at [388].
116 *R. (Al-Skeini)* v. *Secretary of State for Defence* [2005] EWCA Civ 1609 at [121].
117 Ibid at [117].
118 Andrea Carcano, *The Transformation of Occupied Territory in International Law* (Brill 2015) 22–6.

Finally, the Court of Appeal contrasted Turkish control over Northern Cyprus and British control over Basrah on the grounds that Turkey controlled the civilian administration on Northern Cyprus, but the provisional authority governing Iraq was dominated by American personnel and was 'in no sense a subordinate organ or instrument of the UK'.[119] By this logic unless a State exercises total control over the civilian administration, it may not be considered to exercise spatial jurisdiction and by forming coalitions with divided responsibilities the State may avoid the full impact of spatial jurisdiction.

When *Al-Skeini* came before the European Court, the fact that the UK was the supposed belligerent occupier clearly indicated the possible exercise of spatial jurisdiction. The Court even noted that 'the United States and the United Kingdom became occupying powers' in Iraq at the relevant time.[120] It also acknowledged that they 'exercise[d] powers of government temporarily' in Iraq.[121] Yet at no point did the European Court consider whether the UK was exercising spatial jurisdiction in Iraq. It never tested the issue, instead as noted above, it relied on the intermediary form of jurisdiction, personal plus jurisdiction.

The Court has not handled cases of belligerent occupation consistently. In the more recent case of *Chiragov* v. *Armenia*,[122] the Court took a different approach to *Al-Skeini*. That case concerned the district of Lachin, which became part of Azerbaijan's territory after the collapse of the Union of Soviet Socialist Republics (USSR).[123] Armenia and Azerbaijan went to war in the early 1990s over the region of Nagorno-Karabakh, where Lachin is situated. According to the Court, by the end of 1993 ethnic Armenian forces had gained control over almost the entire territory of Nagorno-Karabakh, including Lachin.[124] The applicants were displaced by the conflict and brought a case against Armenia *inter alia* for the loss of peaceful enjoyment of possessions. The Court accepted, as it did previously with Turkey and the TRNC, that the self-proclaimed Nagorno-Karabakh Republic would not exist without the support of Armenia.[125] Thus, the Court concluded that Armenia was heavily

[119] *R. (Al-Skeini)* v. *Secretary of State for Defence* [2005] EWCA Civ 1609 at [119].

[120] *Al-Skeini and Others* v. *United Kingdom* at [143].

[121] Ibid at [144].

[122] *Chiragov* v. *Armenia* (2016) 63 EHRR 9.

[123] Article 5, Minsk Agreement establishing the Commonwealth of Independent States (adopted 8 December 1991, entered into force 22 January 1994) 1819 UNTS 57 states: 'the High Contracting Parties acknowledge and respect each other's territorial integrity and the inviolability of existing borders within the Commonwealth'. Both Azerbaijan and Armenia signed the treaty on 21 December 1991.

[124] *Chiragov* v. *Armenia* (2016) 63 EHRR 9 at [174].

[125] Ibid at [172]–[180].

implicated in the belligerent occupation of territory, which *de jure* belonged to Azerbaijan. The difference in approach between this case and *Al-Skeini* is stark as the Court states:

> The Court first considers that the situation pertaining in Nagorno-Karabakh and the surrounding territories is not one of Armenian State agents exercising authority and control over individuals abroad, as alternatively argued by the applicants. Instead, the issue to be determined on the facts of the case is whether the Republic of Armenia exercised and continues to exercise effective control over the mentioned territories and as a result may be held responsible for the alleged violations [...] to determine whether Armenia has jurisdiction in the present case, it is thus necessary to assess whether it exercises effective control over Nagorno-Karabakh and the surrounding territories as a whole.[126]

Unlike in *Al-Skeini*, the Court completely discounts the possibility of personal jurisdiction in *Chiragov* and correctly assumes that spatial jurisdiction exists in this context.

Just as the Court did not consistently test the State's jurisdiction where control over territory was lost, as noted in the previous chapter in cases like *Azemi* v. *Serbia* and *Ilascu*,[127] the Court is not consistently testing the State's jurisdiction when control is gained over territory. The question is why? Why should the Court treat comparable situations of the armed forces of one State occupying the territory of another State and establishing a governing entity so differently? Why should the Court examine whether spatial jurisdiction exists in *Chiragov*, but not in *Al-Skeini*? The trend at the Court has been to apply the spatial jurisdiction test to cases of prolonged occupation/de facto annexation where both the parties involved are contracting States.[128] However, the Court has never made this an express part of the criteria for finding spatial jurisdiction. Indeed, as noted above, the Court was prepared to accept that effective control of an area could be exercised both on a short term basis and over an area not previously subject to Convention protection in *Issa* v. *Turkey*.[129] Giacca has argued, in the context of economic, social and cultural rights, that a contextual approach should be taken in which 'varying levels of obligations' attach to a State 'depending

[126] Ibid at [169]–[170].

[127] See Chapter 1 – Section 1.4.

[128] See, for example, the TRNC in *Loizidou* v. *Turkey* (Preliminary Objections) (1995) 20 EHRR 99, the Moldovan Republic of Transdniestria in *Ilascu and Others* v. *Moldova and Russia* and Nagorno-Karabakh in *Chiragov* v. *Armenia*.

[129] *Issa* v. *Turkey* (2005) 41 EHRR 27 at [74].

on the degree of control exercised in the territory', thus the effectiveness of occupation becomes the determining factor.[130] This could explain the underlying rationale of both the Court of Appeal and the European Court in *Al-Skeini* and it also offers a tempting compromise. According to this approach, as the insurgency in Iraq undermined the effectiveness of the UK's occupation, it should have led to fewer obligations being imposed on the UK. Although appealing at the level of principle, the uncertainty this would create over the scope and nature of the obligations is deeply undesirable. The State ought to know exactly what its obligations are in a given situation. The differing scope of the obligations between spatial, personal and personal plus jurisdiction is already considerable and introducing further variations within spatial jurisdiction would only exacerbate the situation. Even if this was the Court's position, it should not preclude the Court from testing whether spatial jurisdiction exists.

The Court attempted to explain why it did not test whether spatial jurisdiction existed in *Al-Skeini* in the case of *Hassan* v. *United Kingdom*.[131] The *Hassan* case illustrates the problems that arise in determining the type of jurisdiction being exercised during the early stages of occupation. In *Hassan*, the applicant's brother was captured by UK forces in Basrah in April 2003 and detained in a US-run detention facility, before he was allegedly released. His dead body was found in September 2003 and showed evidence that he had been subject to ill-treatment before his death. The applicant complained that his brother's arrest and detention were unlawful and that the UK had failed to carry out an effective investigation into the circumstances of his detention, ill-treatment and death. The substantive elements of the case will be discussed in later chapters,[132] for now the issue of jurisdiction is paramount.

The British forces had taken control of Basrah by 5 April 2003 and began arresting officials there. It was around this time that Hassan was captured. The UK argued that personal jurisdiction did not apply during the active hostilities phase of an international armed conflict and that because 'major combat operations' were not deemed to be complete until 1 May 2003, it was not in belligerent occupation and was not exercising spatial jurisdiction.[133] Even though the alleged violation in *Hassan* took place during the active

[130] Gilles Giacca, *Economic, Social and Cultural Rights in Armed Conflict* (Oxford University Press 2014) 161.

[131] *Hassan* v. *United Kingdom* App no 29750/09 (ECtHR, 16 September 2014).

[132] See Chapter 5.

[133] *Hassan* v. *United Kingdom* App no 29750/09 (ECtHR, 16 September 2014) at [71].

hostilities phase of the conflict, the Court adopted the same approach as it did in *Al-Skeini*, which took place during the occupation period. The Court stated:

> as in *Al-Skeini*, the Court does not find it necessary to decide whether the United Kingdom was in effective control of the area during the relevant period, because it finds that the United Kingdom exercised jurisdiction over Tarek Hassan on another ground.[134]

The Court went on to find the UK was exercising personal jurisdiction over the applicant's brother stating 'Tarek Hassan was within the physical power and control of the United Kingdom soldiers and therefore fell within United Kingdom jurisdiction'.[135] According to the Court it did not examine whether spatial jurisdiction existed in *Al-Skeini* because another ground for jurisdiction was present. There are two problems with this conclusion. Firstly, it is not borne out by the facts. It was not obvious that *Al-Skeini* was a case of personal jurisdiction because many of the applicants were challenging instantaneous extra-territorial acts of violence, which following the rulings of *Medvedyev* and *Bankovic*, ought not to have given rise to personal jurisdiction.[136] This other ground for jurisdiction could not have been apparent because the Court had to bend its rules on personal jurisdiction to accommodate the claims in *Al-Skeini*. Secondly, it is not at all clear why the Court should automatically discount spatial jurisdiction once personal jurisdiction is apparent. Logic dictates that they can both exist and spatial jurisdiction offers much greater protection to applicants, requiring the occupier to guarantee both positive and negative human rights obligations.[137] The Court should not default to the lower level of protection and should be testing whether spatial jurisdiction exists consistently when there is evidence that a contracting State is in belligerent occupation of territory.

## 2.6 CONCLUSION

This chapter began by introducing different types of extra-territorial jurisdiction and proceeded to analyse the developments in the jurisprudence over time. A remarkable picture emerged with the extra-territorial jurisprudence

[134] Ibid at [75].
[135] Ibid at [76].
[136] *Bankovic and Others* v. *Belgium and Others* at [73]; The Court expressly endorsed this conclusion in *Medvedyev* v. *France* (2010) 51 EHRR 39 at [64].
[137] *Al-Skeini and Others* v. *United Kingdom* at [138]; *Catan and Others* v. *Moldova and Russia* at [106].

mirroring the jurisprudence on losing control of territory, falling into many of the same pitfalls we identified in the previous chapter.

Firstly, the jurisdictional consequences of gaining or losing control of territory remain uncertain. In the previous chapter this was evident in the cases of *Isayeva* and *Azemi*. In this chapter, the cases of *Al-Skeini* and *Hassan* reflected similar issues regarding belligerent occupation and spatial jurisdiction. Secondly, the Court is not being consistent in the tests it applies when analysing jurisdiction. This was evident in the previous chapter's analysis of *Azemi*, *Assanidze* and *Isayeva*. In this chapter, a similar problem was identified in *Al-Skeini*, *Hassan* and other cases. Thirdly, the positive obligations owed by the State are unclear across this area of law. In the previous chapter, the cases of *Ilascu*, *Mozer* and *Ivantoc* illustrated how the scope of the positive obligations owed by the State that had lost control over territory were unclear. Similarly, the obligations owed extra-territorially are to be 'divided and tailored' in the wake of *Al-Skeini*, leaving States in the dark as to what the results will be. This issue will be further analysed in the next chapters.

Although similar pitfalls have been identified between both bodies of jurisprudence, it would be wrong to conclude that these pitfalls are an inevitable by-product of applying human rights law to military operations. The problems identified over the preceding chapters are largely of the Court's own making. While there are many unavoidable issues with applying the Convention to military operations, many of the issues identified here can be ameliorated through consistent interpretation and giving State's clearer guidelines on how the Convention will apply to military operations. The following chapter begins to examine issues that are not as easily avoided, specifically the disparity between the substantive provisions of IHL and the Convention's protection of the right to life.

# 3

# Article 2: Substantive Obligations

## 3.1 INTRODUCTION

The previous chapters identified jurisdictional problems which have arisen from the application of the Convention to military operations both at home and abroad. While these problems remain extant, a great deal of attention has been devoted to them already. There is a need to look beyond the questions of whether the law applies toward addressing the significant and real practical problems arising from the application of the Convention to military operations. The next two chapters address the practical problems arising from the application of Article 2 (right to life) to military operations. This chapter looks at the substantive obligations in Article 2 of the Convention, while the following chapter looks at the procedural obligations. Each chapter presents an extended critique of the Court's interpretation and application of Article 2 in the context of military operations.

The chapter begins by clearly setting out the normal Convention standards applied by the Court, such as the condition that force should only be used when absolutely necessary and the positive obligation to protect persons from foreseeable harms. The chapter expands upon the difficulties States will face in upholding these obligations in practice during military operations, in particular extra-territorial military operations. This chapter shows that the application of Article 2 to military operations is weakening the standards applied by the Court. At times these divergent interpretations appear to arise from the implicit application of IHL, but the influence of IHL is far from consistent. Perhaps the most troubling aspect of this development is the haphazard and often contradictory approach the Court takes when interpreting Article 2, which ranks among the most important rights in the Convention.

## 3.2 OBLIGATIONS UNDER ARTICLE 2

Article 2 of the Convention states:

1. Everyone's right to life shall be protected by law. No one shall be deprived of his life intentionally save in the execution of a sentence of a court following his conviction of a crime for which this penalty is provided by law.
2. Deprivation of life shall not be regarded as inflicted in contravention of this Article when it results from the use of force which is no more than absolutely necessary:
   A. In defence of any person from unlawful violence;
   B. In order to effect a lawful arrest or to prevent the escape of a person lawfully detained;
   C. In action lawfully taken for the purpose of quelling a riot or insurrection.

Article 2 contains two sets of obligations, substantive and procedural. The focus of this chapter is on the substantive obligations of Article 2.[1] There is a further sub-division within these obligations along the lines of positive and negative obligations. Negative obligations demand that the State refrain from doing something, e.g. using force where not absolutely necessary. Positive obligations by contrast demand that the State undertake certain actions to proactively safeguard life.[2] In order to understand the difficulties encountered in applying Article 2 to military operations, it is necessary to first understand what those obligations are and how they apply in normal situations. The law on Article 2 has already been set out in detail in many textbooks,[3] there is little benefit in duplicating that analysis and a brief overview to contextualise the discussion is sufficient for present purposes.

The substantive obligations in Article 2 restrict the use of lethal force, demanding that it have as its aim the defence of people from unlawful violence, effecting a lawful arrest or preventing a person lawfully detained

[1] Procedural obligations are discussed further in Chapter 4.

[2] Alastair Mowbray, *The Development of Positive Obligations under the European Convention on Human Rights by the European Court of Human Rights* (Hart 2004) 7.

[3] Bernadette Rainey, Elizabeth Wicks and Clare Ovey, *Jacobs, White and Ovey: the European Convention on Human Rights* (7th edn, Oxford University Press 2017); David Harris, Michael O'Boyle, Ed Bates, Carla Buckley and Colin Warbrick, *Law of the European Convention on Human Rights* (3rd edn, Oxford University Press 2014); Pieter van Dijk, Fried van Hoof, Arjen van Rijn, Leo Zwaak (eds), *Theory and Practice of the European Convention on Human Rights* (5th edn, Intersentia 2018).

from escaping, quelling a riot or insurrection. The State must refrain using lethal force to achieve these aims unless it is absolutely necessary.[4] A State agent using force must honestly believe at the specific moment the force is used, that it is absolutely necessary to achieve one of these aims.[5] In general, this requires that force is used only in response to an immediate threat.[6]

Beyond the individual instance of using force, the State must also make other means available to respond proportionately to different threats.[7] In advance of using lethal force, the State must exhaust other potential means of achieving the aims of Article 2. These other means must be either ineffective or incapable of achieving the desired outcome in the circumstances. In general, the aim and the means used to achieve it must be balanced against each other.[8] The State has a closely related obligation to plan and control operations where force may be used to ensure no more lethal force than is absolutely necessary is used in any given situation.[9] It should also minimise damage and injury to the greatest extent possible in the circumstances.[10] The State has a positive obligation to protect people within its jurisdiction from avoidable loss of life resulting from the criminal acts of private individuals where the State authorities knew, or ought to have known, of a real and immediate risk to the life of the individual and failed to take reasonable measures, within the scope of their powers, to avoid that risk.[11]

## 3.3 THE STANDARD OF NECESSITY

The requirement that any use of force must be absolutely necessary in the Convention is perhaps the most striking difference between IHL and the Convention.[12] IHL broadly speaking permits any attack as long as it is directed at a military target, and proportionate in the sense that it is not expected to cause excessive damage to civilians when compared to the direct military

4 *Nachova* v. *Bulgaria* (2006) 42 EHRR 43 at [94]–[95].
5 *McCann and Others* v. *United Kingdom* (1996) 21 EHRR 97 at [200].
6 *Dimov and Others* v. *Bulgaria* App no 30086/05 (ECtHR, 6 November 2012) at [78].
7 *Giuliani and Gaggio* v. *Italy* (2012) 54 EHRR 10 at [216].
8 *Gulec* v. *Turkey* (1999) 28 EHRR 121 at [71]–[72].
9 *Ergi* v. *Turkey* (2001) 32 EHRR 18 at [79].
10 *Gul* v. *Turkey* (2002) 34 EHRR 28 at [84].
11 *Osman* v. *United Kingdom* (2000) 29 EHRR 245 at [116].
12 Inter-American Commission on Human Rights, *Report on Terrorism and Human Rights* (OEA/SerL/V/II116 Doc 5 rev 1 corr, 2002) at [109].

advantage anticipated.[13] Article 2 of the Convention severely restricts the situations in which force can be used to three scenarios and only when 'absolutely necessary' as a last resort.[14] The State must always attempt to capture the person where possible instead of using lethal force.[15] Lethal force must be a proportionate response to an immediate risk of imminent harm.[16]

Demanding that a State only use force where it is absolutely necessary during an armed conflict could severely hamper the effectiveness of military operations.[17] Academics have struggled, with varying degrees of success, to bridge the divide between the standards. Some argue that a hybrid, unified use of force rule, based predominantly on the standard of absolute necessity in human rights law, should be applied in all circumstances.[18] Others have come at the problem from the other side, interpreting the principles of military necessity and humanity in IHL as requiring States to use minimal amounts of force and avoid killing wherever possible.[19] One obvious solution in the context of the Convention is to take advantage of its derogation clause, which permits derogations from Article 2 for 'lawful acts of war'. Once a State could establish that its acts were legal under IHL, it would not face liability under the Convention for such actions.[20] No State has made use of this part of the derogation clause to date and this possibility is discussed further below and in Chapter 7. Outside of derogation, reconciling the permissive rules of IHL with the restrictive ones of

[13] Article 51, Protocol Additional to the Geneva Conventions of 12 August 1949, and relating to the Protection of Victims of International Armed Conflicts (adopted 8 June 1977, entered into force 7 December 1979) 1125 UNTS 3 (hereinafter Additional Protocol 1); Louise Doswald-Beck and Jean-Marie Henckaerts (eds), *Customary International Humanitarian Law*, 2 vols. (Cambridge University Press 2004) vol I, 46.

[14] Principle 4, United Nations Committee on Crime Prevention Control, *Basic Principles on the Use of Force and Firearms by Law Enforcement Officials* (7 September 1990); See Charles Garraway, '"To Kill or Not to Kill?" – Dilemmas on the Use of Force' (2010) 14 *Journal of Conflict & Security Law* 499, 502.

[15] Christian Tomuschat, Evelyne Lagrange and Stefan Oeter, *The Right to Life* (Martinus Nijhoff 2010) 240.

[16] *Giuliani and Gaggio* v. *Italy* (2012) 54 EHRR 10 at [216]; Similar rules apply in the Inter-American system – *Alejandre* v. *Cuba* Report No 86/99 IAComHR 29 September 1999.

[17] Tomuschat, Lagrange and Oeter (n. 15) 171.

[18] Francisco Martin, 'Using International Human Rights Law for Establishing a Unified Use of Force Rule in the Law of Armed Conflict' (2001) 64 *Saskatchewan Law Review* 347, 370.

[19] Nils Melzer, *Interpretive Guidance on the Notion of Direct Participation in Hostilities under International Humanitarian Law* (International Committee of the Red Cross 2009) 78–82; Jean Pictet, *Development and Principles of International Humanitarian Law* (Martinus Nijhoff 1985) 75.

[20] Elizabeth Wicks, *The Right to Life and Conflicting Interests* (Oxford University Press 2010) 82.

HRL is no easy task and these endeavours have prompted criticism from many sources.[21] So how has the Court handled this issue?

### 3.3.1 *Interpreting Absolute Necessity*

Some authors argue that the Court applies different standards of necessity in different cases. Both Forowicz and Melzer argue that the standard of absolute necessity has been interpreted more liberally in the context of military operations than in times of peace.[22] Droege presents two further contentions, first that the Court 'does not question the right of government forces to attack opposition forces' and second that the Court does not 'require that lethal force be avoided even in the absence of an immediate threat'.[23]

### 3.3.2 *Necessity of Attack*

The truth of Droege's first contention, that the Court does not question the right of government forces to attack opposition forces, is evident in a few cases. *McCann* v. *United Kingdom* exemplifies the standard human rights approach. In that case, the Court examined an incident in which UK security forces opened fire on suspected terrorists in Gibraltar. The Court stated that it must examine whether the authorities 'minimise, to the greatest extent possible, recourse to lethal force'.[24]

The standard applied in other cases is markedly different.[25] In *Ergi* v. *Turkey*, for example, Turkish security forces set up an ambush to attack insurgents in a village in South-East Turkey. The Court examined whether the operation was

[21] Noam Lubell, 'Parallel Application of International Humanitarian Law and International Human Rights Law: An Examination of the Debate' (2007) 40 *Israel Law Review* 648, 654–5; Jordan Paust, 'The Right to Life in Human Rights Law and the Law of War' (2002) 65 *Saskatchewan Law Review* 411; William Hays Parks, 'Part IX of the ICRC "Direct Participation in Hostilities" Study: No Mandate, No Expertise, and Legally Incorrect' (2010) 42 *International Law and Politics* 769; Leslie Green, 'The Unified Use of Force Rule and the Law of Armed Conflict: A Reply to Professor Martin' (2002) 65 *Saskatchewan Law Review* 427.

[22] Nils Melzer, *Targeted Killing in International Law* (Oxford University Press 2009) 386; Magdalena Forowicz, *The Reception of International Law in the European Court of Human Rights* (Oxford University Press 2010) 331.

[23] Cordula Droege, 'Elective Affinities? Human Rights and Humanitarian Law' (2008) 90 IRRC 501, 533.

[24] *McCann and Others* v. *United Kingdom* (1996) 21 EHRR 97 at [194].

[25] See, for example, *Isayeva, Yusupova, Bazayeva* v. *Russia* (2005) 41 EHRR 39 at [177]; *Isayeva* v. *Russia* (2005) 41 EHRR 38 at [176]; *Abuyeva and Others* v. *Russia* App no 27065/05 (ECtHR, 2 December 2010) at [203]; *Damayev* v. *Russia* App no 36150/04 (ECtHR, 29 May 2012) at [60].

planned and conducted 'in such a way as to avoid or minimise, to the greatest extent possible, any risk to the lives of the villagers'.[26] The focus clearly shifts from minimising recourse to the use of force generally in *McCann*, to minimising the risk to the villagers alone in *Ergi*. The Court does not question whether attempts were made to arrest the insurgents or whether an ambush carried out by heavily armed soldiers was the most appropriate way of securing the arrest of the insurgents. Instead, there is a tacit acceptance of the use of force against the insurgents.

The case of *Ahmet Ozkan* v. *Turkey* reveals a similar focus. In that case, over one hundred members of the Turkish security forces surrounded a village in South-East Turkey and began moving toward the village. When they fired warning shots during their approach, fire was returned from some houses within the village. In response, the security forces fired thousands of rounds of ammunition and dozens of grenades at the village. The Court was again focused on 'minimising incidental loss of civilian life'.[27] It ruled that this 'tactical response' of opening 'intensive fire' was absolutely necessary for protecting life.[28] Gioia observes that 'when the Court was faced with a real combat situation, as opposed to a law-enforcement operation, it never took the lives of the combatants into account'.[29]

At no point does the Court expressly refer to IHL in these judgments, there are no references to the Geneva Conventions or NIACs. However, IHL is clearly influencing the Court's approach. The fundamental distinction between human rights law and IHL is that the protection of human rights is inherent and inalienable for 'all members of the human family'.[30] Civilian and combatant are equally entitled to protection of their human rights.[31] As one author put it, legitimising the use of lethal force against a person merely because of their status is 'anathema to human rights law'.[32] Yet, in these cases we see the Court distinguishing between civilians and others, tacitly accepting

[26] *Ergi* v. *Turkey* (2001) 32 EHRR 18 at [79].

[27] *Ahmet Ozkan and Others* v. *Turkey* App no 21689/93 (ECtHR, 6 April 2004) at [297]; See also *Isayeva, Yusupova, Bazayeva* v. *Russia* (2005) 41 EHRR 39 at [177].

[28] *Ahmet Ozkan and Others* v. *Turkey* App no 21689/93 (ECtHR, 6 April 2004) at [305]–[306].

[29] Andrea Gioia, 'The Role of the European Court of Human Rights in Monitoring Compliance with Humanitarian Law in Armed Conflict' in Orna Ben-Naftali (ed), *International Humanitarian Law and International Human Rights Law* (Oxford University Press 2012) 231.

[30] Preamble, Universal Declaration of Human Rights (adopted 10 December 1948) UNGA Res 217 A(III).

[31] Solon Solomon, 'Targeted Killings and the Soldiers' Right to Life' (2007–2008) 14 *ILSA Journal of International & Comparative Law* 99, 108.

[32] David Kretzmer, 'Rethinking the Application of IHL in Non-International Armed Conflicts' (2009) 42 *Israel Law Review* 8, 25.

the use of force against those others. The reference to minimising incidental loss of civilian life directly mirrors IHL standards.[33]

The issue is not the convergence of standards or the interpretation of the Convention in light of IHL, but rather the way the Court goes about this. This fundamental distinction between IHL and human rights law is discarded in an offhand manner with no discussion. The influence of IHL is not expressly acknowledged and there is no clear demarcation of these cases as being exceptional or unusual. When the Court adjusts its standards in this way, it needs to be clear that it is an exception and clearly define the limits to the exception. As Quenivet correctly observes, the way the Court negates a basic tenet of human rights law here is 'rather frightening' and the failure to define civilian is confusing.[34] This approach undermines the unity and coherence of the standard in Article 2, making the adjustments appear arbitrary. It also risks establishing precedents of lower protection, which could be invoked by States outside of the context of military operations. If the State had derogated from Article 2, the Convention standard could have been interpreted in light of IHL so that targeting combatants was not considered unlawful. The derogation would offer a clear contextual barrier for this unusual interpretation, avoiding the risk of establishing lower levels of protection.

### 3.3.3 *Immediate Threats*

Droege's second contention, that the Court permits the use of lethal force in the absence of an immediate threat, is also reflected in the jurisprudence. The case of *Nachova* v. *Bulgaria*, exemplifies the standard human rights approach. In that case, two conscript soldiers went absent without leave from a construction site. Military police were dispatched to capture the unarmed men and fired upon them as they tried to evade arrest. The two men died from bullet wounds sustained during the attempted arrest. The Court stressed that lethal force could only be used where absolutely necessary and no such necessity existed when the person did not pose a serious threat and was not suspected of having committed a violent offence.[35] The use of force was neither qualitatively, nor temporally, necessary and the Court has reached similar findings elsewhere.[36]

33 Article 57(2)(a), Additional Protocol 1.

34 Noelle Quenivet, 'The Right to Life in International Humanitarian Law and Human Rights Law' in Roberta Arnold and Noelle Quenivet (eds), *International Humanitarian Law and Human Rights Law: Towards a New Merger in International Law* (Brill 2008) 343.

35 *Nachova* v. *Bulgaria* (2006) 42 EHRR 43 at [95].

36 See *Gul* v. *Turkey* and *Erdogan and Others* v. *Turkey* App no 19807/92 (ECtHR, 25 April 2006).

In other cases, the standard applied is different. The case of *Isayeva, Yusupova, Bazayeva* v. *Russia* offers a good illustration. There the city of Grozny in Chechnya was held by Chechen insurgents and besieged by Russian armed forces.[37] During the siege, Russian military jets dropped numerous bombs on a vehicle convoy containing civilians, which was attempting to leave Grozny. In its analysis of whether the use of force was absolutely necessary, the Court stated:

> the Court will assume [...] that the military reasonably considered that there was an attack or a risk of attack from illegal insurgents, and that the air strike was a legitimate response to that attack.[38]

The Court accepts the use of lethal force here in the absence of a definite, immediate threat. The State was permitted to use lethal force where its forces 'reasonably considered', but were not certain, that there was an attack or 'a risk of attack'.[39] The standard applied by the Court is one of reasonable necessity, which is at odds with the normal standard of absolute necessity.[40] Similar issues concerning the immediacy of the threat are evident in other cases, such as *Kelly* v. *United Kingdom*[41] and *Khatsiyeva and Others* v. *Russia*.[42]

### 3.3.4 *Consistency in Applying IHL*

The Court's rulings in the aforementioned cases were clearly influenced by IHL. Permitting attacks on targets that do not pose an immediate threat and distinguishing between civilians and others are clearly influenced by IHL.

37 For an analysis of the genesis of this conflict see Kirill Koroteev, 'Legal Remedies for Human Rights Violations in the Armed Conflict in Chechnya: The Approach of the European Court of Human Rights in Context' (2010) 1 *International Humanitarian Legal Studies* 275, 276–9.

38 *Isayeva, Yusupova, Bazayeva* v. *Russia* (2005) 41 EHRR 39 at [181].

39 Melzer, *Targeted Killing in International Law* (n. 22) 389.

40 Forowicz (n. 22) 334; Claire Landais and Lea Bass, 'Reconciling the Rules of International Humanitarian Law with the Rules of European Human Rights Law' (2015) 97 IRRC 1295, 1300–1.

41 *Kelly* v. *United Kingdom* App no 17579/90 (EComHR, 13 January 1993), where the European Commission held that the use of force was justified when soldiers opened fire on a vehicle that failed to stop at a checkpoint based on a reasonable belief that the drivers were terrorists and that the harm averted by stopping them was greater than the harm inflicted. For some analysis see Ilias Bantekas and Lutz Oette, *International Human Rights Law and Practice* (Cambridge University Press 2013) 632. The Court and Commission seem to have distinguished this case in subsequent jurisprudence, in particular *Aytekin* v. *Turkey* App no 22880/93 (EComHR, 18 September 1997) at [94]–[95]; *Pisari* v. *Russia and Moldova* App no 42139/12 (ECtHR, 21 April 2015) at [56] and *Atiman* v. *Turkey* App no 62279/09 (ECtHR, 23 September 2014).

42 *Khatsiyeva and Others* v. *Russia* App no 5108/02 (ECtHR, 17 January 2008), see Monica Hakimi, 'A Functional Approach to Targeting and Detention' (2012) 110 *Michigan Law Review* 1365, 1389; Gioia (n. 29) 229.

The way that the Court is approaching these issues is problematic. The Court seems to tacitly apply these rules without first determining that the threshold for their application has been satisfied.[43] While the Court has repeatedly referred to the existence of armed conflicts in its judgments,[44] it does not engage in detailed analysis of the nature of the conflict or the point at which IHL begins to apply.[45] The Court has been very inconsistent in its consideration and application of IHL under Article 2.

The inconsistency is perhaps best illustrated in close analysis of cases from Chechnya. In Chapter 1, it was noted that there was an armed insurgency in Chechnya that caused Russia to lose control over parts of Grozny in *Isayeva* v. *Russia*. Notwithstanding this loss of control, the Court considered the situation in Grozny was 'outside wartime' and should be 'judged against a normal legal background'.[46] Yet in the case of *Isayeva, Yusupova, Bazayeva,* discussed above, which arose from the same facts as the *Isayeva* v. *Russia* case, the Court did not judge that case against the normal legal background, but decided to apply a standard closer to IHL instead. In other cases involving aerial strikes that cause civilian deaths, the Court has called on the State to minimise the risk of death to both hostile targets and civilians.[47]

In *Esmukhambetov* v. *Russia*, for example, which has a similar fact pattern to *Isayeva, Yusupova, Bazayeva,* the Court applied the normal standard on absolute necessity. There a Russian plane fired machine guns and dropped

[43] Arnold and Quenivet (n. 34) 335; William Abresch, 'A Human Rights Law of Internal Armed Conflict: The European Court of Human Rights in Chechnya' (2005) 16 EJIL 741, 742.

[44] *Ahmet Ozkan and Others* v. *Turkey* App no 21689/93 (ECtHR, 6 April 2004) at [85], [305]–[306]; *Avsar* v. *Turkey* App no 25657/94 (ECtHR, 10 July 2001) at [285]; *Bankovic and Others* v. *Belgium and Others* (2007) 44 EHRR SE5 at [60]; *Hassan* v. *United Kingdom* App no 29750/09 (ECtHR, 16 September 2014) at [101].

[45] See Anthony Cullen, *The Concept of Non-International Armed Conflict in International Humanitarian Law* (Cambridge University Press 2010) 117–57; This contrasts with the Inter-American bodies, which have repeatedly assessed the threshold issue – *Juan Carlos Abella* v. *Argentina* Report No 55/97 IAComHR 18 November 1997 at [149]–[152] and *Mapiripán Massacre* v. *Colombia* Series C No 134 IACtHR 15 September 2005 at [173]; Laurence Burgorgue-Larsen and Amaya Úbeda de Torres, '"War" in the Jurisprudence of the Inter-American Court of Human Rights' (2011) 33 *Human Rights Quarterly* 148, 153; Christina Cerna, 'The History of the Inter-American System's Jurisprudence as Regards Situations of Armed Conflict' (2011) 2 *International Humanitarian Legal Studies* 3, 37–8.

[46] *Isayeva* v. *Russia* (2005) 41 EHRR 38 at [191]. The Court later appears to contradict this finding in the case of *Al-Skeini* v. *United Kingdom,* where the Court noted that the procedural obligations in Article 2 continued to apply in armed conflict citing *Isayeva* as an example – *Al-Skeini and Others* v. *United Kingdom* at [164].

[47] *Kerimova* v. *Russia* App no 17170/04 (ECtHR, 3 May 2011) at [248]; *Khamzayev and Others* v. *Russia* App no 1503/02 (ECtHR, 3 May 2011) at [180]; *Esmukhambetov and Others* v. *Russia* App no 23445/03 (ECtHR, 29 March 2011) at [146].

several bombs on a village in Chechnya in 1999. The applicant's relatives were killed in the attack and many houses were also damaged. The Court looked at whether Russia had carried out the operation:

> in such a way as to avoid or minimise, to the greatest extent possible, risks of loss of lives, both of persons at whom the measures were directed and of civilians, and to minimise the recourse to lethal force.[48]

The Court considered both the right to life of the combatants and the non-combatants. The inconsistency is arguably compounded by the fact that in *Esmukhambetov* the Court specifically mentioned provisions of IHL as being relevant international law, but did not interpret the Convention in light of them.[49] By contrast in *Isayeva, Yusupova, Bazayeva*, the Court made no direct reference to IHL, but seemed to implicitly interpret Article 2 in light of it.

Krahenmann has argued that the Court's approach in *Esmukhambetov* was 'controversial',[50] but it is difficult to see how the Court applying its normal standards to a situation it deemed 'outside wartime' is controversial. The true controversy is the lack of consistency in the Court's approach to similar cases and the inconsistency in the concurrent application of IHL with human rights law. The divergences from the Convention norms seem to occur randomly. Elements of IHL norms seem to be assimilated into Convention norms and applied inconsistently to a variety of conflict and non-conflict situations from low-level insurgency in Northern Ireland,[51] to a NIAC in Chechnya,[52] without any detailed consideration of whether the threshold for the application of IHL is reached or the implications of this for Convention norms.

### 3.3.5 *Abandoning Absolute Necessity?*

The State's authorities undoubtedly faced extremely challenging situations in the aforementioned cases and this has clearly influenced the Court's response. However, if the Court decides that it is necessary to interpret the absolute necessity criterion flexibly in these cases, it must be clear about why it is doing so, the circumstances in which this will occur, and the alternative

48 Ibid.

49 Ibid at [76].

50 Sandra Krahenmann, 'Positive Obligations in Human Rights Law during Armed Conflicts' in Robert Kolb and Gloria Gaggioli (eds), *Research Handbook on Human Rights and Humanitarian Law* (Elgar 2013) 171.

51 *Kelly* v. *United Kingdom* App no 17579/90 (EComHR, 13 January 1993).

52 Philip Leach, 'The Chechen Conflict: Analysing the Oversight of the European Court of Human Rights' [2008] EHRLR 732, 733–4.

standards by which the Court will assess the State's use of force. There is little consistency in the circumstances when absolute necessity is set aside. While the Court appeared to follow a 'reasonable necessity' standard in *Isayeva, Yusupova, Bazayeva,* the Court did not elaborate on this alternative standard. What grounds need to be present for the State to reasonably consider the use of force necessary? How certain must the State be of the risk of an attack before it can act? The alternative appears to have been developed extemporaneously without any detailed consideration.

The Court has also altered how the absolute necessity test applies to decisions to resort to the use of force. This is evident from two judgments relating to hostage situations – *Finogenov* v. *Russia* and *Tagayeva* v. *Russia*. In *Finogenov* v. *Russia* around forty Chechen separatists took control of a Moscow theatre holding approximately 900 people hostage over two days.[53] They set bombs around the theatre and were wearing suicide bomb-vests. In an attempted rescue, Russian military special forces pumped a narcotic gas into the theatre to incapacitate the terrorists before storming the building. The facts of *Tagayeva* are somewhat similar. In *Tagayeva* v. *Russia*,[54] the Court addressed the Beslan school siege, where Chechen separatists took hundreds of people hostage in a school in North Ossetia in September 2004. The separatists were heavily armed and set up bombs around the school, threatening to kill the hostages if Russian troops were not withdrawn from Chechnya and demanding recognition of Chechnya as an independent State. Both cases raised extensive issues under Article 2 from resort to the use of force, to the adequacy of investigations and the positive obligation to protect people from violence.

The situations in *Finogenov* and *Tagayeva* show the difficulties that can arise in applying the normal human rights standards to military operations. In the face of these difficulties the Court's tendency has been to weaken the protections of human rights law. In both cases, the use of force against the hostage takers went completely unquestioned. In *Finogenov* hostage takers were shot dead while unconscious from the gas,[55] the Court again referred to *Ergi* and the need to safeguard civilians, rather than the more general obligation to avoid using force unless absolutely necessary from *McCann*.[56] In *Tagayeva*, the Court made an initial statement that it had to examine whether the authorities had planned and controlled the operation so as to 'minimise, to

53 *Finogenov and Others* v. *Russia* (2015) 61 EHRR 4.
54 *Tagayeva* v. *Russia* App no 26562/07 (ECtHR, 13 April 2017).
55 *Finogenov and Others* v. *Russia* (2015) 61 EHRR 4 at [22].
56 Ibid at [265].

the greatest extent possible, recourse to lethal force',[57] but the Court's attention was directed toward avoiding and minimising the 'risk to the hostages' and 'casualties among the hostages' rather than minimising recourse to the use of force generally.[58] The Court at one point even appeared to tacitly endorse the use of indiscriminate weapons against the hostage takers.[59]

When the Court came to consider the decisions to resort to the use of force in each case, the application of the absolute necessity test could have undermined any decisions to confront the hostage takers directly. However, the Court was understandably keen to give the State leeway in its decision making over whether to enter the buildings and use force against the hostage takers or continue negotiating. In *Finogenov*, the Court considered that the hostage taking incident was 'truly exceptional' and as the authorities were not in control of the situation in the building, the Court was prepared to grant them a 'margin of appreciation' in so far as the 'military and technical aspects of the situation' were concerned.[60] It would instead apply greater scrutiny to 'subsequent phases of the operation [...] where no serious time constraints existed and the authorities were in control of the situation'.[61] The Court unfortunately used some very loose language when referring to the absolute necessity test stating:

> the Court may occasionally depart from that rigorous standard of 'absolute necessity'. As the cases of *Osman*, *Makaratzis*, and *Maiorano and Others* [...] show, its application may be simply impossible where certain aspects of the situation lie far beyond the Court's expertise and where the authorities had to act under tremendous time pressure and where their control of the situation was minimal.[62]

Besides the issue of whether the Court is permitted to ignore parts of the Convention, the statement is problematic for other reasons. What will justify this 'occasional departure' in future? The hostage taking situation in *Finogenov* was clearly an exceptional situation, but the other cases referred to *Osman* v. *United Kingdom*,[63] *Makaratzis* v. *Greece*[64] and *Maiorano* v. *Italy*[65]

57 *Tagayeva* v. *Russia* App no 26562/07 (ECtHR, 13 April 2017) at [562].
58 Ibid at [589] and [602].
59 Ibid at [588].
60 *Finogenov and Others* v. *Russia* (2015) 61 EHRR 4 at [213].
61 Ibid at [212]–[214].
62 Ibid at [211].
63 *Osman* v. *United Kingdom* (2000) 29 EHRR 245.
64 *Makaratzis* v. *Greece* (2005) 41 EHRR 49.
65 *Maiorano* v. *Italy* App no 28634/06 (ECtHR, 15 December 2009).

were nowhere near as exceptional. Both the *Osman* and *Maiorano* cases were about authorities allegedly failing to take adequate measures to protect people from unlawful violence. *Makaratzis* concerned a car chase in which the State used their firearms extensively to attempt to stop a driver. These were unusual situations, but none of them involved situations in which the absolute necessity standard was 'impossible to apply'. The preconditions set out by the Court – time pressure and lack of State control over the situation – are also quite common, paving the way for much more frequent 'departures' from the standard of absolute necessity.

The Court seemed to moderate its language in *Tagayeva* when referring to this part of *Finogenov* stating:

> As the body tasked with supervision of the human rights obligations under the Convention, the Court would need to differentiate between the political choices made in the course of fighting terrorism, that remain by their nature outside of such supervision, and other, more operational aspects of the authorities' actions that have a direct bearing on the protected rights. The absolute necessity test formulated in Article 2 is bound to be applied with different degrees of scrutiny, depending on whether and to what extent the authorities were in control of the situation and other relevant constraints inherent in operative decision-making in this sensitive sphere.[66]

There is no reference to occasional departure from absolute necessity or the impossibility of applying the standard, instead the Court refers opaquely to 'different degrees of scrutiny' without elaborating on what these degrees of scrutiny entail. The State is exempted from having to show their use of force was absolutely necessary, but not compelled to show its decisions met any other standards. Skinner suggests that the Court will allow a balancing of individual rights against collective interests to guide the way States can respond to a situation like *Finogenov*.[67] Nonetheless the lack of clarity concerning this approach is concerning and it is open to abuse by States seeking to justify behaviour that would otherwise violate the Convention.

The partly dissenting opinion of Judge Pinto de Albuquerque in *Tagayeva* is ironic. The judge praised the application of the strict criteria of 'absolute necessity',[68] despite the clear departure from that standard. He also praised

66 *Tagayeva* v. *Russia* App no 26562/07 (ECtHR, 13 April 2017) at [481].

67 *Finogenov and Others* v. *Russia* (2015) 61 EHRR 4 at [213]; Stephen Skinner, 'Deference, Proportionality and the Margin of Appreciation in Lethal Force Case Law under Article 2 ECHR' [2014] EHRLR 32.

68 *Tagayeva* v. *Russia* App no 26562/07 (ECtHR, 13 April 2017), Partly Dissenting Opinion of Judge Pinto de Albuquerque at [1].

the Court for remaining 'faithful to the Court's standards on the use of lethal force in large-scale anti-terrorist operations' and 'refusing to apply the paradigm of the law on armed conflicts to them', despite the Court tacitly accepting the use of force against hostage takers and applying the standard in *Ergi*,[69] which, as noted above, appears to be directly influenced by the law of armed conflict.

This section has shown significant divergences from the human rights paradigm in the Court's jurisprudence on military operations. The Court's jurisprudence has distinguished between civilians and others, tacitly accepting the use of force against those others and permitted the use of force against people in the absence of immediate threats. It has also declined to apply the absolute necessity test to decisions made by the State on whether to use force in certain circumstances. The Court appears to be interpreting the Convention in light of IHL without directly acknowledging its influence or consistently applying it.

## 3.4 PROPORTIONALITY

The Court has also dealt with cases concerning the indiscriminate use of force during military operations, which is an interesting case study on the application of IHL. The tacit influence of IHL was arguably recognisable in the cases on absolute necessity above, with references to civilians and incidental loss of life. Its influence is perhaps even more obvious in the cases concerning the indiscriminate use of force. By way of introducing this jurisprudence, the Court finds substantive violations of Article 2 when evaluating how attacks are undertaken by States during military operations. In these cases, assessments of proportionality in the use of force and operational planning and control are often intertwined. The use of a weapon that is inherently incapable of distinguishing between targets and others may be considered a disproportionate use of force. The fact that such a weapon was considered appropriate for a given operation may also indicate a failure to properly plan and control the operation. The context is paramount in these cases and a weapon that may be appropriate in one context may be completely inappropriate in another.[70]

[69] *Tagayeva* v. *Russia* App no 26562/07 (ECtHR, 13 April 2017) at [573].

[70] Yoram Dinstein, *The Conduct of Hostilities under the Law of International Armed Conflicts* (Cambridge University Press 2004) 62; the Court, for example, criticised the failure to equip security forces with riot control gear in *Gulec* v. *Turkey* (1999) 28 EHRR 121 at [71].

### 3.4.1 *Implicit Use of IHL*

The level of influence IHL has on the Court has been the subject of debate among academics. Quenivet claims the Court has used IHL to aid its interpretation of Article 2 in the context of armed conflict.[71] It was noted above that the Court applies similar standards to IHL in some cases, indeed the Court itself admitted this possibility in its *Varnava* v. *Turkey* judgment when it stated 'Article 2 must be interpreted in so far as possible in light of the general principles of international law, including the rules of international humanitarian law'.[72] The case of *Hassan* v. *United Kingdom* provides perhaps the most striking use of IHL in the Court's history. In that case, which will be discussed in much greater detail in Chapter 5, the Court considered whether the internment of a person by UK forces in Iraq in 2003 breached Article 5, which only permits lawful detention in a finite set of clearly defined situations. The Court expressly interpreted this provision in light of IHL to allow the UK to intern civilians and detain prisoners of war.[73] Reidy and Heintze point toward the Court's use of IHL terminology in its judgments as further evidence,[74] again noted above in the references to civilians and incidental loss of life.

Others consider that the Court is engaged in a subtler use of IHL. They suggest the Court is applying IHL '*sub silentio*' when interpreting the Convention.[75] Orakhelashvili contends that the Court is engaged in the implicit application of IHL standards 'cloaked in the Convention-specific categories of legitimacy, necessity, and proportionality'.[76] Critics also argue that if the Court was applying IHL in its judgments it would result in different outcomes.[77] They highlight cases where the Court should have applied IHL, but

[71] Quenivet (n. 34) 335.

[72] *Varnava and Others* v. *Turkey* App no 16064/90 (ECtHR, 18 September 2009) at [185].

[73] *Hassan* v. *United Kingdom* App no 29750/09 (ECtHR, 16 September 2014) at [96]–[107], esp. [104].

[74] Hans-Joachim Heintze, 'On the Relationship between Human Rights Law Protection and International Humanitarian Law' (2004) 86 IRRC 789, 810; Aisling Reidy, 'The Approach of the European Commission and Court of Human Rights to International Humanitarian Law' (1998) 38 IRRC 513, 521.

[75] Abresch (n. 43) 746; Quenivet (n. 34) 332; Eriko Tamura, 'The Isayeva Cases of the European Court of Human Rights: The Application of International Humanitarian Law and Human Rights Law in Non-International Armed Conflicts' (2011) 10 *Chinese Journal of International Law* 129, 137; Forowicz (n. 22) 331.

[76] Alexander Orakhelashvili, 'The Interaction between Human Rights and Humanitarian Law: Fragmentation, Conflict, Parallelism, or Convergence?' (2008) 19 EJIL 161, 174.

[77] Abresch (n. 43) 752; Bill Bowring, 'Fragmentation, Lex Specialis and the Tensions in the Jurisprudence of the European Court of Human Rights' (2009) 14 *Journal of Conflict and Security Law* 485, 493; Noam Lubell, 'Challenges in Applying Human Rights Law to Armed Conflict' (2005) 87 IRRC 737, 743.

clearly did not use it.[78] Other authors are more circumspect about the extent of the Court's use of IHL in its judgments. They point toward the Court's obvious hesitation and reluctance to explicitly refer to IHL in its judgments, even if it seems to have some underlying influence.[79]

The Court's reticence in applying IHL seems to be motivated in part by legitimate concerns over the scope of its mandate.[80] The Convention states that 'the jurisdiction of the Court shall extend to all matters concerning the interpretation and application of the Convention',[81] at times this has been viewed as a restriction on the Court's capacity to consider other treaties.[82] However, the American Convention on Human Rights contains a very similar limitation – 'The jurisdiction of the Court shall comprise all cases concerning the interpretation and application of the provisions of this Convention',[83] but this has not held back the Inter-American bodies from interpreting the American Convention in light of IHL. The Inter-American human rights bodies have adopted a much more open approach toward interpreting the American Convention on Human Rights in light of IHL,[84] in particular by analysing the status of participants in conflict situations to determine whether they were combatants.[85] Even so it seems that the European Court pays lip-service to this constraint of its mandate while it continues to implicitly apply IHL.[86] A derogation from Article 2 could serve to ameliorate this situation. It could open the door for use of force against combatants and provide a clear justification for interpreting Convention norms in light of IHL. The Court would be obliged to consider whether the State's actions in killing or inflicting

78 Heintze (n. 74) 807–8 citing the failure to utilise law governing belligerent occupation in TRNC cases.

79 Lubell, 'Challenges' (n. 77) 743; Burgorgue-Larsen and Úbeda de Torres (n. 45) 167.

80 See discussion of mandate in Introduction.

81 Article 32(1), European Convention on Human Rights 1950.

82 *Markovic* v. *Italy* (2007) 44 EHRR 52 at [108]–[109].

83 Article 62(3), American Convention on Human Rights (adopted 22 November 1969, entered into force 18 July 1978) 1144 UNTS 144.

84 Burgorgue-Larsen and Úbeda de Torres (n. 45) 163; Emiliano Buis, 'The Implementation of International Humanitarian Law by Human Rights Courts: The Example of the Inter-American Human Rights System' in Quenivet and Arnold (n. 34) 286; Juan Pablo Perez-Leon Acevedo, 'The Role of the Inter-American Court of Human Rights in dealing with Armed Conflicts and Post-Conflict Reconstruction: Jurisprudential Analysis and Some Comparative Considerations' (2009) 7 *International Journal of Civil Society Law* 7, 9.

85 See, for example, *Arturo Ribón Avilán* v. *Colombia* Report No 26/97 IAComHR 30 September 1997 at [133]–[134]; *Abella* v. *Argentina* Report No 55/97 IAComHR 18 November 1997 at [161].

86 Forowicz (n. 22) 339.

life-threatening injuries were consistent with the State's other obligations under international law, which would include IHL.[87]

### 3.4.2 *Indiscriminate Attacks*

The implicit use of IHL is readily recognisable in the Court's case law on indiscriminate attacks. Under IHL indiscriminate attacks are considered unlawful. These attacks are characterised by a number of features: (a) they are not directed at a specific military objective, (b) they employ methods or means of combat which cannot be directed at a specific military objective, or (c) they employ methods or means of combat the effects of which cannot be limited as required by IHL.[88] While appropriate targeting is demanded in the first scenario, the others aim specifically at the regulation of weapons. Dinstein notes that IHL distinguishes between weapons that are intrinsically incapable of distinguishing between civilian and military targets, which are always unlawful, and weapons that can be used lawfully, but are used indiscriminately in certain situations.[89] These prohibitions on indiscriminate attacks have been mirrored in the Court's interpretation of Article 2.[90]

IHL can assist the Court in assessing certain situations where it has limited rules or jurisprudence covering the specific area. The benefits of using IHL in such circumstances have been expressly recognised in the Inter-American system.[91] However, the Court has not applied consistent rules, based on IHL or otherwise, to its case law on indiscriminate attacks. When it evaluates indiscriminate attacks in the course of military operations, it has not differentiated between armed conflict situations and other military operations. It has also applied unusual interpretations of the term indiscriminate in its jurisprudence.

87 See discussion in Chapter 7. Abresch (n. 43) 746; Michael O'Boyle and Jean Paul Costa, 'The ECtHR and IHL' in Christos Rozakis (ed), *The European Convention on Human Rights: A Living Instrument* (Bruylant Press 2011) 117–18; See by analogy Article 5 detention measures also Douglass Cassel, 'Pretrial and Preventive Detention of Suspected Terrorists: Options and Constraints under International Law' (2008) 98 *The Journal of Criminal Law and Criminology* 811, 821; *Serdar Mohammed* v. *Ministry of Defence* [2014] EWHC 1369 at [284].

88 Article 51(4), Additional Protocol 1.

89 Dinstein (n. 70) 55.

90 O'Boyle and Costa (n. 87) 121.

91 The Inter-American Commission for example justified resort to IHL on the grounds that 'the American Convention contains no rules that either define or distinguish civilians from combatants and other military targets, much less, specify when a civilian can be lawfully attacked or when civilian casualties are a lawful consequence of military operations' – *Abella* v. *Argentina* Report No 55/97 IAComHR 18 November 1997 at [161].

In *Isayeva* v. *Russia*, the Court examined an aerial attack in Chechnya. Chechen insurgents took over the village of Katyr-Yurt, which resulted in Russian security forces attacking the village. Russian forces used a variety of weapons including 'Grad' multiple missile-launchers, free falling FAB-250 and FAB-500 heavy aviation bombs and thermobaric (vacuum) bombs. Members of the applicant's family were killed when a bomb exploded near the minibus they were travelling in as they attempted to flee the village. The Court was critical of the weapons used by the Russian forces during the attack stating:

> The massive use of indiscriminate weapons stands in flagrant contrast with [the aim of protecting civilians from unlawful violence] and cannot be considered compatible with the standard of care prerequisite to an operation of this kind involving the use of lethal force by State agents.[92]

Note that the Court criticises the use of 'indiscriminate weapons', not the indiscriminate use of the weapons. The Court has been similarly critical of the use of high explosive aerial bombs as indiscriminate weapons in other cases.[93] In these cases, the weapons themselves – free-falling aerial bombs – are not inherently indiscriminate.[94] They are capable of being targeted at a specific military objective. If the bomb had hit only the rebel fighters in *Isayeva*, its use would arguably have been perfectly justified under Article 2.[95] The Court has clearly confused inherently indiscriminate weapons with weapons that are used indiscriminately.

Returning to the *Finogenov* case, the Court examined an incident in which Russian security forces pumped a narcotic gas into a theatre attempting to incapacitate hostage takers and rescue the hostages. Approximately 125 hostages died from exposure to the gas and the applicants, who were relatives of the deceased hostages, alleged that the gas was a lethal weapon, which had been used indiscriminately in violation of Article 2. The Court held that these actions did not violate Article 2. Firstly, although this was clearly not an armed conflict situation, the Court purported to 're-affirm' and apply the principle

92 *Isayeva* v. *Russia* (2005) 41 EHRR 38 at [191].

93 In *Abuyeva* v. *Russia*, the Court criticised Russia's use of 'indiscriminate and highly lethal weaponry' – *Abuyeva and Others* v. *Russia* App no 27065/05 (ECtHR, 2 December 2010) at [199]; In *Kerimova* v. *Russia*, the Court criticised the State for using a 'high-explosive indiscriminate type of weapon' – *Kerimova* v. *Russia* App no 17170/04 (ECtHR, 3 May 2011) at [253].

94 Agnieszka Jachec-Neale, 'The Right to Take Life: Killing and Death in Armed Conflict' in Jon Yorke (ed), *The Right to Life and the Value of Life: Orientations in Law, Politics and Ethics* (Ashgate 2010) 139–40.

95 The Court's findings in *Ahmet Ozkan and Others* v. *Turkey* App no 21689/93 (ECtHR, 6 April 2004) would support such an argument.

on indiscriminate attacks from *Isayeva*. Thus, the Court purports to tacitly apply standards based on IHL without first determining whether the threshold for its application has been met. However, it is the Court's later statements which are the real cause for concern. The Court stated:

> In the present case, however, the gas used by the Russian security forces, while dangerous, was not supposed to kill, in contrast, for example, to bombs or air missiles. The general principle stated in the *Isayeva* case, condemning the indiscriminate use of heavy weapons in anti-terrorist operations, can be reaffirmed, but it was formulated in a different factual context, where the Russian authorities used airborne bombs to destroy a rebel group which was hiding in a village full of civilians. Although the gas in the present case was used against a group consisting of hostages and hostage-takers, and although the gas was dangerous and even potentially lethal, it was not used 'indiscriminately' as it *left the hostages a high chance of survival, which depended on the efficiency of the authorities' rescue effort.*[96] (emphasis added)

Instead of re-affirming *Isayeva*, the Court distinguished it on the ground that the Court was dealing with different factual contexts. It did not differentiate the cases on the grounds that *Isayeva* was arguably a situation of armed conflict and *Finogenov* was not. Instead the Court claimed there was a difference in how weapons were used in each case and adopted a completely different definition of indiscriminate.[97] The Court misquotes *Isayeva* in *Finogenov* claiming that it had condemned 'the indiscriminate use of heavy weapons' when in fact it had condemned 'the massive use of indiscriminate weapons'.[98] However, the Court went on to suggest that *Finogenov* should be differentiated because the gas was 'not supposed to kill'. The lethality or otherwise of the weapon is clearly not at issue. The real problem in both *Finogenov* and *Isayeva* was the use of weapons where they would affect civilians and military targets without distinction.

The Court observes that the gas could be used in a manner that discriminated between targets and civilians. This claim is open to question,[99] but the

[96] *Finogenov and Others* v. *Russia* (2015) 61 EHRR 4 at [232].

[97] Others have questioned the merits of the distinction made by the Court, but argue it is offset by the closer scrutiny of other aspects of the case – Rainey, Wicks and Ovey, (n. 3) 146.

[98] *Isayeva* v. *Russia* (2005) 41 EHRR 38 at [191].

[99] Under Article 51(4), Additional Protocol 1 some weapons are considered by their nature indiscriminate weapons either because the weapon is incapable of being targeted at a military objective or because the effects of the weapon cannot be limited as required by IHL. Even assuming the gas was capable of being targeted, the effects of the chemicals could not be controlled afterwards.

truth is that the gas clearly wasn't used discriminately.[100] The Court's claim that the gas was not used indiscriminately because the people subjected to it had a chance of surviving cannot be correct. The aftermath of an attack does not alter the nature of the initial attack. If a blindfolded gunman opened fire on a crowd, would the fact that some of his victims survived because the emergency services acted quickly mean that they were not the subjects of an indiscriminate attack? The assessment of whether the effects of a weapon can be limited must be made at the time of the action or before, rather than *ex post facto*. The use of this weapon would have violated Article 2 had the standard in *Isayeva* been applied. A significant number of people died from exposure to the gas, meaning it was a potentially lethal use of force, which was directed at both persons who were a threat, the hostage takers, and those who posed no threat to life, the audience, making this a situation in which force was used against persons when it was not absolutely necessary.[101] Even if one accepts the argument that this was a non-lethal weapon, it created a potentially life-threatening situation, which also triggers the application of Article 2.[102] Thus, while the Court tacitly applies rules based on IHL, it does not seem to follow the finer details of IHL, e.g. the distinction between inherently indiscriminate weapons and weapons which are not inherently indiscriminate but are used indiscriminately.

The trend from previous cases is evident again in *Tagayeva*. In that case, 330 people were killed and hundreds injured when Russian security forces attempted to rescue the hostages of the Beslan school siege. The applicants alleged that Russia had used force indiscriminately against both hostages and hostage takers. Weapons including tank shells, flamethrowers and grenade launchers were used during the storming of the building and the applicants claimed these weapons could not be considered appropriate for either rescuing the hostages or effecting arrests of the terrorists.[103]

The State argued that lethal force was applied 'directly and precisely' at the hostage takers and not a single death 'among the hostages' was attributed to the security forces.[104] It argued that the situation warranted departure from the absolute necessity test per *Finogenov* or alternatively, if the

[100] The Russian government later acknowledged this in its pleadings in *Tagayeva* v. *Russia* App no 26562/07 (ECtHR, 13 April 2017) at [579].

[101] International Committee of the Red Cross, *'Incapacitating Chemical Agents' Law Enforcement, Human Rights Law and Policy Perspectives 24–26 April 2012* (Montreux, Switzerland 2012) 52–3.

[102] *Makaratzis* v. *Greece* (2005) 41 EHRR 49 at [49].

[103] *Tagayeva* v. *Russia* App no 26562/07 (ECtHR, 13 April 2017) at [576].

[104] Ibid at [579]–[580].

absolute necessity test was applied, it was satisfied because the force was only directed at the hostage takers.[105] To the Court's credit it did not entertain the departure from the absolute necessity test suggested. It concluded that 'State agents used indiscriminate weapons upon the building while the terrorists and hostages were intermingled' and ruled that the State had not satisfied the absolute necessity test.[106] Nonetheless, the Court's approach illustrates many of the failings of its previous jurisprudence. The Court repeatedly adverted to 'the use of indiscriminate weapons', rather than the indiscriminate use of the weapons,[107] which was again the central issue. The Court also fixated on whether the building was 'clear of hostages' before the 'indiscriminate weapons' were used.[108] It tacitly accepted the use of indiscriminate weapons against the hostage takers and failed to question the propriety of using such weapons where the objective is to minimise the recourse to the use of force more generally and State's aim should be to arrest rather than kill the hostage takers.

## 3.5 POSITIVE OBLIGATION TO PROTECT DURING MILITARY OPERATIONS

When a State knows, or ought to have known, of a real and immediate risk to the life of an individual, it must take measures within the scope of its powers that judged reasonably might have been expected to avoid that risk.[109] This is the positive obligation to protect under Article 2, which has already been discussed incidentally in some of the cases above. This section examines how this obligation operates to protect both civilians and soldiers during military operations.

### 3.5.1 *Protection of Civilians*

There is some correlation between the positive obligation under Article 2 and IHL. The obligations under IHL demand that the State remove civilians and civilian objects from the vicinity of military objectives, avoid locating military objectives within or near densely populated areas, and taking other necessary precautions to protect the civilian population against the dangers resulting

[105] Ibid at [581].
[106] Ibid at [605].
[107] Ibid at [584] and [588].
[108] Ibid at [590].
[109] *Osman* v. *United Kingdom* (2000) 29 EHRR 245 at [115]; The Inter-American Court has inferred a similar obligation holding that a State can be held responsible where it did not take the necessary steps in order to prevent the particular violation from taking place – *Velásquez-Rodríguez* v. *Honduras* Series C No 4 IACtHR 29 July 1988 at [30]–[31].

from military operations.[110] There are some very striking alignments with the positive obligation in Article 2 and IHL. The case of *Esmukhambetov* v. *Russia* (discussed above) is a clear example of the Court implicitly relying on IHL when interpreting Article 2. The correlation between factors considered under IHL and the Court's assessment is profound.

The relevant IHL rules on targeting and precaution are set out in Article 57(2) of the first Additional Protocol to the Geneva Conventions 1977.[111] Firstly, the State must verify the objectives being attacked are military objectives. In *Esmukhambetov*, the Court was critical of the State's failure to produce evidence that there were illegal fighters in the area or that they were planning an attack.[112] It also criticised the State's failure to adequately identify military targets.[113] Secondly, the State must choose means and methods to avoid or minimise incidental loss of civilian life. In this regard, the Court criticised Russia for failing to prepare the operation: 'in such a way as to avoid or minimise, to the greatest extent possible, risks of loss of lives, both of persons at whom the measures were directed and of civilians'.[114] The Court also directly refers to and criticises Russia's 'choice of means' in this case.[115] IHL also demands that effective advance warning is given of attacks that may affect the civilian population, unless circumstances do not permit.[116] The Court was critical of the State's failure to take 'any steps with a view to informing the villagers of the attack beforehand and to securing their evacuation'.[117] Similar approaches are identifiable in other cases.[118]

The Court also directly referred to IHL in *Pasa and Erkan Erol* v. *Turkey*.[119] In that case the Turkish gendarmerie placed several landmines near their station to protect it from attacks. The area where they placed the mines was

110 Article 58, Additional Protocol 1.

111 Dinstein (n. 70) 125–8; Doswald-Beck and Henckaerts (n. 13) 55–60. Forowicz argues the Court also borrows terminology from these provisions in certain cases such as *Ergi* v. *Turkey* – Forowicz (n. 22) 328–9.

112 *Esmukhambetov and Others* v. *Russia* App no 23445/03 (ECtHR, 29 March 2011) at [145].

113 Ibid at [148]; See also *Kerimova* v. *Russia* App no 17170/04 (ECtHR, 3 May 2011) at [250].

114 *Esmukhambetov and Others* v. *Russia* App no 23445/03 (ECtHR, 29 March 2011) at [146].

115 Ibid at [147]–[148]; *Gulec* v. *Turkey* (1999) 28 EHRR 121 at [71].

116 Article 57(2)(c), Additional Protocol 1.

117 *Esmukhambetov and Others* v. *Russia* App no 23445/03 (ECtHR, 29 March 2011) at [149].

118 *Kerimova* v. *Russia* App no 17170/04 (ECtHR, 3 May 2011); *Abuyeva and Others* v. *Russia* App no 27065/05 (ECtHR, 2 December 2010); *Isayeva* v. *Russia* (2005) 41 EHRR 38; *Ergi* v. *Turkey* (2001) 32 EHRR 18; *Ahmet Ozkan and Others* v. *Turkey* App no 21689/93 (ECtHR, 6 April 2004).

119 *Pasa and Erkan Erol* v. *Turkey* App no 51358/99 (ECtHR, 12 December 2006) [only available in French].

used as pasture by local farm animals. The gendarmerie placed two rows of barbed wire around the mines, warning signs at 20 metre intervals and advised locals of their location orally and in writing. The applicant's son followed some grazing animals onto the minefield and lost his leg when one of the mines exploded. The Court made a direct reference to the prohibition of anti-personnel mines under IHL, observing that the mines were particularly dangerous to young children and their use was prohibited under the Ottawa Convention, to which Turkey was a party.[120] The Court found a violation of Article 2 because the protective measures taken by the authorities were insufficient to prevent people from accessing the area.[121]

One potentially onerous aspect of the positive obligation is that it requires States to protect people both from risks arising from State agents and from third parties. In *Albekov and Others* v. *Russia*, several people were killed by landmines planted in the forest near their homes. It was unclear who was responsible for planting the landmines there, but the Court stated it:

> does not consider it necessary to decide on this issue since, in any event, the Government does not deny that the authorities were aware that mines had been laid in the area. Accordingly [...] the Court finds that the domestic authorities were under a positive obligation to protect the residents from the risks involved.[122]

The Court reached a similar finding in *Ergi*, discussed above, where the Court demanded that the operation was planned and conducted to avoid or minimise any risk to the lives of the villagers. The State had to not only protect civilians from the risk of fire from State agents, but also from the insurgents they were engaging.[123] These rulings reflect similar obligations in IHL, in particular the rule that 'the civilian population and individual civilians shall enjoy general protection against the dangers arising from military operations'.[124] This can represent an onerous burden on the State and the practicalities of enforcing such an obligation will be discussed further in this section and in the next chapter.[125]

[120] Ibid at [32].

[121] Ibid at [34]. See Daniel Reitiker, 'Strange Bedfellows? The Cross-Fertilization of Human Rights and Arms Control' (2014) 3(2) *Cyprus Human Rights Law Review* 130, 137–43.

[122] *Albekov and Others* v. *Russia* App no 68216/01 (ECtHR, 9 October 2008) at [85].

[123] *Ergi* v. *Turkey* (2001) 32 EHRR 18 at [79].

[124] Article 13(1), Protocol Additional to the Geneva Conventions of 12 August 1949, and relating to the Protection of Victims of Non-International Armed Conflicts (adopted 8 June 1977, entered into force 7 December 1978) 1125 UNTS 609.

[125] See Chapter 4.

Although both IHL and the Convention coalesce in this area of law, the Court has been inconsistent in their application of the positive obligations to military operations. In *Nakayev* v. *Russia*, the applicant lived in Chechnya in 1999. He was permanently disabled following the explosion of a shell in the yard of a house where he was staying. The incident occurred during a Russian counter-insurgency operation in the area. He alleged that the Russian forces had subjected the area to indiscriminate shelling. However, the applicant did not report the incident to the authorities for many years. The Court noted that the State's own criminal investigation into the incident established that:

> a number of armed clashes, including exchanges of gunfire, had taken place between Russian forces and illegal armed groups in the area of the applicant's residence in 1999. As a result of the bombardment of Martan-Chu the applicant was injured [...] The projectile, which had hit the yard [...] and wounded the applicant, had been launched by one of the parties to the conflict. However, it was impossible to establish which party had launched the projectile.[126]

The Court did not find a violation of the positive obligation under Article 2 in this case, although it did find a violation of the procedural obligation. In its view, the applicant had not made 'an arguable claim of the State's responsibility for the attack in question'.[127]

In *Udayeva and Yusupova* v. *Russia*, the applicants lived in Urus-Martan, an urban area near Grozny, Chechnya. In October 2000, during the conflict with Chechen insurgents, Russia held control of Urus-Martan and had several military units stationed around the area. The applicants' sons were killed when a shell exploded near them while they were walking home from school. The source of the shell was unclear and the State refused to disclose evidence to the Court or co-operate with the Court's investigation. Russia claimed that the military unit stationed in Urus-Martan had been subjected to shelling by an illegal armed group that day.[128] The applicants gathered extensive witness statements from local citizens who claimed the shell was fired by a nearby Russian tank. The Court stated that there was a 'lack of information and evidence pertaining to the nature of the incident', and that it was not proven beyond reasonable doubt that the Russian forces were implicated.[129] They further stated that there was:

[126] *Nakayev* v. *Russia* App no 29846/05 (ECtHR, 21 June 2011) at [17].
[127] Ibid at [80].
[128] *Udayeva and Yusupova* v. *Russia* App no 36542/05 (ECtHR, 21 December 2010) at [15].
[129] Ibid at [78]–[79]; The Court reached a similar finding in *Sirin Yilmaz* v. *Turkey* App no 35875/97 (ECtHR, 29 July 2004).

> no indication that the authorities knew or ought to have known at the time of the existence of a real and immediate risk to the lives the applicants' sons and that they failed to take measures to avoid that risk.[130]

The Court did conclude that the State had failed to carry out an effective investigation in this case. The Court appeared to apply IHL implicitly in the context of the NIAC in Chechnya in *Esmukhambetov* and other cases, but completely ignored the rules of IHL relating to precautions in attack in the similar contexts of *Udayeva* and *Nakayev*.

The Court frequently focuses on a single aspect of Article 2 and ignores other relevant issues, which can give rise to inconsistencies in its approach. In *Finogenov*, for example, the focus on planning and control proved detrimental to the assessment of absolute necessity, in *Nakayev* and *Udayeva*, the fixation on establishing a violation of the procedural obligation in Article 2 meant the Court did not properly consider the relevant positive obligations. The Court ought to take a more holistic approach toward the application of the Convention to ensure it applies the law fairly and consistently.

It is difficult to reconcile *Nakayev* and *Udayeva* with the approach in *Ergi* and *Albekov*. Russia's responsibility for the incident ought not to be relevant to the application of the positive obligation, which covers the actions of State agents and the insurgents. The relevant issue was whether the risk was foreseeable and in this respect the Court's conclusion in *Udayeva and Yusupova* seems implausible. There are two plausible explanations for the events in both these cases. First, insurgents were trying to shell a Russian military unit stationed near a civilian area, or *vice versa*, and missed their target. Second, insurgents and Russian forces were exchanging fire with each other near a civilian area and a stray shell was responsible for the damage. In either situation, there was a strong possibility that the inhabitants of the nearby villages could be hit and the risk was clearly foreseeable. Chevalier-Watts argues that the correct application of the positive obligation in Article 2 would require the State to evacuate an area that could be shelled by enemy forces,[131] while Krahenmann argues that the positive obligation must be interpreted so that the conduct of hostilities close to inhabited areas must be avoided.[132] Neither of these approaches were adopted by the Court meaning its analysis of comparable situations where civilians are at risk from the effects of explosive devices utilised by parties to a conflict remains problematic.

[130] *Udayeva and Yusupova* v. *Russia* App no 36542/05 (ECtHR, 21 December 2010) at [78].

[131] Juliet Chevalier-Watts, 'Military Operations and the Right to Life: The Uneasy Bedfellows' (2011) 5 *Human Rights and International Legal Discourse* 207, 225.

[132] Krahenmann (n. 50) 171.

### 3.5.2 *An Obligation to Protect Soldiers?*

The following sections look at the entitlements of soldiers to receive protection from human rights law during military operations. The positive obligation in Article 2 applies to everyone within the State's jurisdiction, including soldiers deployed on military operations abroad. It also applies in principle to any activity, whether public or not, in which the right to life may be at stake.[133] There is no directly comparable legal obligation on a State to protect its own soldiers under IHL.[134] The extra-territorial application of this obligation has yet to come directly before the Court, but it is increasingly coming before other courts.[135] The issue warrants serious consideration as it cuts to the heart of the practicality of applying human rights law to military operations. As noted in the previous chapters, States will struggle to satisfy positive obligations in the absence of the institutional support of a functioning State. Demanding greater protection of soldiers' lives will also impact upon the effectiveness of military operations.[136]

The application of this positive obligation was the subject of a case before the UK Supreme Court (UKSC) in *Smith and Others* v. *Ministry of Defence*, which is likely to have a significant bearing on any similar cases before the Court.[137] The appellants argued that their relatives had been killed in Iraq because the British government failed to provide them with necessary equipment. Although the case also dealt with a question concerning the tort of

[133] *Oneryildiz* v. *Turkey* (2005) 41 EHRR 20 at [71]; *LCB* v. *United Kingdom* (1999) 27 EHRR 212 at [36].

[134] Some authors have attempted to interpret the principle of necessity in IHL, which demands that the least possible expenditure of personnel and resources are used to achieve the submission of the enemy, as implying a duty upon States to avoid putting soldiers at unnecessary risk whenever possible. However, this is far from a mainstream view and any such obligation would be much narrower in scope than the positive obligations in Article 2 – Solomon (n. 31) 104–5; Peter Rowe, 'The Obligation of a State under International Law to Protect Members of its own Armed Forces during Armed Conflict or Occupation' (2006) 9 *Yearbook of International Humanitarian Law* 3, 16–22.

[135] In England and Wales see for example the cases of *R. (Smith)* v. *Oxfordshire Assistant Deputy Coroner* [2010] UKSC 29; *Multiple Claimants* v. *Ministry of Defence* [2003] EWHC 1134; *Mulcahy* v. *Ministry of Defence* [1996] QB 732; *R. (Long)* v. *Secretary of State for Defence* [2014] EWHC 2391 (Admin). The Court also accepted the friendly settlement of a case related to the rights of soldiers in theatre – *Pritchard* v. *United Kingdom* App no 1573/11 (ECtHR, 18 March 2014).

[136] *R. (Long)* v. *Secretary of State for Defence* [2014] EWHC 2391 (Admin) at [81]–[87].

[137] *Smith and Others* v. *Ministry of Defence* [2013] UKSC 41.

negligence, our focus is on the case taken under Article 2 as given effect through the Human Rights Act 1998.[138]

The applications concerned the deaths of two soldiers who were killed by improvised explosive devices (IEDs) planted by the roadside while they were driving Land Rovers in 2005 and 2006 respectively. A piece of equipment known as an electronic counter measure (ECM), which helps to detect IEDs, was not fitted to the Land Rover involved in the first incident. The Land Rover involved in the second incident did have an ECM, but it lacked a specific component, 'element A', which would have assisted in detecting the IED. The appellants argued that the failure to properly equip the Land Rovers or provide better armoured vehicles violated the positive obligation in Article 2.

The UKSC began with the question of jurisdiction. It applied the judgment in *Al-Skeini* and held that the UK soldiers operating in Iraq came within the State's Article 1 jurisdiction.[139] It reasoned that as State agents bring others within the jurisdiction of the State through their actions extra-territorially, those State agents must themselves be within the jurisdiction of the State.[140] The majority considered that:

> a finding that in all circumstances deaths or injuries in combat that result from the conduct of operations by the armed forces are outside the scope of Article 2 would not be sustainable. It would amount, in effect, to a derogation from the State's substantive obligations under that article.[141]

Deploying the soldiers overseas did not automatically amount to a violation of Article 2.[142] The UKSC recognised that soldiers could die as a result of systemic and operational failures on the part of the State, e.g. failure to provide equipment and such failures could not be immune from scrutiny under Article 2.[143] Courts should be slow to question operational decisions in the field.[144] At the same time, procurement decisions, relating as they do

[138] The State has historically been shielded from such cases by a series of immunities. Section 10 of the Crown Proceedings Act 1947, for example, gave immunity to the Ministry of Defence from actions pursued in tort. This was repealed in the Crown Proceedings (Armed Forces) Act 1987. For a good overview of the legal protections from suit in this area and how they have changed over time see Anthony Forster, 'British Judicial Engagement and the Juridification of the Armed Forces' (2012) 88 *International Affairs* 283.

[139] For a more detailed discussion of jurisdiction see Chapters 1 and 2.

[140] *Smith and Others* v. *Ministry of Defence* [2013] UKSC 41 at [50]–[52].

[141] Ibid at [58].

[142] Ibid at [62].

[143] Ibid at [63].

[144] Ibid at [64].

to political choices concerning the allocation of resources, are less amenable to judicial scrutiny.[145] The court had to determine whether there was a middle ground between each of these limitations. It stated:

> It will be easy to find that allegations are beyond the reach of article 2 if the decisions that were or ought to have been taken about training, procurement or the conduct of operations were at a high level of command and closely linked to the exercise of political judgment and issues of policy. So too if they relate to things done or not done when those who might be thought to be responsible for avoiding the risk of death or injury to others were actively engaged in direct contact with the enemy. But finding whether there is room for claims to be brought in the middle ground, so that the wide margin of appreciation which must be given to the authorities or to those actively engaged in armed conflict is fully recognised without depriving the article of content, is much more difficult. No hard and fast rules can be laid down. It will require the exercise of judgment. This can only be done in the light of the facts of each case.[146]

The case was put to trial to determine whether it fell within this 'middle ground' and has not been determined at the time of writing. The scope for scrutiny of State decisions here seems to be waifer thin, but nonetheless, a subsequent case, *R (Long)* v. *Secretary of State for Defence*, fell within this middle ground.[147] That case concerned events in Iraq in 2003 where six British soldiers were isolated from other units in an Iraqi police station after they were confronted by an angry mob. The mob broke into the station and killed the soldiers. The soldiers had been ordered to carry iridium satellite phones with them while off base. The phones were in short supply, but available. The order was routinely disobeyed and the six soldiers were not equipped with the phone, which could have been used to call for assistance, when they were confronted by the mob.

The case brought by the soldiers' relatives centred on the effectiveness of the investigation carried out by the UK authorities, but the Court of Appeal made some interesting remarks concerning *Smith* v. *MOD*. The court determined that the case concerned neither a decision about training, procurement or the conduct of operations, nor was it a decision relating to 'things done or not done when those who might be thought to be responsible for avoiding the risk of death or injury to others were actively engaged in direct contact with the enemy'.[148] There was no attempt by the State to justify failing to

145 Ibid at [65].

146 Ibid at [76].

147 *R. (Long)* v. *Secretary of State for Defence* [2015] EWCA Civ 770.

148 Ibid at [11].

equip the soldiers with iridium phones or allegation that this failure resulted from a decision taken under pressure in difficult circumstances.[149] This was a systemic insufficiency of control and not mere negligent control by an individual.[150] Article 2 was therefore engaged and an investigation into why a practice developed whereby this order was routinely ignored was required in the circumstances.[151]

These cases are part of *Al-Skeini's* legacy. The UKSC had previously held that jurisdiction only arose while soldiers were on their bases in foreign countries.[152] However, following the Court's ruling in *Al-Skeini*,[153] the UKSC came under pressure to depart from this narrow interpretation.[154] The UKSC is simply setting out the next logical consequence of the *Al-Skeini* judgment. The European Court of Human Rights would likely follow suit if confronted with a similar case. The application of Article 2 could perhaps have been discounted on the basis of the *Bankovic* ruling in the past.[155] However, it is now beyond doubt that the Convention applies to soldiers during extra-territorial military operations, including combat. Rowe rightly observed that: 'to argue that the right to life has no application at all to the soldiers of a state during an armed conflict or an occupation, in the absence of any permitted derogation, is not consistent with the logic nor with the current jurisprudence of relevant human rights bodies'.[156]

### 3.5.3 *Interpreting the Positive Obligation to Protect Soldiers*

The cases of *Smith* v. *MOD* and *Long* present significant difficulties for the Court in defining the scope of this obligation and the so-called 'middle ground' and for States attempting to apply the positive obligation during military operations, which will be discussed in the following sections.

149 Ibid at [31].

150 Ibid at [29].

151 Ibid at [31].

152 This arose from the House of Lords and Court's findings in *Al-Saadoon and Mufdhi* v. *United Kingdom (Merits)* (2010) 51 EHRR 9. It had been applied in other UK cases such as *R. (Smith)* v. *Oxfordshire Assistant Deputy Coroner* [2010] UKSC 29.

153 See in particular *Al-Skeini and Others* v. *United Kingdom* (2011) 53 EHRR 18 at [136] where the Court rejects the notion of control over buildings in which people are held as triggering jurisdiction.

154 Richard Mullender, 'Military Operations, Fairness and the British State' (2014) 130 *Law Quarterly Review* 28, 29; Gordon Junor, 'A Soldier's (Human) Rights When Fighting Abroad: The Supreme Court Decides' (2013) 37 *Scots Law Times* 251, 251–2.

155 *R. (Smith)* v. *Oxfordshire Assistant Deputy Coroner* [2010] UKSC 29 at [303]–[309].

156 Rowe, 'The Obligation of a State' (n. 134) 15–16.

At the outset it could be argued that few issues will fall within the middle ground identified by the UKSC and Court of Appeal and therefore this is not a significant problem. However, we have already seen two cases of this in *Smith* and *Long*, others will likely follow.[157] The bar to bringing a case is lowered by the fact that there is no need to show that proper equipment, for example, would have saved the soldiers' lives. It only needs to be shown, as the complainants did in *Long*, that there was a failure to take reasonable measures, which could have had a real prospect of avoiding the deaths.[158] This is counterbalanced by the idea that the Court must avoid imposing positive obligations on the State in connection with the planning for and conduct of military operations in situations of armed conflict which are unrealistic or disproportionate.[159] This is certainly consistent with the approach in *Al-Skeini*, discussed in the previous chapter. Is it possible to provide some protection to soldiers while simultaneously avoiding placing a disproportionate burden on the State? Before discussing this further, it is important to recognise how military operations subvert the positive obligation paradigm.

The normal positive obligation under Article 2 stipulates that as the risk to an individual becomes more real and immediate, we expect the State to offer greater levels of protection from the harm.[160] However, States consciously put soldiers in harm's way during military operations. As a result, our expectations are practically inverted for the military and as the risk increases to military forces, there is a corresponding lower expectation of protection.[161] We would expect that a State could reasonably foresee certain risks to soldiers within a base and to take measures to protect soldiers within it, even though they are comparatively safe there. Yet during a pitched battle between opposing armies with air support, artillery and armoured units, the soldiers are perhaps at the greatest risk, but we do not expect the State to offer the greatest level of protection in that situation.[162]

157 Landais and Bass, (n. 40) 1298.

158 *R. (Long)* v. *Secretary of State for Defence* [2015] EWCA Civ 770 at [32].

159 *Smith and Others* v. *Ministry of Defence* [2013] UKSC 41 at [76].

160 This is implicit in the Court's reasoning in *Osman* v. *United Kingdom* (2000) 29 EHRR 245 at [116].

161 That does not mean that there are no expectations of protection at all, as Solomon rightly points out the soldier's job is not to die for his country, but to fight for it and the co-application of HRL and IHL ought to prevent soldiers being sent on suicide missions, see Solomon (n. 31) 112. The UKSC referred to this point in *Smith and Others* v. *Ministry of Defence* [2013] UKSC 41 at [171].

162 *R. (Smith)* v. *Oxfordshire Assistant Deputy Coroner* [2010] UKSC 29 at [122]–[125].

The levels of State control over different situations have a bearing,[163] but the Court accepts that the situation of soldiers is unique in *Stoyanovi* v. *Bulgaria*. In that case, the family members of a soldier who died in a parachuting accident brought a case under Article 2 alleging that the State was responsible for his death and had failed to properly investigate it. The Court's analysis differentiated the situation of the military, acknowledging that engaging in dangerous activities was effectively what the armed forces did and it is 'a situation which differs from those "dangerous" situations of specific threat to life which arise exceptionally from risks posed by violent, unlawful acts of others or man-made or natural hazards'.[164] The Court's focus was therefore on ensuring that there was a correct framework for the operations and that risks are reduced to a 'reasonable minimum'.[165] The Court ruled that there was no violation of Article 2.

In principle human rights law should protect the right to life of each person equally, unless some specific risk or danger triggers a specific obligation for the State to protect. However, military operations once again subvert this paradigm as arbitrary distinctions can exist between the levels of protection the State offers to different people, which are often unrelated to the level of risk the individuals face. In Iraq, for example, civilian police co-opted to work for the UK were always transported in heavily armoured vehicles as a matter of policy.[166] By contrast, rank and file members of the army were often transported in less protective Land Rovers. Each person in this situation is a State agent participating in an extra-territorial military operation. Why should one group receive greater protection than another? The increased levels of protection do not even correspond to the levels of risk faced by the individuals. The rank and file soldiers were arguably at greater risk on active patrol in Land Rovers than the police were moving between training posts. There is an element of arbitrariness here, which is difficult to reconcile with a human rights approach.

The Court appears to accept distinctions in treatment predicated on consent to the risk of harm. In *Chember* v. *Russia*, a conscript soldier suffered severe injuries completing a punishment for failing to properly clean his barracks. The Court found that Russia had violated his rights under Article 3.

[163] *Smith and Others* v. *Ministry of Defence* [2013] UKSC 41 at [64].

[164] *Stoyanovi* v. *Bulgaria* App no 42980/04 (ECtHR, 9 November 2010) at [61].

[165] Ibid

[166] See 'Statement by Paul Robert Kernaghan' (Chilcott Inquiry, 9 June 2010) <www.iraqinquiry.org.uk/media/46162/kernaghan-statement-final.pdf> accessed 4 August 2018.

The Court specified that the military should make special dispensations to protect conscripted soldiers from the dangers of military service:

> The State has a primary duty to put in place rules geared to the level of risk to life or limb that may result not only from the nature of military activities and operations, but also from the human element that comes into play when a State decides to call up ordinary citizens to perform military service. Such rules must require the adoption of practical measures aimed at the effective protection of conscripts against the dangers inherent in military life and appropriate procedures for identifying shortcomings and errors liable to be committed in that regard by those in charge at different levels.[167]

The Court singles out conscript soldiers here as it has in other cases.[168] There is a sense that while enlisted soldiers voluntarily assume their roles in the military, conscripted soldiers are forced to join the military.[169] As such, enlisted soldiers consciously waive some of their rights, whereas conscripts are forced to do so and therefore deserve more protection. It remains to be seen whether such differentiation would also occur during active operations.

So how can the Court interpret the positive obligation in the context of extra-territorial military operations to avoid imposing an impossible or disproportionate burden on the authorities? The Court could adopt specific limitations to the positive obligation in Article 2 here by taking advantage of the leeway it generated in *Al-Skeini* to 'divide and tailor' the Convention obligations when applying them extra-territorially.[170] Milanovic argues that the Court should limit the positive obligations imposed on States where they are not exercising territorial control, but merely personal jurisdiction outside their home territory.[171] There are some problems with utilising *Al-Skeini* in this way. The judgment implied that when a State was exercising personal jurisdiction it was under an obligation to uphold the rights and freedoms that are relevant to the situation of that individual. The positive obligation to safeguard in Article 2 is clearly relevant in this situation and it may be difficult to avoid its application.

167 *Chember* v. *Russia* App no 7188/03 (ECtHR, 3 July 2008) at [50]; *R. (Smith)* v. *Oxfordshire Assistant Deputy Coroner* [2010] UKSC 29 at [100]. See also Rowe, 'The Obligation of a State' (n. 134) 9.

168 See *Yilmaz* v. *Turkey* App no 21899/02 (ECtHR, 17 June 2008) at [57].

169 Courts could also potentially draw similar distinctions between new recruits and fully trained soldiers, see *R. (Smith)* v. *Oxfordshire Assistant Deputy Coroner* [2010] UKSC 29 at [118].

170 For further discussion of this topic see Chapter 2.

171 Marko Milanovic, *Extraterritorial Application of Human Rights Treaties: Law, Principles, and Policy* (Oxford University Press 2011) 215–19.

The second, perhaps more likely option, lies in interpreting the margin of appreciation given to States when dealing with positive obligations. It could offer a wide margin of appreciation to States in respect of their policy decisions on procurement, equipment etc. and a wide margin of appreciation to operational decisions made by commanders on the ground. This could effectively narrow the middle ground on which *Long* and *Smith* were founded. The Court has historically been very slow to find breaches of the positive obligation for threats emanating from third parties,[172] though in those cases the State was absolved of responsibility because it did not know about or reasonably foresee the danger, which may not be a readily available defence for deployed military forces.[173]

The Court also has a mixed record when it comes to granting a wider margin of appreciation to the military because of its unique characteristics. Rowe points out that the Court has remained vigilant over the concessions it grants the military in certain cases, showing a reluctance to grant them specific concessions and a wider margin of appreciation, for example, in cases under Articles 8 and 10.[174] On the other hand, the Court has stressed in cases like *Engel and Others* v. *Netherlands* that one had to bear in mind the 'particular characteristics of military life and its effects on the situation of individual members of the armed forces' when interpreting and applying the rules of the Convention to the military.[175] It has also demonstrated a willingness to offer lower levels of human rights protections to the armed forces for other articles.[176] It is difficult to speculate how this would pan out, but as Landais and Bass note it is significant that the Court communicated the case of *Pritchard* v. *United Kingdom*,[177] which involved the death of a British soldier at the hands of a third party while he was travelling in an unarmoured jeep in Iraq in 2003, to the British government.[178] While the case was eventually subject to a friendly

[172] See for example *Osman* v. *United Kingdom* (2000) 29 EHRR 245 and *Van Colle* v. *United Kingdom* (2013) 56 EHRR 23.

[173] See *Akkoc* v. *Turkey* (2002) 34 EHRR 51; *Kontrova* v. *Slovakia* App no 7510/04 (ECtHR, 31 May 2007).

[174] Peter Rowe, *Control Over Armed Forces Exercised by the European Court of Human Rights* (Geneva Centre for the Democratic Control of Armed Forces Working Paper No. 56, 2002) 64–6; *Lustig-Prean* v. *United Kingdom* (2000) 29 EHRR 548.

[175] *Engel and Others* v. *Netherlands* (1979–1980) 1 EHRR 647 at [54].

[176] See *Chember* v. *Russia* App no 7188/03 (ECtHR, 3 July 2008) where the Court held that many acts, which would be violations of Article 3, may not reach the threshold of ill-treatment when they occur in the armed forces. See also *Sen and Others* v. *Turkey* App no 45824/99 (ECtHR, 8 July 2003) where the Court held military forces could expect lower levels of protection of their freedoms of expression and religion; *Grigoriades* v. *Greece* (1999) 27 EHRR 464.

[177] *Pritchard* v. *United Kingdom* App no 1573/11 (ECtHR, 30 August 2011).

[178] Landais and Bass (n. 40) 1298.

settlement, the fact that it was not rejected at the admissibility stage shows the Court is prepared to entertain such cases. Overall though the Court has been extremely cautious in extending this positive obligation to the police, it will likely be even more cautious and flexible when it comes to the military.[179]

### 3.5.4 *State Application of Positive Obligations*

The positive obligation in Article 2 presents significant difficulties for States attempting to uphold their obligations during many military operations. It remains unclear what kind of margin of appreciation will be granted to the State and how flexible the Court will be in applying this obligation, for example, to active combat operations. As such the exact scope of the positive obligation remains unclear. The difficulties are apparent if you consider the example of the first UK soldier killed in Iraq in 2003.[180]

In March 2003, Sergeant Steven Roberts was killed in a friendly fire incident. He was inadvertently hit when a vehicle-mounted machine gun opened fire on someone throwing stones at him. During the initial deployment of troops in Iraq, around 30 per cent of the battle group deployed there did not have enhanced body armour. This armour contained ceramic plates and offered better protection than standard combat body armour. As a result, British commanders in Iraq selected which troops should receive enhanced body armour and which soldiers would have to make do with combat body armour.[181] This meant armour was redistributed among the soldiers. Sergeant Roberts initially had enhanced body armour, but as a tank commander was ordered to surrender his enhanced body armour and wear combat body armour instead.

The board of inquiry examining Sergeant Roberts' death concluded that had he been wearing enhanced body armour, he would not have been fatally injured.[182] This seems to surpass the threshold established in *Long* with the inquiry showing that proper equipment, equipment which had been present and taken away, would have prevented the death. Soldiers in active combat

[179] Landais and Bass (n. 40) 1299.

[180] Rowe considers alternative scenarios in his article – Rowe, 'The Obligation of a State' (n. 134) 7–8.

[181] 'Iraq death due to kit shortage' (*BBC News*, 31 July 2006) 23 <http://news.bbc.co.uk/1/shared/bsp/hi/pdfs/sgtroberts31_07_06.pdf> accessed 4 August 2018.

[182] Ibid at 26; See also reports of the coroner's narrative verdict at the inquest into the death of Sergeant Roberts where the coroner stated: 'Sgt Roberts lost his life because he did not have that basic piece of equipment' – Stewart Payne 'Unforgiveable armour delay caused death', *The Daily Telegraph* (London, 19 December 2006).

operations are obviously going to be at risk from enemy small arms fire and while the risk is not completely avoidable, it can be reduced by equipping the soldiers with bullet proof helmets and body armour. The positive obligation would therefore require the State to provide body armour.

The problem here is that the State did provide body armour, it just wasn't the variety that would have prevented this injury and death. Does that mean that the State is liable for failing to provide him with enhanced body armour? This appears to be a policy decision on defence procurement, which may involve balancing complex political, social and economic interests.[183] The UKSC in *Smith* said such decisions were not amenable to judicial review and the Court has historically been extremely reluctant to substitute its views for those of the State's authorities.[184] While the Court may examine the reasons given by the State for the lack of protective equipment,[185] it seems unlikely that the State would be held liable for such a decision. Yet if the Court critiques decisions further along, such as the decision to redistribute armour, which seems to fall within the scope of *Long*, this amounts to an indirect assessment of the policy decisions on procurement. The decision to redistribute is a direct consequence of the earlier procurement decision and if a breach is found on this basis, the only way to resolve it is to change the procurement decision. Soldiers seldom have the perfect equipment for the job for a variety of reasons and the extension of the positive obligation in Article 2 may cause serious difficulties for States deploying troops without the perfect equipment. The distribution of armour represents one among a myriad of other procurement and deployment decisions a State will make during a military operation. The boundaries of the positive obligation in this field are not clear and the scope of the State's liability is disturbingly wide.

## 3.6 CONCLUSION

This chapter continued to analyse some of the themes identified in the previous chapters, uncertainty over the scope and content of obligations and inconsistent application of the law to similar situations. The chapter also looked in much greater detail at how the Court engages with IHL in its

183 *R. (Smith)* v. *Oxfordshire Assistant Deputy Coroner* [2010] UKSC 29 at [127].

184 *Oneryildiz* v. *Turkey* (2005) 41 EHRR 20 at [107]; *Buckley* v. *United Kingdom* App no 20348/92 (ECtHR, 29 September 1996) at [75]; *Hatton* v. *United Kingdom* App no 36022/97 (ECtHR, 8 July 2003) at [100]; The courts in England and Wales have been even more circumspect see *R. (Gentle)* v. *Prime Minister* [2008] UKHL 20.

185 Rowe, 'The Obligation of a State' (n. 134) 15.

judgments. It illustrated how the Court has glossed over some fundamental distinctions between human rights law and IHL by distinguishing between different categories of persons, civilians and others and accepting the use of force when not absolutely necessary. The implicit use of IHL standards in human rights law was perhaps most evident in the cases pertaining to indiscriminate attacks.

While Article 2 has come to incorporate many of the rules in IHL when it is applied to some military operations, this influence has not been overt or uniform. It has resulted in a great deal of arbitrariness and uncertainty over IHL's application. The apparent absorption and application of rules from IHL in the Convention's jurisprudence has not been accompanied by any clear assessment from the Court of whether the armed conflict threshold has been reached.

It is also unclear on what basis the Court treats certain cases differently or subjects them to different standards. At times the Court applies standards which mirror IHL, at other times the standard Convention approach is adopted. The result is a dilution of the Convention standards in some military operations cases without any clear rationale for this occurrence. This is exacerbated by the absence of a holistic approach toward the analysis of Article 2 cases more generally. The Court tends to fixate on establishing a single violation of the Convention, for example a failure to properly investigate, while overlooking other clear violations of the Convention, such as the clear breaches of the positive obligations in the cases of *Nakayev* and *Udayeva* identified above. This generates inconsistencies between factually similar cases where the Court's focus is directed toward establishing a violation under another head of Article 2.

The Court needs to take a more comprehensive and integrated approach toward the interpretation of Article 2. It needs to openly and transparently engage with IHL and acknowledge when it influences Convention norms. The Court would do well to follow the approach of the Inter-American bodies, which are much more open in their application of IHL. As it stands the Court's implicit application of IHL lacks transparency and encourages arbitrariness and inconsistency in the interpretation of Article 2. The Court's approach in *Hassan* is a welcome change which will hopefully continue, even if it is opposed by some judges at the Court, such as judge Pinto de Albuquerque.

This openness in interpretation must also carry through to the other side of Article 2, the procedural obligations, which form the subject of the next chapter. The Court arguably has much more autonomy to act in this area given the relative absence of procedural obligations arising under IHL. Yet the difficulties identified in this chapter are largely mirrored in respect of the procedural obligations, the Court must strike a fair balance between the rights of the victim and ensuring the State is not held to a disproportionate burden in the circumstances. In this sense, the Court faces another gargantuan task, trying to translate highly specialised and largely institution-dependent obligations into the alien world of military operations. As the Court has struggled to interpret substantive aspects of Article 2 transparently and consistently, it also struggles with procedural obligations.

# 4

# Article 2 Procedural Obligations

## 4.1 INTRODUCTION

The procedural obligations in Article 2, which are obligations related to the investigation of deaths or life-threatening injuries, present a unique challenge to States attempting to uphold them during military operations. The obligations require extensive institutional support from police, forensic investigators, prosecutors etc. to properly enforce them and they have proven to be a fertile source of applications to the Court related to both domestic and extra-territorial military operations.[1] These obligations represent another key fault line between IHL and human rights law, which must be examined. Human rights law seeks a review of every use of lethal force by State agents, while IHL implicitly accepts the use of force by State agents and the infliction of life-threatening injuries. As any obligation to thoroughly investigate all deaths or life-threatening injuries in the context of a military operation has the potential to be quite onerous for the State, this chapter looks at how to mitigate the impact of the obligations and reconcile the obligations in Article 2 with IHL. It outlines some of the benefits concurrent application and derogation can bring to this area of law, but also recognises some of the shortcomings these options present.

This chapter builds on a number of themes discussed in the previous chapters. It continues to examine the scope of the State's obligations during military operations, in particular the extent to which the obligations to investigate apply to the acts of third parties during military operations. It identifies and analyses the problems arising from the application of the Convention during

[1] See, for example, the domestic military operations cases like *Ogur* v. *Turkey* (2001) 31 EHRR 40 and *Jordan* v. *United Kingdom* (2003) 37 EHRR 2, and extra-territorial cases like *Al-Skeini and Others* v. *United Kingdom* (2011) 53 EHRR 18 and *Jaloud* v. *Netherlands* (2015) 60 EHRR 29.

military operations where institutional support is limited. The chapter considers how the discrete elements of the procedural obligations in Article 2 apply during military operations and whether it is genuinely possible for States to carry out prompt, independent, transparent and effective investigations in the context of military operations domestically and extra-territorially. The chapter identifies further inconsistencies in the Court's approach, at times granting concessions to the unusual circumstances presented by military operations and at other times holding very firmly to the same standards it would demand of an investigation at home.

## 4.2 THE PROCEDURAL OBLIGATIONS IN ARTICLE 2

The Court identified what triggers a duty to investigate in *Angelova and Iliev* v. *Bulgaria*. In that case, the applicant's son died after he was severely beaten and stabbed by a group of teenagers. The subsequent investigation and prosecution was poor and the Court found a procedural violation of Article 2. It stated that there must be some form of effective investigation when there is 'reason to believe that an individual had sustained life-threatening injuries in suspicious circumstances'.[2] The essential purpose of the procedural obligation to investigate is to secure the effective implementation of the domestic laws safeguarding the right to life and, in those cases involving State agents or bodies, to ensure their accountability for deaths occurring under their responsibility.[3]

The State must act of its own volition in investigating once the death or life-threatening injury is brought to its attention.[4] The investigating officers must be institutionally, hierarchically and practically independent from the State agents under investigation.[5] While the form of the investigation may vary,[6] it must be capable of determining whether a use of force was justified in the circumstances, identifying and, if necessary, punishing those responsible.[7] The authorities must take 'reasonable steps available to them' to secure evidence, e.g. witness statements, forensic evidence, autopsy, records of injury etc.[8] The investigation must be carried out expeditiously and the next of kin must be involved to the 'extent necessary to safeguard their interests'.[9] There must also

2 *Angelova and Iliev* v. *Bulgaria* (2008) 47 EHRR 7 at [94].
3 *Nachova* v. *Bulgaria* (2006) 42 EHRR 43 at [110].
4 *Ergi* v. *Turkey* (2001) 32 EHRR 18 at [82].
5 *Jordan* v. *United Kingdom* (2003) 37 EHRR 2 at [106].
6 *Kelly and Others* v. *United Kingdom* App no 30054/96 (ECtHR, 4 May 2001).
7 *Ogur* v. *Turkey* (2001) 31 EHRR 40 at [88].
8 *Edwards* v. *United Kingdom* (2002) 35 EHRR 19 at [71].
9 Ibid at [73].

be sufficient public scrutiny of the investigation or its results, although the scope of this obligation will vary from case to case.[10]

The procedural obligations under Article 2 have been held to directly apply to military operations and armed conflicts, whether international or non-international.[11] The Court expressly acknowledged this in its admissibility decision in *Georgia* v. *Russia (II)* stating: 'the procedural obligation under Article 2 of the Convention continued to apply even where the security conditions were difficult, including in the context of armed conflict'.[12]

## 4.3 GENERAL SCOPE OF THE PROCEDURAL OBLIGATIONS

The procedural obligations are presumed to apply domestically, but as the chapters on jurisdiction observed, the situation is less straightforward extra-territorially.[13] The type of jurisdiction exercised by the State may alter the scope of the procedural obligations. We can draw a broad distinction between two situations, firstly where the State exercises spatial jurisdiction extra-territorially i.e. effective control over another State's territory and secondly where the State exercises personal jurisdiction, wherein a person is placed under the effective authority and control of a State agent, or personal plus jurisdiction, the former situation, but in the broader context of exercising all or some of the public powers normally exercised by the territory's government.

In the first situation, all the Convention obligations apply, including the procedural obligations in Article 2.[14] The State would be obliged to investigate all cases where a person has sustained life-threatening injuries in suspicious circumstances. Crucially in the context of military operations, this could include where the death or life-threatening injury is caused by the actions of third parties.[15] This obligation is evident from cases like *Menson* v. *United Kingdom*, where the Court stated that 'the absence of any direct State responsibility for the death of a person does not exclude the applicability of Article 2'.[16]

[10] *Slimani* v. *France* (2006) 43 EHRR 49 at [29].
[11] Andrea Gioia, 'The Role of the European Court of Human Rights in Monitoring Compliance with Humanitarian Law in Armed Conflict' in Orna Ben-Naftali (ed), *International Humanitarian Law and International Human Rights Law* (Oxford University Press 2012) 201–3.
[12] *Georgia* v. *Russia (II)* (2012) 54 EHRR SE10 at [72].
[13] See Chapter 2.
[14] *Loizidou* v. *Turkey (Preliminary Objections)* (1995) 20 EHRR 99 at [62].
[15] *Ergi* v. *Turkey* (2001) 32 EHRR 18 at [82]; *Kolevi* v. *Bulgaria* App no 1108/02 (ECtHR, 5 November 2009) at [191]; *Angelova and Iliev* v. *Bulgaria* (2008) 47 EHRR 7 at [93].
[16] *Menson* v. *United Kingdom* (2003) 37 EHRR CD220; *Pereira Henriques* v. *Luxembourg* App no 60255/00 (ECtHR, 9 May 2006).

In the second situation, the State has the obligation to secure the rights that are relevant to the situation,[17] which may alter the scope of the procedural obligations such that the State is not obliged to investigate all cases. One can reasonably infer from the *Al-Skeini* case, discussed in the previous chapters, that the State would only be obliged to investigate where the State agent has exercised some effective control over, or had used force against, the person who has died or suffered a life threatening injury.[18] Thus, these forms of jurisdiction would be unlikely to encompass deaths caused by third parties because they rely on the actions of State agents to create the jurisdictional link to the contracting State.

Where the State exercises spatial jurisdiction, it could face an extremely onerous burden during military operations. This is a key fault line between IHL and HRL, as human rights law seeks a review of every use of lethal force by State agents, while IHL is based on the premise that force will be used and humans intentionally killed. HRL works to limit the development and use of a shoot-to-kill policy, while IHL is directed toward controlling how such a policy is implemented.[19] Watkin argues an automatic investigation into every use of force by State agents is not feasible and that not every death can or should be subject to the exhaustive review process normally associated with the application of peacetime human rights norms.[20] If the obligation is considered excessive when solely applicable to the use of force by State agents, it will be even more excessive if the State also has to investigate deaths caused by third parties.[21]

In many of the cases involving the extra-territorial use of force the exact party responsible may not be clear. In *Jaloud* v. *Netherlands*, for example, where Dutch and Iraqi soldiers opened fire on a vehicle passing through a checkpoint in Iraq in 2004, it was not clear whether Dutch or Iraqi soldiers were responsible for the fatal injuries.[22] This would have meant that an Article 2-compliant investigation was required even though a third party may have been responsible.

[17] *Al-Skeini and Others* v. *United Kingdom* (2011) 53 EHRR 18 at [137].

[18] Ibid at [136].

[19] Kenneth Watkin, 'Controlling the Use of Force: A Role for Human Rights Norms in Contemporary Armed Conflict' (2004) 98 AJIL 1, 32; Jacob Turkel, *The Public Commission to Examine the Maritime Incident of 31 May 2010: Second Report: Israel's Mechanisms for Examining and Investigating Complaints and Claims of Violations of the Laws of Armed Conflict According to International Law* (2013) 100–3; David Kretzmer, 'Rethinking the Application of IHL in Non-International Armed Conflicts' (2009) 42 *Israel Law Review* 8, 36.

[20] Watkin (n. 19) 32–3; Turkel (n. 19) 100–3.

[21] House of Commons Defence Committee, *UK Armed Forces Personnel and the Legal Framework for Future Operations: Twelfth Report of Session 2013–14* (The Stationery Office 2014) Evidence 24–5.

[22] *Jaloud* v. *Netherlands* (2015) 60 EHRR 29 at [12].

While the procedural obligations can be challenging to satisfy domestically, the situation is even more difficult extra-territorially. As noted in previous chapters, human rights law is heavily dependent on having a functioning nation State for its proper operation and once the precept of the functioning State is removed, the scope, content and even the very application of the law becomes extremely fluid. When armed forces are deployed abroad, they lack the same level of support from civilian institutions they enjoy on home territory.[23] Consider the difficulties presented by discharging the procedural obligation during the Iraq invasion of 2003.

The UK was a belligerent occupier of part of Iraq from May 2003 to June 2004 and let's assume that it exercised spatial jurisdiction there. Discharging the procedural obligation in this context would naturally fall to Royal Military Police (RMP). The number of RMP available during that period varied due to troop rotations from a high point of 250 to a low of 70 RMP. These soldiers had a variety of tasks, including close protection, guarding and maintaining law and order within the Army itself. Only a small fraction of these were designated investigators in the Special Investigations Branch (SIB),[24] and their job was to investigate possible crimes perpetrated by armed forces personnel. The SIB could not serve as a surrogate police force for a State emerging from conflict, that was clearly not their function.

During that period from May 2003 to June 2004, 656 people were killed in Basrah alone.[25] Obliging the UK to investigate every death, including those by third parties, would have placed an impossible burden on the tiny RMP force. The SIB deployed there reported that even minor increases in the numbers of fatalities they had to investigate created significant problems.[26] To give some perspective on those figures, in the same year in England and Wales, with its police force of approximately 135,000 and all its facilities and resources, they had to investigate 772 homicides.[27] It would have

[23] Michael Schmitt, 'Investigating Violations of International Law in Armed Conflict' (2011) 2 *Harvard National Security Journal* 31, 54–5.

[24] *R. (Ali Zaki Mousa)* v. *Secretary of State for Defence (CA)* [2011] EWCA Civ 1334 at [28].

[25] Figures taken from statistics at 'Iraq Body Count' <www.iraqbodycount.org/database> accessed 1 August 2018.

[26] Her Majesty's Inspectorate of Constabulary, *HMIC Royal Military Police Special Investigation Branch Inspection Re-inspection* (Ref: J284574, 2007) 7.

[27] Amardeep Dhani and Peter Kaiza, *Police Service Strength, England and Wales, 31 March 2011* (Home Office Statistical Bulletin HOSB: 13/11, 2011), 26; Homicide statistics: Kevin Smith and others, *Homicides, Firearm Offences and Intimate Violence 2010/11: Supplementary Volume 2 to Crime in England and Wales 2010/11* (Home Office Statistical Bulletin HOSB: 02/12, 2012) 32.

been simply impossible for the State to satisfy the obligation in Iraq with the resources it had deployed.[28]

Yet, it was entirely foreseeable that law and order would collapse in Iraq post-conflict, so to what extent should the lack of personnel and resources deployed serve as an excuse for the inability to properly uphold Convention obligations? This is a difficult question to answer. The Court has been unreceptive to pleas that a lack of resources could excuse a failure to discharge a Convention obligation in the past.[29] The danger in allowing such an excuse is that it could incentivise States to limit their troop deployments and claim an inability to uphold Convention obligations because of that. At the same time, questions concerning how resources are allocated and divided lie largely in a policy sphere that the Court is not eager to engage with, as noted in the previous chapter.[30] It is also safe to say that at the time the UK Ministry of Defence did not fully appreciate or plan for the human rights obligations they would be held to years later in cases like *Al-Skeini*, *Al-Saadoon* and *Al-Jedda*.[31] They had received advice from the Attorney General that the Convention applied to some aspects of the conflict.[32] However, a number of issues were unresolved at that point, and still remain largely unresolved today, including the scope and content of the State's extra-territorial obligations.[33] In this context, the deployment of a small contingent of RMP is perhaps more understandable.

## 4.4 MODIFYING THE PROCEDURAL OBLIGATION

As noted in previous chapters, where the Court is dealing with duties/positive obligations on the State it is keen to avoid imposing impossible or disproportionate burdens on the State.[34] In respect of the procedural obligation, the Court specifically noted that 'Article 2 must be applied realistically, to take account of specific problems faced by investigators'.[35] The nature and degree

[28] Cusack notes that satisfying a similar obligation would have also been impossible for the UK's US allies in Iraq with the resources available to them – Colin Cusack, 'We've Talked the Talk, Time to Walk the Walk: Meeting International Human Rights Law Standards for U.S. Military Investigations' (2013) 217 *Military Law Review* 48, 67.

[29] *Burdov* v. *Russia* (2009) 49 EHRR 2 at [70].

[30] See Chapter 2 – Sections 2.5.1 and 2.5.2.

[31] William Gage, *The Baha Mousa Public Inquiry Report* (The Stationery Office 2011) 667 and 809.

[32] The Baha Mousa Public Inquiry, *Attorney-General's Advice Ruling*, 1 April 2010 at [38].

[33] This was discussed extensively in Chapter 2.

[34] See, for example, *Giuliani and Gaggio* v. *Italy* (2012) 54 EHRR 10 at [245]; *Osman* v. *United Kingdom* (2000) 29 EHRR 245 at [116] and the discussions of positive obligations in Chapters 2 and 3.

[35] *Al-Skeini and Others* v. *United Kingdom* (2011) 53 EHRR 18 at [168].

of scrutiny of the procedural obligation may also depend on the practical realities of investigation work.[36] It is clear that an obligation to investigate all of the deaths and life-threatening injuries in a specific territory during, or shortly after, an armed conflict has the potential to be a disproportionate burden on the State, which the Court would be keen to avoid. This section discusses how the impact of this obligation could be mitigated.

### 4.4.1 *Derogation*

The most obvious solution appears to be derogation. Article 15 refers to there being 'no derogation from Article 2, except in respect of deaths resulting from lawful acts of war'. By inference States could derogate from Article 2 for lawful acts of war, thereby modifying the substantive obligation under Article 2 so that only unlawful acts of war were penalised under Article 2. This would in turn mean that the procedural obligations would only be triggered where an unlawful act of war resulted in a death or life-threatening injury, alleviating some of the discrepancies arising from the different types of jurisdiction.

While the term war naturally implies international armed conflict, there is scope to broaden the definition to include NIACs.[37] As noted in the previous chapter, the Court's engagement with IHL in the context of Article 2 leaves much to be desired.[38] Utilising such a derogation would force the Court to actively consider how IHL influences the Convention norms because derogations must be consistent with the State's other obligations under international law.[39]

There are some issues with derogation here, which are discussed in detail in Chapter 7, but it suffices at this point to note that States have never derogated from Article 2 in the past and that because it is only possible to derogate

[36] *Velcea and Mazare* v. *Romania* App no 64301/01 (ECtHR, 1 December 2009) at [105]; *Velikova* v. *Bulgaria* App no 41488/98 (ECtHR, 18 May 2000) at [80].

[37] Joan Fitzpatrick, *Human Rights in Crisis: The International System for Protecting Human Rights During States of Emergency* (University of Pennsylvania Press 1994) 57; Louise Doswald-Beck, 'The Right to Life in Armed Conflict: Does International Humanitarian Law Provide all the Answers?' (2006) 88 IRRC 881, 882. For a similar discussion in the context of the American Convention on Human Rights see Robert Norris and Paula Reiton, 'The Suspension of Guarantees: A Comparative Analysis of the American Convention on Human Rights and the Constitutions of the States Parties' (1980) 30 *American University Law Review* 189, 195; See further discussion of this topic in Chapter 7 – Section 7.4.1.

[38] See Chapter 3 – Section 3.3.4.

[39] Christine Byron, 'A Blurring of the Boundaries: The Application of International Humanitarian Law by Human Rights Bodies' (2006–2007) 47 *Virginia Journal of International Law* 839; Noam Lubell, 'Challenges in Applying Human Rights Law to Armed Conflict' (2005) 87 IRRC 737, 742–4. These issues are also discussed further in Chapter 7.

from Article 2 for lawful acts of war, military operations short of armed conflict would still fall under standard Article 2 rules in the event of a derogation. Applying this rule would also force the Court to determine whether an armed conflict existed. While the Court has recognised the existence of conflicts, it has not engaged in specific analysis of whether the threshold for the existence of an armed conflict has been reached.[40] While there are significant advantages to derogating, States may not use these powers.[41]

### 4.4.2 *Sharing the Procedural Obligation*

Another option to alleviate the investigatory burden on the military is for the State to share it. The Court does not seem to have any objection to the investigatory burden being shared between different bodies. This is evident from *Pearson v. United Kingdom*, where the Court observed that the essential purpose of the procedural obligations is to ensure accountability and there did not need to be:

> one unified procedure satisfying all requirements: the aims of fact-finding and accountability may be carried out by or shared between several authorities, as long as the various procedures provide for the necessary safeguards in an accessible and effective manner.[42]

The Court seemed particularly well disposed to the sharing of the procedural obligation in the context of war crimes in the case of *Maktouf and Damjanovic v. Bosnia and Herzegovina*. The Court looked at how the burden to investigate was shared between the State courts and Entity courts in Bosnia. The Court stated that:

> given the large number of war crimes cases in post-war Bosnia and Herzegovina, it is inevitable that the burden must be shared between the State Court and Entity courts. If not, the respondent State would not be able to honour its Convention obligation to bring to justice those responsible for serious violations of international humanitarian law in a timely manner.[43]

While the bodies in each of the above cases were domestic authorities, the principle of sharing the obligation expounded by the Court could be

[40] See Chapter 3 – Section 3.3.4.

[41] In the long term this may change, it is argued in Chapter 7 that claims that the State is not exercising jurisdiction during military operations foreign or domestic, or that IHL displaces HRL, are becoming increasingly untenable before the Court. This could prompt more States to derogate in the future.

[42] *Pearson v. United Kingdom* (2012) 54 EHRR SE11 at [71].

[43] *Maktouf and Damjanovic v. Bosnia and Herzegovina* (2014) 58 EHRR 11 at [82].

applicable in other contexts. The State could revert some of the investigation duties to the domestic institutions where the institutional capacity is greater, thereby relieving the burden on forces in the field. The British courts applied the principle from *Pearson* to a military operation in the case *R. (Long)* v. *Secretary of State for Defence*, discussed in the Chapter 3, with an internal military Board of Inquiry discharging part of the investigatory obligation and a coronial inquest discharging the remainder.[44] However, as these investigations are often carried out long after the events, they can suffer from problems with promptness.[45]

The State could also potentially rely on a local administration established in an occupied territory to assist in fulfilling its investigatory obligations.[46] In fact, as the discussion below indicates, it may be obliged to do this by limitations to the deployed force's jurisdiction. In principle, the Court did not see any reason to dismiss the sharing of the procedural obligations between Dutch and Iraqi authorities during a military operation in *Jaloud* v. *Netherlands*, although it did find that aspects of the Iraqi investigation were deficient, which will be discussed further below. The burden could also be shared with international partners in certain circumstances. Investigations into enforced disappearances can benefit from the assistance of the International Commission on Missing Persons. Investigations into war crimes can be assisted by the International Criminal Court, which would be especially relevant where the State is unable to discharge its obligation to investigate.[47]

### 4.4.3 *Co-application of IHL and the Convention*

The Court could also alleviate the burden created by the procedural obligation by interpreting the Convention in light of IHL. This could considerably alter the legal paradigm,[48] in a similar way to the derogation discussed above.

44 *R. (Long)* v. *Secretary of State for Defence* [2015] EWCA Civ 770 at [52]–[55].

45 In the Inter-American system, for example, the Commission was able to rely on extensive reports from the truth and reconciliation commission established in El Salvador in the case of *Ignacio Ellacurias* v. *El Salvador* Report No 136/99 IAComHR 22 December 1999 at [75]–[78]; Although note the difficulties the UK has encountered in establishing a Convention-compliant investigation into historical human rights abuses in Iraq discussed further below.

46 Note the Court allowed Turkey to rely upon the local administration established in the TRNC to assist in satisfying its human rights obligations – *Cyprus* v. *Turkey* (2002) 35 EHRR 30 at [102].

47 The Rome Statute of the International Criminal Court allows the ICC to investigate where the State is unwilling or unable to exercise its duty to do so see Article 17(1)(a), Rome Statute of the International Criminal Court (adopted 17 July 1998, entered into force 1 July 2002) 2187 UNTS 3 (Rome Statute).

48 Schmitt (n. 23) 54–5.

Under this approach, the right to life would be interpreted such that deprivations of life or the infliction of life threatening injuries that are legal under IHL would not trigger the procedural obligation.[49] As noted in the introduction, the ICJ interpreted the right to life in the ICCPR harmoniously with IHL stating:

> whether a particular loss of life [...] is to be considered an arbitrary deprivation of life contrary to Article 6 of the Covenant, can only be decided by reference to the law applicable in armed conflict.[50]

There is a difference in the wording of the right to life in the ICCPR and the Convention. The ICCPR prohibits arbitrary deprivation of life, while the Convention sets out a finite list of specific circumstances in which force can be used. Yet, the same is true of Article 9 of the ICCPR, which prohibits arbitrary arrest or detention and Article 5 of the European Convention, which contains a finite list of situations in which people can be deprived of their liberty. This difference did not prevent the Court from interpreting Article 5 in light of IHL in *Hassan* v. *United Kingdom*.

In *Hassan*, the applicant's brother had been subject to internment by UK forces in Basrah while they were in occupation of the territory. The applicant alleged that his detention was arbitrary, unlawful and lacked procedural safeguards in violation of Article 5. The Court stated 'even in situations of international armed conflict, the safeguards under the Convention continue to apply, albeit interpreted against the background of the provisions of international humanitarian law'.[51] It then proceeded to interpret Article 5 in light of IHL, holding that security detention was permissible under Article 5, but that the legitimacy of the detention must be reviewed by an impartial body, offering fair procedures and ensuring the detention was not arbitrary.[52] This judgment is discussed extensively in Chapter 5, for now it suffices to note that if the Court can read the finite list of circumstances in which the State can detain someone as including a right to detain someone under IHL, it could also read the finite list of circumstances in which a person can be deprived of the right to life as including deprivations of life consistent with IHL.

49 Turkel (n. 19) 109.

50 *Legality of the Threat or Use of Nuclear Weapons*, Advisory Opinion, ICJ Reports 1996, p. 226 8 July 1996 at [25]; Jean-Marie Henckaerts, 'Concurrent Application of International Humanitarian Law and Human Rights Law: A Victim Perspective' in Noelle Quenivet and Roberta Arnold (eds), *International Humanitarian Law and Human Rights Law: Towards a New Merger in International Law* (Brill 2008) 265.

51 *Hassan* v. *United Kingdom* App no 29750/09 (ECtHR, 16 September 2014) at [104].

52 Ibid at [106].

The procedural obligation in Article 2 could be applied to ensure criminal activities occurring in the context of military operations, such as grave breaches of the Geneva Conventions, war crimes, crimes against humanity and genocide, are subject to Article 2-compliant investigations and prosecutions.[53] This could provide a number of benefits.

As noted in the introduction, the absence of a forum in which to enforce individual claims of IHL violations is a key factor driving applicants to take cases to the Court in the first place.[54] The object of IHL may be to protect individuals from the excesses of armed conflict, but individual victims have been marginalised in the process of redressing IHL violations. Weak enforcement of IHL norms and the lack of political will to utilise means of enforcement, such as universal jurisdiction, has meant that many violations go unpunished.[55] Even when violations are addressed, the use of criminal sanctions has resulted in a focus on punishing the perpetrator, rather than compensating the victim.[56] While it is possible for individuals to seek reparations for

[53] Generally speaking the procedural obligation is an obligation of means rather than results, but Schabas argues that the Convention may oblige States to have recourse to prosecutions – William Schabas, 'Synergy or Fragmentation? International Criminal Law and the European Convention on Human Rights' (2011) 9 *Journal of International Criminal Justice* 609, 619. The Inter-American bodies stress the need for criminal prosecution of human rights abuses in many cases – *Ignacio Ellacurias* v. *El Salvador* Report No 136/99 IAComHR 22 December 1999 at [191]–[196]; *Santo Domingo Massacre* v. *Colombia* Series No. 259 IACtHR 30 November 2012 at [157]; Fernando Felipe Basch, 'The Doctrine of the Inter-American Court of Human Rights Regarding States' Duty to Punish Human Rights Violations and Its Dangers' (2007) 23 *American University International Law Review* 195. Others have cautioned against the idea that Article 2 should demand prosecutions, see Natasa Mavronicola, 'Taking Life and Liberty Seriously: Reconsidering Criminal Liability Under Article 2 of the ECHR' (2017) 80(6) *Modern Law Review* 1026, 1048.

[54] Noelle Quenivet, 'The Right to Life in International Humanitarian Law and Human Rights Law' in Roberta Arnold and Noelle Quenivet (eds), *International Humanitarian Law and Human Rights Law: Towards a New Merger in International Law* (Brill 2008) 9; Theodor Meron, 'The Humanization of Humanitarian Law' (2000) 94 AJIL 239, 247; Emiliano Buis, 'The Implementation of International Humanitarian Law by Human Rights Courts: The Example of the Inter-American Human Rights System' in Noelle Quenivet and Roberta Arnold (eds), *International Humanitarian Law and Human Rights Law: Towards a New Merger in International Law* (Brill 2008) 269–70.

[55] M. Cherif Bassiouni, 'Searching for Peace and Achieving Justice: The Need for Accountability' (1996) 59 *Law & Contemporary Problems* 9, 17–18.

[56] Henckaerts (n. 50) 249. The ICC aims to redress some of this bias by creating a permanent institution to prosecute international crimes occurring throughout the world. It also took some steps toward re-focusing on and offering reparations to victims of IHL, see Article 75, Rome Statute.

IHL violations,[57] such actions have had limited success in practice.[58] Utilising the accountability framework provided by the procedural obligations in the Convention could act as a catalyst for more widespread and effective enforcement of IHL.

The Convention seems to envisage Article 2 operating in this fashion during armed conflicts. Article 15 contemplates the continued application of Article 2 to unlawful acts of war.[59] The application of the procedural obligations in this context would be no more than the State is already obliged to do by other provisions of international law. There is a strong argument that States have a duty under customary international law to investigate and prosecute international crimes.[60] The Geneva Conventions require States to search for, try or extradite people who are suspected of committing grave breaches of their provisions.[61] The Rome Statute of the International Criminal Court demands that States investigate and prosecute international crimes, including war crimes, crimes against humanity and genocide.[62] Although Schabas cautions that the criminal acts under IHL would still have to coincide with violations of the Convention for the procedural obligation to investigate to arise.[63]

57 Article 3, Hague Convention (IV) Respecting the Laws and Customs of War on Land and Its Annex: Regulations concerning the Laws and Customs of War on Land (adopted 18 October 1907, entered into force 26 January 1910) 205 CTS 277. This article does not specify who should be the recipient of reparations. At the time of drafting it was presumed to be States given that the notion of an individual as a subject of international law did not become widespread until later.

58 Emanuela-Chiara Gillard, 'Reparation for Violations of International Humanitarian Law' (2003) 85 IRRC 529, 536–7.

59 See the discussion in Chapters 3 and 7.

60 Harmen van der Wilt and Sandra Lyngdorf, 'Procedural Obligations Under the European Convention on Human Rights: Useful Guidelines for the Assessment of "Unwillingness" and "Inability" in the Context of the Complementarity Principle' (2009) 9 *International Criminal Law Review* 39, 69; Louise Doswald-Beck and Jean-Marie Henckaerts (eds), *Customary International Humanitarian Law*, 2 vols. (Cambridge University Press 2004) vol I, 607.

61 Article 49, Geneva Convention for the Amelioration of the Condition of the Wounded and Sick in Armed Forces in the Field (adopted 12 August 1949, entered into force 21 October 1950) 75 UNTS 31 (Geneva Convention I); Article 50, Geneva Convention for the Amelioration of the Condition of Wounded, Sick and Shipwrecked Members of Armed Forces at Sea (adopted 12 August 1949, entered into force 21 October 1950) 75 UNTS 85 (Geneva Convention II); Article 129, Geneva Convention Relative to the Treatment of Prisoners of War (adopted 12 August 1949, entered into force 21 October 1950) 75 UNTS 135 (Geneva Convention III); Article 146, Geneva Convention Relative to the Protection of Civilian Persons in Time of War (adopted 12 August 1949, entered into force 21 October 1950) 75 UNTS 287 (Geneva Convention IV).

62 This obligation is implicit in the complementarity principle established in Article 17, Rome Statute. To date only seven Council of Europe States have not ratified the Rome Statute: Armenia, Azerbaijan, Monaco, Russia, Turkey, Ukraine.

63 Schabas (n. 53) 622.

### 4.4.4 *Flexible Interpretation of Article 2*

The harmonious interpretation of IHL with the Convention will be of limited benefit for military operations short of armed conflicts. In such circumstances, applicants will have to rely on flexible interpretations of Article 2. The Court is clearly open to interpreting the Convention flexibly in this context, as noted above it stated that it would apply the procedural obligations 'realistically' in *Al-Skeini*. It made similar remarks in *Jaloud* v. *Netherlands* stating it was:

> prepared to make reasonable allowances for the relatively difficult conditions under which the Netherlands military and investigators had to work. In particular, it must be recognised that they were engaged in a foreign country which had yet to be rebuilt in the aftermath of hostilities, whose language and culture were alien to them, and whose population [...] clearly included armed hostile elements.[64]

The approach is pragmatic and sensible. Although, as noted in Chapters 2 and 3, adopting this standard of what is 'realistic' introduces a great deal of uncertainty into the law. Equally, as the following sections will illustrate, the Court pays lip-service to the idea of flexible interpretation without necessarily making concessions for the difficulties faced by the States. What is clear is that there are a number of options available to the Court to ensure that the potentially onerous procedural obligations in Article 2 are mitigated.

## 4.5 INDEPENDENCE

The struggle to guarantee the independence and impartiality of those investigating the acts of military forces has been a recurring theme in human rights law.[65] The Court has sought to limit the scope for military forces to cover up illegal behaviour and Article 2 demands that where a State agent is implicated in its violation, those investigating the violation must be independent from those implicated.[66]

[64] *Jaloud* v. *Netherlands* (2015) 60 EHRR 29 at [226].

[65] See, for example, *Jordan* v. *United Kingdom* (2003) 37 EHRR 2. It has equally occupied the Inter-American system, see for example, the Commission's criticism of the Honor Commission's investigations in El Salvador – *Ignacio Ellacurias* v. *El Salvador* Report No 136/99 IAComHR 22 December 1999 at [142], or the recommendations to remove certain crimes from military jurisdiction in *Arturo Ribón Avilán* v. *Colombia* Report No 26/97 IAComHR 30 September 1997 at [191].

[66] This uncompromising approach toward the independence of investigators is evident in other cases also see *Charalambous and Others* v. *Turkey* App no 46744/07 (ECtHR, 3 April 2012) at [57] and *Gulec* v. *Turkey* (1999) 28 EHRR 121 at [81]–[82].

The independence criterion requires multiple elements. The investigators must be hierarchically, institutionally and practically independent from the alleged perpetrators. Hierarchical independence requires that the chain of command controlling the investigators must be independent from that of the accused parties.[67] In *Al-Skeini*, the Court stated that the military police investigating the incidents had to be institutionally separate from the soldiers implicated. Finally, practical independence demands that investigators have access to their own resources and be self-reliant.[68]

The Court has found many violations of the independence criterion during domestic military operations, for example, in Turkey,[69] Northern Ireland[70] and Russia.[71] While the problems arising from the independence criterion domestically have not been completely resolved in these countries,[72] the case law has resulted in significant institutional reforms.[73] There has also been significant academic comment on the independence criterion in the domestic sphere.[74] By contrast, the application of the independence criterion to extra-territorial investigations has received little attention and the following sections address that issue.

### 4.5.1 *Independence during Extra-Territorial Military Operations*

The application of the independence criterion to extra-territorial military operations has the potential to cause significant problems for the armed forces. The high level of interdependence between different parts of the

67 In *Jordan* v. *United Kingdom*, for example, a violation was found because there was a hierarchical link between the officers in the investigation and the officers subject to investigation.

68 Alastair Mowbray, 'Duties of Investigation under the European Convention on Human Rights' (2002) 51 ICLQ 437, 440.

69 See, for example, *Ipek* v. *Turkey* App no 25760/94 (ECtHR, 17 February 2004) at [174]; *Gulec* v. *Turkey* (1999) 28 EHRR 121.

70 *Kelly and Others* v. *United Kingdom* App no 30054/96 (ECtHR, 4 May 2001); *Jordan* v. *United Kingdom* (2003) 37 EHRR 2; *McShane* v. *United Kingdom* App no 43290/98 (ECtHR, 28 May 2002).

71 See, for example, *Abuyeva and Others* v. *Russia* App no 27065/05 (ECtHR, 2 December 2010) at [212]; *Turluyeva* v. *Russia* App no 63638/09 (ECtHR, 20 June 2013) at [109]; *Askhabova* v. *Russia* App no 54765/09 (ECtHR, 18 April 2013) at [153].

72 See, for example, *Aslakhanova and Others* v. *Russia* App no 2944/06 (ECtHR, 18 December 2012).

73 Silvia Borelli and Sandra Lyngdorf, *The Impact of the Jurisprudence of the European Court of Human Rights on Domestic Investigations and Prosecutions of Serious Human Rights Violations by State Agents* (DOMAC/7, May 2010) 22–6.

74 Juliet Chevalier-Watts, 'Effective Investigations under Article 2 of the European Convention on Human Rights: Securing the Right to Life or an Onerous Burden on a State?' (2010) 21 EJIL 701; David Harris, Michael O'Boyle, Ed Bates, Carla Buckley and Colin Warbrick, *Law of the European Convention on Human Rights* (3rd edn, Oxford University Press 2014) 214ff.

military can make it difficult for them to satisfy every aspect of the independence criterion during extra-territorial military operations. Military police may need other units to provide security while they investigate incidents or share facilities with other units, compromising their practical independence. Deployed forces may have extremely limited facilities to house their troops, making separating military police from regular soldiers difficult. Demanding such strict separation during an active conflict could also compromise the security of the troops, potentially leading to a violation of the positive obligation to protect soldiers.

In 2006, the UK inspectorate of constabularies reviewed the operations of the RMP's investigators in Iraq, and the report offers a good insight into some of practical difficulties faced by the investigators in Iraq. The report showed that military police were typically deployed in small numbers with even fewer members of Special Investigations Branch tasked with investigations. An investigation team of four was always available for deployment in Iraq if requested by a commanding officer.[75] The units had little capacity to conduct investigations on their own initiative. The team had sufficient post-mortem facilities and capacity to conduct forensic examinations,[76] but deploying the team and its ancillaries (pathologist, radiologist, ballistics expert and forensic warrant officer), along with a protection force required significant co-ordination and resources.[77] The team was heavily reliant on other soldiers providing security while they investigated, which clearly compromised their practical independence.

As noted above, the Court is open to making concessions for practical problems on the ground. However, in practice the Court's approach to the independence criterion has been inconsistent. In *Al-Skeini*, the Court did not alter the standards it had set on independence in previous jurisprudence, notwithstanding the difficulties identified above. It stressed the importance of the independence criterion stating that it was 'particularly important that the investigating authority was, and was seen to be, operationally independent of the military chain of command'.[78]

The focus was on institutional and hierarchical independence. In three of the cases joined to *Al-Skeini*, the investigations were deemed inadequate because they had been carried out by the commanding officers of the soldiers

[75] Her Majesty's Inspectorate of Constabulary, *HMIC Royal Military Police Special Investigation Branch Inspection* (Ref: J276389, 2006) 13.

[76] Ibid 25.

[77] Ibid 8 and 11.

[78] *Al-Skeini and Others v. United Kingdom* (2011) 53 EHRR 18 at [169].

implicated. Those investigations remained entirely within the military chain of command and were limited to taking statements from the soldiers involved.[79] In the other two cases, although the RMP investigated the deaths, they were found not to be operationally independent of the military chain of command and were not sufficiently independent of the soldiers implicated for the purposes of Article 2.[80] Thus while the Court seemed to accept that concessions needed to be made for the circumstances, it declined to make them, stressing the importance of upholding the independence criterion.

The Court did make concessions in the case of *Jaloud* v. *Netherlands*. In that case, the applicant's son was shot as he drove through a checkpoint in South-Eastern Iraq in April 2004. The checkpoint was manned by Dutch and Iraqi soldiers. The Dutch military dispatched investigators to review the shooting shortly after it occurred. The applicant alleged that the investigators were not sufficiently independent from the alleged perpetrators for the purposes of Article 2. His complaint related to the fact that the investigators shared living quarters with the soldiers alleged to have carried out the shooting. The Court acknowledged that they did share quarters and that independence can be compromised where the investigators and alleged perpetrators 'maintain close relations with one another'.[81] However, the Court stated that:

> no circumstances have been suggested, or become apparent, that might lead the Court to find that this in itself affected the independence of the Royal Military Constabulary unit to the point of impairing the quality of its investigations.[82]

The Court went on to find a violation of the procedural obligation on different grounds, discussed further below. This finding is problematic because the function of the independence criterion is not just to secure actual independence, but also to ensure public confidence in the State's monopoly on the use of force.[83] Just as the State must avoid bias and any appearance of bias to secure public confidence and satisfy Article 6,[84] so too should the independence requirements of Article 2 require both actual independence and the avoidance of any appearances of a lack of impartiality.[85] In this instance, the Court seems to only care about the former, but not the latter. Some

79 Ibid at [153] and [171].
80 Ibid at [172].
81 *Jaloud* v. *Netherlands* (2015) 60 EHRR 29 at [188].
82 Ibid at [189].
83 *Giuliani and Gaggio* v. *Italy* (2012) 54 EHRR 10 at [300].
84 *Micallef* v. *Malta* (2010) 50 EHRR 37 at [93].
85 *Ramsahai* v. *Netherlands* (2008) 46 EHRR 43 at [321] and [325].

commentators have expressed concerns over the consistency of the Court's approach between *Jaloud* and *Al-Skeini* arguing that the Court has failed to clarify the scope of the procedural obligation.[86]

### 4.5.2 *Adapting Investigation Procedures*

The UK tried to tackle many of the problems with their investigation procedures after *Al-Skeini*. This remedial process revealed significant difficulties with ensuring independence and offers some cautionary lessons for other States, like the Netherlands, who may also have to deal with the issue. The *Al-Skeini* judgment demanded that the UK conduct effective investigations into the deaths of the applicants' relatives. A special team, the Iraq Historic Allegations Team (IHAT), had been set up in 2010 to determine whether cases were properly investigated in Iraq and to determine what further action, if any, needed to be taken. It was already investigating both Article 2 and 3 violations and was given the task of investigating the *Al-Skeini* cases as well. However, the IHAT was subject to a number of judicial review challenges over its compliance with the procedural obligations of Articles 2 and 3.[87] The IHAT was staffed, in part, by provost branch staff of the army, which is generally responsible for guarding, policing and custody issues. The Court of Appeal ruled that because provost branch members were involved in matters surrounding the detention and internment of suspected persons in Iraq, 'the practical independence of IHAT is, at least as a matter of reasonable perception, substantially compromised'.[88]

The IHAT was then reformed so that Royal Navy Police and civilian police replaced the provost branch staff. A further judicial review action challenging the restructured IHAT came before the Divisional Court in the UK in 2013. The Divisional Court considered there was no issue with the independence of the re-organised IHAT,[89] but that there were broader issues with IHAT's compliance with the procedural obligations in Articles 2 and 3. The IHAT's investigations were deemed too slow to comply with Article 2.[90] Furthermore,

[86] Friederycke Haijer and Cedric Ryngaert, 'Reflections on Jaloud v. the Netherlands Jurisdictional Consequences and Resonance in Dutch Society' (2015) 19 *Journal of International Peacekeeping* 174, 182–3.

[87] See *R. (Ali Zaki Mousa)* v. *Secretary of State for Defence (HC No.2)* [2010] EWHC 3304 (Admin); *R. (Ali Zaki Mousa)* v. *Secretary of State for Defence (CA)*.

[88] *R. (Ali Zaki Mousa)* v. *Secretary of State for Defence (CA)* at [38].

[89] *R. (Ali Zaki Mousa)* v. *Secretary of State for Defence (HC No.3)* [2013] EWHC 1412 (Admin) at [108]–[109].

[90] Ibid at [164].

as they were structured like formal police investigations, they were not accessible enough to victims' families or the public to satisfy the transparency requirements in Article 2.[91] The Divisional Court suggested modifying the UK's current coronial inquisition system and utilising it for the outstanding cases before the IHAT. A judge was appointed to oversee the whole process and deal with further judicial review requests to help avoid further delays. The Divisional Court also set parameters for the new investigation.[92]

The IHAT investigations drew heavy criticism from several British newspapers who described it as a 'witch hunt'.[93] In 2017, a House of Commons Select Committee on Defence decried the cost of the investigations, the failure to mount a single prosecution and the impact it had on soldiers' lives.[94] This prompted the British Secretary of State for Defence to announce that the IHAT would close in 2017 with outstanding work passed to a Service Police Legacy Investigation led by a senior Royal Navy Police Officer.[95] This led to the cessation of the majority of its investigations.[96]

In the action plan to address the *Al-Skeini* judgment submitted to the Committee of Ministers of the Council of Europe, the UK stated that the *Al-Skeini* case related to the particular circumstances of the past operations in Iraq and it had no implications for its current operations elsewhere, including in Afghanistan.[97] This is probably a mistake and the judgment will likely have broader implications, not only for the UK forces, but also for the military forces of other contracting States.[98] Other States are facing similar problems, such as the Netherlands in the *Jaloud* case and lessons should be learned from the UK's experience of attempting to remedy the investigations in the *Al-Skeini* cases.

91 Ibid at [187]–[188].

92 Ibid at [4]–[8].

93 Ryan Sabey, 'Legal Witch-Hunt of British Army Veterans Set to Be Over in MONTHS after It Sparked Outrage', *The Sun* (London, 14 July 2018); Nicholas Soames, 'Mr Cameron MUST Stop These Vile Witch-Hunts against Our Brave Troops: From a Former Armed Forces Minister Who's Winston Churchill's Grandson, a Blistering Call to Arms...', *The Daily Mail* (London, 20 January 2016); Robert Mendick, 'Senior Police Repeatedly Warned Bosses about Iraq Inquiry Witch Hunt... but Were Ignored for Years', *The Telegraph* (London, 4 March 2018).

94 House of Commons Defence Committee, *Who Guards the Guardians? MOD Support for Former and Serving Personnel* (The Stationery Office 2017) 13.

95 Sam Lister, 'Investigation into historic allegations against British troops in Iraq to end following "scathing" report', *Independent* (London, 10 February 2017).

96 Samira Shackle, 'Why we may never know if British troops committed war crimes in Iraq', *Guardian* (London, 7 June 2018).

97 Committee of Ministers, *Item reference: 1144th meeting DH (June 2012) – Revised Action plan/Action report 2 May 2012* (DH – DD(2012) 438, 2012) 3.

98 Stuart Hendin, 'Detainees in Afghanistan: The Balance Between Human Rights and International Humanitarian Law for Foreign Military Forces' (2008) 14 *Tilburg Law Review* 249, 263–4; *Serdar Mohammed* v. *Ministry of Defence* [2014] EWHC 1369.

States should utilise the full breadth of their policing resources, as the UK did by incorporating Navy police, to help ensure the independence of their investigations. There is also scope for utilising more civilian police from the contracting State during extra-territorial military operations, at the very least in an advisory capacity. This is already standard practice in countries like Australia and utilising the skills, resources and experience offered by the civilian police could provide valuable insights and assistance to military forces, not to mention another avenue to ensure hierarchical and institutional independence.[99]

States need to avoid using *ad hoc* solutions as the UK did with the IHAT and try to develop more coherent and permanent solutions aimed at investigating extra-territorial deaths during military operations. Expanding the jurisdiction and powers of existing mechanisms, such as the coronial system in the UK, to cover deaths in theatre may provide a ready-made solution.

Practical developments ensuring investigative independence need to be backed up by legal developments and appropriate oversight. The UK has adopted legislation, which creates a legal duty upon the commanding officer of the military police to ensure that all investigations carried out by the force are free from improper interference.[100] Further provisions ensure that service police forces are regularly inspected to evaluate the independence and effectiveness of their investigations.[101]

The independence criterion is likely to remain a difficult hurdle for States to overcome extra-territorially. The Court must accept that the State may not be able to realise the same level of independence that it can domestically for a variety of reasons. While the State must demonstrate that it is doing its utmost to achieve independence and mobilising all the resources at its disposal to achieve that aim, the Court must also be flexible when the military forces are clearly acting in good faith.

## 4.6 CONDUCT OF INVESTIGATIONS

Conducting investigations during military operations often creates significant practical problems for States both domestically and extra-territorially. The logistics of getting the necessary investigators to the scene can be

99 'Statement by Paul Robert Kernaghan' (Chilcott Inquiry, 9 June 2010) 9 <www.iraqinquiry.org.uk/media/46162/kernaghan-statement-final.pdf> accessed 2 August 2018; Although investigators need to have a specialised understanding of how the military operates and its capabilities see Turkel (n. 19) 142.

100 s.3, Armed Forces Act 2011.

101 s.4, Armed Forces Act 2011.

problematic.[102] Investigators may also have little time to analyse crime scenes and protecting investigators on-site can be extremely challenging.[103] It is also foreseeable that crime scenes could be taken over by enemy forces, precluding investigations.[104] These difficulties do not absolve the State of the obligation to investigate,[105] but they may impact upon the effectiveness of the investigation. The circumstances may place restrictions on 'certain aspects of the investigation'.[106] The Court noted in *Al-Skeini* and reiterated in *Jaloud* that:

> where the death to be investigated under Article 2 occurs in circumstances of generalised violence, armed conflict or insurgency, obstacles may be placed in the way of investigators and [...] concrete constraints may compel the use of less effective measures of investigation or may cause an investigation to be delayed.[107]

The Court is prepared take into account the fact that the circumstances may have impeded the search for conclusive evidence.[108] In this context, the authorities must take 'reasonable steps available to them to secure the evidence concerning the incident'.[109] The Court has stressed the need to impose realistic obligations on the State noting, for example, the breakdown of civil infrastructure, shortages of pathologists and facilities for autopsies in *Al-Skeini*.[110]

While the Court claims not to be overly prescriptive in the way investigations must be carried out, it has often found violations of Article 2 as a direct result of very specific shortcomings. Chevalier-Watts notes there is an increasing tendency for the Court to be prescriptive about the specific measures States must take to properly investigate, even in the context of military operations.[111] The Court has arguably held States to unreasonable standards in some cases. The Court often compares the forensic tests undertaken in the context

[102] Her Majesty's Inspectorate of Constabulary (n. 75) 11; Cusack (n. 28) 67.

[103] Her Majesty's Inspectorate of Constabulary (n. 75) 8.

[104] United Nations Human Rights Council, *Report of the Committee of Independent Experts in International Humanitarian and Human Rights Laws to Monitor and Assess any Domestic, Legal or other Proceedings Undertaken by both the Government of Israel and the Palestinian side, in the light of General Assembly Resolution 64/254, including the Independence, Effectiveness, Genuineness of these Investigations and their Conformity with International Standards* (A/HRC/15/50, 2010) at [32].

[105] *Yasa* v. *Turkey* (1999) 28 EHRR 408 at [104].

[106] *Tagayeva* v. *Russia* App no 26562/07 (ECtHR, 13 April 2017) at [504].

[107] *Al-Skeini and Others* v. *United Kingdom* (2011) 53 EHRR 18 at [164].

[108] *Yasa* v. *Turkey* (1999) 28 EHRR 408 at [104].

[109] *Nachova* v. *Bulgaria* (2006) 42 EHRR 43 at [113].

[110] *Al-Skeini and Others* v. *United Kingdom* (2011) 53 EHRR 18 at [168].

[111] Chevalier-Watts (n. 74) 717; *Jularic* v. *Croatia* App no 20106/06 (ECtHR, 20 January 2011).

of military operations with best practices and, unsurprisingly, finds violations of Article 2 where the State has not met high standards.[112]

In *Kaya* v. *Turkey*,[113] the applicant's brother was killed by Turkish security forces in disputed circumstances. The security forces claimed they were attacked by PKK terrorists and that he was killed in the clash. The applicant claimed his brother was unarmed and that the security forces planted a weapon on him post-mortem. The Turkish government flew a doctor to the scene and he carried out an 'on-the-spot' autopsy. The applicant alleged that the authorities had not conducted an effective investigation. The Court noted that:

> the on-the-spot post-mortem and forensic examination were conducted in an area prone to terrorist violence, which may have made it extremely difficult to comply with standard practices.[114]

Despite acknowledging the difficult circumstances, the Court carried out an extensive critique of the investigation specifically criticising the 'perfunctory' autopsy and the failure to conduct detailed examinations of the crime scene. The Court ultimately found Turkey responsible for a violation of Article 2 stating:

> The Court notes that loss of life is a tragic and frequent occurrence in view of the security situation in south-east Turkey. However neither the prevalence of violent armed clashes nor the high incidence of fatalities can displace the obligation under Article 2 to ensure that an effective, independent investigation is conducted into deaths arising out of clashes involving the security forces, more so in cases such as the present where the circumstances are in many respects unclear.[115]

The Court's approach of accepting that the autopsy was carried out in difficult circumstances and then singling it out for criticism is incongruous.

### 4.6.1 *Legal Barriers to Investigation*

The legal frameworks governing the deployment of troops extra-territorially can limit the State's ability to satisfy the procedural obligations under Article 2.[116] States typically negotiate Memoranda of Understanding (MOU)

[112] Mowbray (n. 68) 441–2; *Ramsahai* v. *Netherlands* (2008) 46 EHRR 43 at [326].
[113] *Kaya* v. *Turkey* (1999) 28 EHRR 1.
[114] Ibid at [89].
[115] Ibid at [91].
[116] This issue is not germane to the procedural obligations in Article 2 and the gap in human rights oversight over personnel deployed on foreign territory has surfaced in other cases before the Court, see, for example, *Behrami* v. *France* (2007) 45 EHRR SE10.

or Status of Forces Agreements (SOFAs) with a receiving State before deploying troops on their territory to resolve practical legal issues.[117] These agreements typically confer privileges and immunities upon their forces for acts carried out while they are deployed. The model UN SOFA for peacekeeping forces, for example, demands that military personnel are not subject to the criminal jurisdiction of the receiving State,[118] which is a common theme in many SOFAs. Deployed troops remain subject to the sending State's jurisdiction at all times, meaning that they must comply with their own domestic law.[119] While these agreements often demand that deployed troops respect local laws,[120] the jurisdiction clauses act as a procedural bar to local authorities exercising authority over the deployed troops.

This can result in deployed troops falling between two different investigative jurisdictions, immune from the local legal process, while investigators from the sending State are also prevented from exercising jurisdiction in the receiving State's territory. In *Jaloud* v. *Netherlands*, for example, the applicant claimed that the forensic tests carried out following his son's death did not meet the standards required by Article 2. Part of the State's defence was that it could not properly investigate the death because it lacked the authority to investigate anyone other than Netherlands personnel and it was not in a position to seize items or arrest people other than Netherlands personnel in the State.[121] The Court did not seem sufficiently cognisant of the issues this created for the investigation in its judgment.

The body of the applicant's son was transferred to a local hospital in Iraq following the shooting and a post-mortem examination was carried out by an Iraqi physician. The Dutch authorities were specifically excluded by the Iraqi authorities from attending the autopsy. The Government argued that the autopsy had been as effective as it could have been in the circumstances, but the Court criticised the autopsy for being extremely brief, lacking in detail and not containing any pictures.[122] It also questioned why alternative arrangements

117 Aurel Sari, 'The Status of Foreign Armed Forces Deployed in Post-Conflict Environments: A Search for Basic Principles' in Carsten Stahn, Jennifer Easterday and Jens Iverson (eds), *Jus Post Bellum: Mapping the Normative Foundations* (Oxford University Press 2014) 472 and 491.

118 s.47(b), *United Nations Model Status of Forces Agreement for Peacekeeping Operations* 9 October 1990 UNGA A/45/594.

119 See *inter alia Al-Skeini and Others* v. *United Kingdom* (2011) 53 EHRR 18 at [121].

120 s.6, *UN Model SOFA*; Article 3, *EU SOFA* 31 December 2003 European Council (2003/C 321/02); Article 2, *NATO SOFA* (adopted 19 June 1951) 199 UNTS 67.

121 '*Jaloud* v. *Netherlands Hearing*' (European Court of Human Rights, 19 February 2014) <www.echr.coe.int/Pages/home.aspx?p=hearings&w=4770808_19022014&language=lang&c=&py=2014> accessed 3 August 2018.

122 *Jaloud* v. *Netherlands* (2015) 60 EHRR 29 at [214].

were not considered for the autopsy.[123] As pointed out in the concurring opinion, the Dutch forces lacked the facilities for such an examination and it is not clear that they possessed any legal authority to carry out such examinations in Iraq.[124]

The Court was also critical that bullet fragments taken from the body of the applicant's son were not stored and examined in proper conditions.[125] These fragments were given to the Iraqi police who sent them to Baghdad for analysis and they were eventually handed over to the military advisors. It is not clear that the Dutch forces could have examined these fragments under their own authority.[126]

While there are strong policy reasons for maintaining the immunities in SOFAs, there are also ways of circumventing the barrier they create. The sending State could, for example, waive its jurisdiction or the receiving State could grant the sending State explicit powers to investigate on its territory. It is also possible that States may deliberately seek to curtail their mandates in order to avoid having to uphold procedural obligations in the Convention. Contracting States will need to bear this in mind for future deployments and the Convention may demand that they adapt SOFAs to permit them to carry out human rights compliant investigations on foreign territory.

The above analysis shows that the Court pays lip service to the notion of a flexible interpretation of the procedural obligation in the context of military operations, but often holds States to high standards in spite of legal restrictions, tenuous security situations and a lack of resources. As one commentator observed, it has not presented understandable reasoning of how it balanced human rights obligations against the requirements of the local and operational context.[127]

## 4.7 TRANSPARENCY

Article 2 demands that there is adequate participation of the victim's relatives and public scrutiny of the investigation to ensure public confidence and transparency in the authorities' adherence to the rule of law.[128] Investigators should inform the victim's relatives of their rights *vis-à-vis* the investigation and any

[123] Ibid at [215].

[124] *Jaloud* v. *Netherlands* (2015) 60 EHRR 29, Concurring Opinion of Judges Casadevall, Berro-Lefevre, Šikuta, Hirvelä, López Guerra, Sajó and Silvis.

[125] *Jaloud* v. *Netherlands* (2015) 60 EHRR 29 at [219].

[126] Haijer and Ryngaert (n. 86) 183.

[127] Ibid.

[128] *Kolevi* v. *Bulgaria* App no 1108/02 (ECtHR, 5 November 2009) at [194].

important developments in the case. Further, there should be some kind of publication of a report on the investigators findings.[129] The degree of scrutiny applied to an investigation may vary from case to case.[130]

### 4.7.1 *State Secrecy*

The Court regularly states that investigations must be accessible to the victim's relatives to the extent necessary to safeguard their legitimate interests.[131] States have some discretion to limit access and investigators may not be required to give applicants access to investigation files, or copies of all documents during an ongoing inquiry.[132] The level of transparency demanded under Article 2 may prove extremely difficult to achieve in the context of military operations. The State may wish to restrict access to certain information to avoid adversely affecting international relations and national security.[133] It may also wish to maintain the secrecy of its weapons capabilities or restrict access to protect secret intelligence sources.[134]

In *Finogenov* v. *Russia*,[135] the Russian security forces used a gas during a rescue attempt, which resulted in many civilian casualties. The State refused to disclose the formula of the gas and Russian law demanded that specific technical methods of anti-terrorist operations be kept secret. Although this limited the transparency of the investigation, the Court stated that it 'recognises the need to keep certain aspects of security operations secret',[136] and 'there may be legitimate reasons for keeping the formula of the gas secret'.[137] A balance must be struck between protecting legitimate restrictions and avoiding too many concessions to States claiming national security concerns as a means of concealing their wrongdoing. The use of State secrecy legislation as a means of guaranteeing impunity for human rights violations is well documented.[138]

[129] *McKerr* v. *United Kingdom* (2002) 34 EHRR 20 at [141].
[130] *Bati* v. *Turkey* (2006) 42 EHRR 37 at [137].
[131] *Giuliani and Gaggio* v. *Italy* (2012) 54 EHRR 10 at [303]; *Ogur* v. *Turkey* (2001) 31 EHRR 40 at [92].
[132] *McKerr* v. *United Kingdom* (2002) 34 EHRR 20 at [121].
[133] In the US, for example, the default position is non-disclosure of investigation materials Cusack (n. 28) 75.
[134] Watkin (n. 19) 33; United Nations Human Rights Council (n. 104) at [32].
[135] *Finogenov and Others* v. *Russia* (2015) 61 EHRR 4, see discussion in Chapter 3.
[136] Ibid at [266].
[137] Ibid at [200].
[138] *Bámaca Velásquez* v. *Guatemala* Series C No 70 IACtHR 25 November 2000 at [93(a)]; *El-Masri* v. *Macedonia* (2013) 57 EHRR 25 at [191]; The State used secrecy legislation to conceal extraordinary rendition in *Nasr and Ghali* v. *Italy* App no 44883/09 (ECtHR, 23 February 2016).

The Court struck the right balance in the Grand Chamber judgment of *Janowiec and Others* v. *Russia*. In that case, Russia abruptly discontinued an investigation into the so-called Katyn massacre, which involved the deaths of hundreds of Polish people during World War 2. Russia classified the decision to discontinue the investigation as top secret. It refused to disclose the contents of the decision, claiming that its top-secret status meant it was legally precluded from transferring the information to an international organisation like the Court.[139] The Court found there was a violation of Article 38, which obliges States to furnish all necessary facilities to the Court when investigating cases. It noted the domestic decisions did not specify the exact nature of the security concerns justifying their secret classification. While the Court was reluctant to challenge the judgments of national security authorities, it was apparent that there was insufficient legal oversight of the decision. The domestic courts had not balanced the national security claims against the legitimate public interest in the disclosure of the documents.[140] The Court strikes the right balance between the conflicting interests here, indicating that it will respect decisions on classification as long as they are subject to sufficient domestic scrutiny.

### 4.7.2 *Political Compromises*

The participation of victims' relatives in the investigation may also be hampered by post-conflict political compromises. In *Varnava* v. *Turkey*, the applicants were relatives of nine Cypriots who disappeared during military operations in Cyprus in 1974. The applicants alleged that eight of the disappeared were Greek-Cypriot soldiers captured by Turkish soldiers. The ninth was a civilian allegedly last seen in Turkish custody whose body was later discovered in a mass grave in 2007, a medical examination indicated he had suffered gunshot wounds.

After the Cypriot conflict, the United Nations established an agency to investigate missing persons, the United Nations Committee on Missing Persons (CMP). It had a limited mandate aimed at determining whether missing persons were dead or alive, recovering and identifying remains, and providing some information on causes of death. Its work was completely confidential with relatives only notified once remains had been identified.[141] In spite of its

139 *Janowiec and Others* v. *Russia* (2014) 58 EHRR 30 at [192].

140 Ibid at [214].

141 The CMP's workings are discussed in *Karefyllides* v. *Turkey* App no 45503/99 (ECtHR, 1 December 2009) and *Charalambous and Others* v. *Turkey* App no 46744/07 (ECtHR, 3 April 2012).

limited scope, Turkey pleaded that the CMP did enough to satisfy its obligations under Article 2.

The Court considered that although the CMP did not allow the victims' relatives an opportunity to participate to a degree which satisfied Article 2, it nonetheless represented a 'politically-sensitive approach' and was 'the only solution which could be agreed under the brokerage of the UN'. Despite acknowledging that it was the only possible solution in the circumstances, the Court considered this could have 'no bearing on the application of the provisions of the Convention'.[142] The scope of investigations under the CMP was deemed too narrow to satisfy Article 2 and regardless of the extenuating circumstances could not satisfy Turkey's obligations under Article 2.

If the political compromise reached regarding investigations was the only one possible, is it fair to criticise the State for failing to adequately investigate? It should be noted that the length of time since the disappearances in Cyprus in 1974 and the limited nature of attempts at investigation since may have scuppered any goodwill the Court had toward Cyprus in this case. The Court was comparatively more accommodating when dealing with investigation problems arising from political settlements in post-conflict Bosnia, as the following sections demonstrate.

## 4.8 PROMPTNESS

Article 2 demands that investigations are carried out promptly, meaning they must begin promptly and 'proceed with reasonable expedition'.[143] Where delays in the commencement or completion of investigations are attributable to different parties, the Court apportions blame between them. In *Nakayev* v. *Russia*, for example, the applicant alleged that he was injured when the Russian military shelled his village, but failed to report the incident to the authorities for a number of years. The Court refused to hold the State responsible for the failure to commence the investigation promptly, but nonetheless held the State responsible for subsequent delays attributable to it.[144]

The failure to promptly carry out investigations related to military operations has led to numerous violations of Article 2. The Court has found violations as a result of different acts or omissions of the State, including failure

[142] *Varnava and Others* v. *Turkey* App no 16064/90 (ECtHR, 18 September 2009) at [193].

[143] *McCaughey* v. *United Kingdom* App no 43098/09 (ECtHR, 16 July 2013) at [130].

[144] *Nakayev* v. *Russia* App no 29846/05 (ECtHR, 21 June 2011) at [68]–[75]; *Mezhidov* v. *Russia* (2011) 53 EHRR 11 at [69].

to start an investigation quickly enough,[145] dropping investigations prematurely,[146] closing and re-opening case files repeatedly,[147] long periods of inactivity,[148] and in some cases combinations of these.[149] Carrying out investigations both domestically and extra-territorially, whether during or in the immediate aftermath of a conflict, can be extremely challenging. The different contexts raise specific challenges, which impact upon the State's ability to carry out prompt investigations.

### 4.8.1 *Concessions for Delay*

The clash between making concessions for difficult circumstances and upholding the standards of Article 2 is also evident in the context of delays impacting investigations. It was noted above that the Court has repeatedly emphasised the need to be flexible when assessing investigations undertaken during military operations. In the context of the PKK insurgency in Turkey, the Court stated that it must take into account how the violence in South-East Turkey impeded the search for evidence.[150] In the context of the Chechnya conflict, in *Luluyev and Others* v. *Russia*, the Court stated that 'it must be accepted that there may be obstacles or difficulties which prevent progress in an investigation in a particular situation'.[151] It may be difficult in practice to determine whether delays have arisen because of challenging circumstances or deliberate delay by the authorities. While the Court makes positive remarks about making concessions, this rhetoric seldom results in it not finding a violation of the procedural obligations.

The case of *Bazorkina* v. *Russia* illustrates the kind of problems investigators can face. In that case, the applicant's son was arrested by Russian forces in Chechnya in 2000. The applicant saw a television report in which her son was interrogated by Russian soldiers and ordered to be shot by a commander. She reported the incident immediately, but the investigation only commenced seventeen months later. Russia argued the conditions in Chechnya hampered the commencement of the investigation, as investigators were killed, abducted and had their offices bombed by insurgents.

[145] *Tas* v. *Turkey* (2001) 33 EHRR 15.
[146] *Yasa* v. *Turkey* (1999) 28 EHRR 408.
[147] *Akhmadova and Sadulayeva* v. *Russia* App no 40464/02 (ECtHR, 10 May 2007) at [104].
[148] *Dovletukayev and Others* v. *Russia* App no 7821/07 (ECtHR, 24 October 2013) at [221].
[149] *Aslakhanova and Others* v. *Russia* App no 2944/06 (ECtHR, 18 December 2012).
[150] *Yasa* v. *Turkey* (1999) 28 EHRR 408 at [104].
[151] *Luluyev* v. *Russia* (2009) 48 EHRR 45 at [92].

The Court appeared sympathetic in its judgment, but nonetheless found a violation stating:

> While accepting that some explanation for these delays can be found in the exceptional circumstances that have prevailed in Chechnya and to which the Government refers, the Court finds that in the present case they clearly exceeded any acceptable limitations on efficiency that could be tolerated in dealing with such a serious crime.[152]

The delays were clearly too long in this case, but it aptly illustrates the obstacles investigators can face with hundreds of cases to investigate while they are constantly under attack. The Court needs to be conscious of these difficult circumstances and show leniency toward investigators in similar circumstances.

### 4.8.2 *Post-Conflict Situations*

The Court has shown a willingness to make concessions for investigations in some post-conflict States. In *Jularic* v. *Croatia*, the applicant's husband was abducted by armed men and shot. The incident occurred during the Croatian Homeland War and Serbian forces had occupied the territory where the death occurred. Although she notified Croatian authorities immediately, Croatia did not regain control over the area until 1998. Once they did there was progress in the investigation. The Court was prepared to make concessions for the extenuating circumstances noting that 'the Court will examine only the part of the inquiry that took place after January 1998 since before then the Croatian authorities had had no real authority in the town of Vukovar'.[153] It made further concessions for delays because 'the respondent State needed some time to organise its judicial system in the newly regained territories'.[154] Nonetheless, the Court found that delays between January 1998 and October 2001 were inexcusable even in light of the extenuating circumstances.[155]

In *Charalambous and Others* v. *Turkey*, the applicants' relatives went missing during the conflict in Cyprus in 1974. Their bodies were identified between 2005 and 2009. However, as the CMP's investigation procedures were confidential, the authorities were not directly informed of this development. Turkey argued that they only became aware that the applicants wanted a further investigation when they took a case to the Court and had investigated

152 *Bazorkina* v. *Russia* (2008) 46 EHRR 15 at [121].
153 *Jularic* v. *Croatia* App no 20106/06 (ECtHR, 20 January 2011) at [46].
154 Ibid at [47].
155 See also *Jelic* v. *Croatia* App no 57856/11 (ECtHR, 12 June 2014).

further from then. The Court recognised that there was no formal channel of communication between the CMP and Turkish authorities and criticised the lack of a 'pro-active response' in seeking information on identified remains or organising communication channels. However, while the Court was critical of the lack of initiative, they considered that:

> in a case concerning deaths which took place decades before it cannot be said that it undermines any subsequent steps or offends against the requirement of expedition.[156]

The concession offered is in keeping with the idea that the significance of promptness and expedition is diminished in historical cases.[157] The Court only offers a concession in that context, so the flexibility offered is limited. Equally, the Court has not advanced a principled basis on which to differentiate between cases like *Jularic* and *Charalambous*. The cut-off point at which a more lenient approach to promptness is justified is not clear from the jurisprudence, nor is it clear why tardiness is more acceptable in the latter case of *Charalambous* than in *Jularic*.

In *Palic* v. *Bosnia and Herzegovina*, the applicant's husband, a military commander in a UN safe zone in Bosnia in 1995, disappeared after going to negotiate terms of surrender with opposition forces. The applicant alleged that the Bosnian authorities had failed to adequately investigate his disappearance. Although the events took place in 1995, the Court only looked at the adequacy of the investigation from July 2002 when Bosnia ratified the Convention. The investigation was sporadic, interviews only began in 2005 and in 2006, an investigatory commission was established and arrest warrants were issued. The body of the applicant's husband was not identified until August 2009 and a suspect was only charged in December 2009. The Court made a number of concessions for promptness because of the post-conflict situation. It stated:

> In such a post-conflict situation, what amounts to an impossible and/or disproportionate burden must be measured by the very particular facts and context. In this connection, the Court notes that more than 100,000 people were killed, almost 30,000 people went missing and more than two million people were displaced during the war in Bosnia and Herzegovina.[158]

The Court considered the political and institutional changes in Bosnia after the war and concluded that 'the domestic legal system should have become

[156] *Charalambous and Others* v. *Turkey* App no 46744/07 (ECtHR, 3 April 2012) at [61].

[157] *Brecknell* v. *United Kingdom* (2008) 46 EHRR 42 at [69]–[72]; *Janowiec and Others* v. *Russia* App no 55508/07 (ECtHR, 16 April 2012) at [133].

[158] *Palic* v. *Bosnia and Herzegovina* App no 4704/04 (ECtHR, 15 February 2011) at [70].

capable of dealing effectively with disappearances and other serious violations of international humanitarian law by 2005'.[159] Thus instead of holding Bosnia to a full procedural obligation from ratification in 2002, the Court only began assessing promptness from the point when it considered the domestic legal system was capable of dealing with the case. The *Palic* decision could be a particularly important precedent for States in belligerent occupation of foreign territory. A State may be able to request some leeway from the Court to defer investigations until it has established sufficient institutional support to carry out investigations properly.[160]

## 4.9 CONCLUSION

This chapter provided another potent illustration of how dependent human rights law is on having a functioning nation State for its proper operation. The procedural obligations under Article 2 may have the greatest impact on the State's military of any of the Convention obligations. They can potentially influence everything from the legal agreements governing a force's presence on foreign territory, to how many troops are deployed and where they are stationed.

The Court has struggled to articulate practicable limits to these obligations, trying to avoid impunity while also attempting to avoid imposing unrealistic or impossible burdens on the State. The lack of clarity over the scope of the procedural obligations was apparent, in particular whether and when the obligations extended to acts of third parties during extra-territorial military operations.

The Court has also shown itself willing to make concessions for the unusual circumstances arising in military operations, but has not consistently followed through on that promise. At times the Court has bent its rules, such as its rules on independence in *Jaloud* or its rules on promptness in *Palic*. At other times it has very strictly enforced its rules notwithstanding particularly challenging circumstances, such as its rules on autopsies and forensic examinations in *Jaloud* or its rules on promptness in *Charalambous and*

159 Ibid; See also *Fazlic and Others* v. *Bosnia and Herzegovina* App no 66758/09 (ECtHR, 3 June 2014) at [39].

160 IHL would demand that the State assume responsibility for maintaining law and order in the territory and presumably investigating crime once the territory comes under the State's control, see Article 43, Hague Convention (IV) Respecting the Laws and Customs of War on Land and Its Annex: Regulations concerning the Laws and Customs of War on Land (adopted 18 October 1907, entered into force 26 January 1910) 205 CTS 277.

*Others* v. *Turkey*. The result is further inconsistency in the jurisprudence concerning military operations and a lack of clarity for the State concerning their obligations, which the Court needs to address.

The chapter also presented some options for the Court to mitigate the impact of this obligation on contracting States, noting the clear benefits that derogation and co-application would bring to the interpretation of Article 2. Interpreting Article 2 in light of IHL could practically limit the scope of the procedural obligation toward a more manageable burden on the State. Equally, the State itself must also take a much more pro-active role in making the procedural obligation more practicable. As noted in the previous chapters, derogating from Article 2 for lawful acts of war would help to smooth the sharper edges of the obligations in Article 2 for the States' military forces. Both of these issues are discussed further in Chapters 5 and 7. The contracting States also need to proactively adapt their military forces and domestic investigation bodies so that they are in a better position to satisfy the procedural obligations. States should utilise the full breadth of their policing resources, both civilian and military, creatively to satisfy the obligations.

This marks the end of the discussion of the right to life and in the following chapter the focus shifts toward norm conflict and the protections against arbitrary detention in the Convention. The chapter continues to build on the themes developed throughout the book with a strong focus on practical issues surrounding the co-application of IHL and the Convention.

# 5

# Norm Conflict

## 5.1 INTRODUCTION

This chapter looks at the Court's approach toward the resolution of norm conflicts between IHL and the Convention. The preceding chapters have identified clashes between IHL and Convention norms, but the Court itself has not directly acknowledged those conflicts in its judgments. However, there have been a few cases where the Court has been directly confronted with clear conflicts between IHL norms and the Convention. These cases of norm conflict have typically revolved around Article 5 and in particular the conflict between Article 5 and the provisions of IHL that permit security detention or internment.

Article 5(1) creates a finite list of circumstances in which a person can be deprived of their liberty. These include situations where a person has been convicted of a criminal offence or failed to comply with a court order. By creating a finite list, the construction of Article 5 mirrors the construction of Article 2, which contains a finite list of circumstances in which the use of force is permitted. It differs from provisions in other human rights treaties, such as the ICCPR and the American Convention on Human Rights, which instead of creating a finite list of circumstances simply prohibit arbitrary arrest or detention.[1]

While the provisions in each of the international treaties have similar aims, the utilisation of a finite list creates particular problems because common types of detention during military operations, such as internment, are not

[1] Article 7(3), American Convention on Human Rights (adopted 22 November 1969, entered into force 18 July 1978) 1144 UNTS 144 and Article 9(1), International Covenant on Civil and Political Rights (adopted 16 December 1966, entered into force 23 March 1976) 999 UNTS 171.

included in the finite list.[2] Internment is an exceptional measure of control that may be ordered for security reasons in armed conflict, or for the purpose of protecting State security or public order in certain non-conflict situations.[3] This may present conflicting obligations to the State – an obligation to maintain security within a piece of territory under its control and an obligation to protect the human rights of its inhabitants, including their liberty and security.

When the State has not derogated from Article 5, conflicts can arise between Article 5 and provisions permitting internment, in particular provisions of IHL.[4] Security detention during armed conflict is *prima facie* a violation of Article 5(1).[5] As such, a norm conflict arises between IHL and the Convention,[6] which threatens the coherency of international law. The answer to a given legal question: 'can a State legally detain an individual?' becomes subjective depending on whom you ask and what rule system you focus on.[7] If a State relies on IHL to detain people, the Court needs to resolve the conflict between the IHL norm permitting security detention (or a UNSCR conferring that power) and the Convention norm prohibiting it. It represents a

[2] Françoise Hampson, 'The Relationship between International Humanitarian Law and Human Rights Law from the Perspective of a Human Rights Treaty Body' (2008) 90 IRRC 549, 564. A similar problem was identified in Chapter 3 with the finite circumstances in which force can be used.

[3] Jelena Pejic, 'Procedural Principles and Safeguards for Internment/Administrative Detention in Armed Conflict and Other Situations of Violence' (2005) 87 IRRC 375, 376; The UK used internment in Northern Ireland in situations short of a NIAC – *Ireland* v. *United Kingdom* (1979–1980) 2 EHRR 25.

[4] Article 21, Geneva Convention Relative to the Treatment of Prisoners of War (adopted 12 August 1949, entered into force 21 October 1950) 75 UNTS 135 and Article 42, Geneva Convention Relative to the Protection of Civilian Persons in Time of War (adopted 12 August 1949, entered into force 21 October 1950) 75 UNTS 287.

[5] *R. (Al-Jedda)* v. *Secretary of State for Defence* [2007] UKHL 58 at [27].

[6] Koskenniemi defines a norm conflict as 'a situation where two rules or principles suggest different ways of dealing with a problem' – Martti Koskenniemi, *Fragmentation of International Law: Difficulties Arising from the Diversification and Expansion of International Law* (International Law Commission 2006) at [25]; Milanovic states that 'a relationship of conflict exists between two norms if one norm constitutes, has led to or may lead to, a breach of the other' – Marko Milanovic, 'A Norm Conflict Perspective on the Relationship between International Humanitarian Law and Human Rights Law' (2009) 14 *Journal of Conflict and Security Law* 459, 465. There are also different types of norm conflicts, broad and narrow conflicts, and genuine and apparent conflicts the discussion of which is beyond the scope of this chapter. See Erich Vranes, 'The Definition of "Norm Conflict" in International Law and Legal Theory' (2006) 17 EJIL 395; Jure Vidmar and Erika De Wet (eds), *Hierarchy in International Law: The Place of Human Rights* (Oxford University Press 2012); Jan Mus, 'Conflicts between Treaties in International Law' (1998) 45 *Netherlands International Law Review* 208.

[7] Koskenniemi (n. 6) at [483].

fundamental difference between IHL and human rights law with regard to the deprivation of liberty.[8] As security detention is prevalent during military operations, determining a coherent solution to this conflict is of paramount importance to the Court. This chapter looks at the different ways the Court can approach this problem and the Court's judgments on this issue.

## 5.2 APPROACHES TO NORM CONFLICT RESOLUTION

There are many options available to the Court to resolve norm conflicts. Most conflicts can be averted through interpretation. If this fails, a court can try to prioritise the enforcement of one norm over another.[9] In support of this approach, the International Law Commission presented a series of legal maxims as a means of establishing priority between norms and resolving conflicts. It presented three central maxims 'lex posterior derogat lege priori' – later law supersedes earlier law,[10] 'lex superior derogat legi inferiori' – the superior law supersedes the inferior law, and 'lex specialis derogat legi generali' – the specific law supersedes the general law.[11] However, these maxims were originally developed to settle norm conflicts in domestic legal systems and they are ill-suited to application in public international law.[12] With the exception of the *lex specialis* principle, the other principles cited by the International Law Commission appear to have had little consistent influence on the European Court of Human Rights' approach toward resolving conflicts.

### 5.2.1 *Lex Posterior*

The Court appeared to favour the *lex posterior* approach in the case of *Slivenko v. Latvia*,[13] which concerned a Russian family that was living in Latvia at the time that Latvia regained independence from the USSR. The applicants were the wife and daughter of a retired military officer who was forced to leave Latvia under the terms of a bi-lateral treaty between Latvia and Russia. The applicants had their permanent residence status in Latvia withdrawn and they

8 Alexander Orakhelashvili, 'The Interaction between Human Rights and Humanitarian Law: Fragmentation, Conflict, Parallelism, or Convergence?' (2008) 19 EJIL 161, 176.

9 Milanovic (n. 6) 465–6; Koskenniemi (n. 6) at [35].

10 Koskenniemi (n. 6) at [225].

11 Koskenniemi (n. 6) at [56].

12 The *lex posterior* maxim has been applied inconsistently and at times the previous treaty has superseded the latter treaty – Dinah Shelton, 'Normative Hierarchy in International Law' (2006) 100 AJIL 291, 293fn.

13 *Slivenko and Others v. Latvia* App no 48321/99 (ECtHR, 23 January 2002).

challenged their deportation. This gave rise to a conflict between the treaty, which demanded separation of the family, and Article 8 of the Convention, which protects the right to private and family life and favoured keeping the family together. The bi-lateral treaty which motivated the State's action in *Slivenko* was adopted in April 1994,[14] Latvia ratified the European Convention in 1997.[15] The government contended that the bi-lateral treaty was essential to Latvia's sovereignty and national security and should be treated as creating a 'quasi-reservation' in respect of the Convention. However, the Court ruled that the Convention took precedence stating that the:

> ratification of the Convention by a State presupposes that any law then in force in its territory should be in conformity with the Convention. [...] the same principles must apply as regards any provisions of international treaties which a Contracting State has concluded prior to the ratification of the Convention and which might be at variance with certain of its provisions.[16]

Koskenniemi presents the case as an example of *lex posterior* in action with the Court ruling that the Convention controlled the content and/or application of an earlier bilateral treaty, or at least determined how the latter was to be interpreted and applied by the national authorities.[17]

However, the Court has also allowed the Convention to be superseded by earlier customary rules of international law. In *Al-Adsani* v. *United Kingdom*,[18] the applicant brought civil proceedings in England against the Emir of Kuwait alleging that the Emir had abducted him and subjected him to torture. The applicant received a default judgment against the Emir. However, he was prevented from pursuing his claim against the government of Kuwait because of domestic laws giving effect to the principle of sovereign immunity, which prevents States from being subject to another State's jurisdiction.[19] The applicant alleged that he was denied access to a court in violation of Article 6 because he was barred from pursuing his claim by sovereign immunity from English civil jurisdiction. Thus, the rights in the Convention were in conflict with a rule of customary international law, which preceded the adoption of the Convention.

The application of the *lex posterior* principle ought to have led to the Convention taking precedence over the customary rule, but the Court ruled

14 Ibid at [11].
15 Ibid at [54].
16 Ibid at [60]–[61].
17 Koskenniemi (n. 6) at [247].
18 *Al-Adsani* v. *United Kingdom* (2002) 34 EHRR 11.
19 Ibid at [54].

the opposite was the case. It stated that the Convention must be interpreted in light of relevant rules of international law.[20] The measures taken by the State reflected generally recognised rules of international law and did not amount to a disproportionate restriction on the right of access to a court in Article 6.[21] At no point did the Court explicitly say that it was applying the *lex posterior* principle in *Slivenko*, nor was this countervailing principle acknowledged in *Al-Adsani*. Therefore it is not possible to conclude that this principle has any direct bearing on the Court's approach to conflict resolution.

### 5.2.2 *Lex Superior*

International law lacks a centralised system, a single legislator and formal hierarchical integration.[22] As a result, the *lex superior* maxim has limited value in norm conflict resolution, because there is little hierarchically superior law.[23] Two rules function to create some hierarchical law: Article 103 of the UN Charter and Article 53 of the Vienna Convention on the Law of Treaties. Article 103 of the UN Charter states:

> In the event of a conflict between the obligations of the Members of the United Nations under the present Charter and their obligations under any other international agreement, their obligations under the present Charter shall prevail.

The ICJ has interpreted Article 103 to mean that Charter obligations prevail over conflicting obligations from another international treaty, regardless of whether that treaty pre-dates the Charter and whether it is a regional treaty.[24] As Article 25 of the UN Charter obliges UN members to accept and carry out the decisions of the Security Council, the power of Article 103 also extends to obligations arising from UNSCRs. Article 53 of the Vienna Convention on the Law of Treaties stipulates that 'a treaty is void if, at the time of its conclusion, it conflicts with a peremptory norm of general international law'. These peremptory norms can function, in theory at least, to invalidate other treaty-based norms.

[20] Ibid at [55].

[21] Ibid at [56]; See also *Fogarty* v. *United Kingdom* (2002) 34 EHRR 12 and *McElhinney* v. *Ireland* (2002) 34 EHRR 13.

[22] Milanovic (n. 6) 483.

[23] Shelton (n. 12) 291.

[24] *Case concerning Military and Paramilitary Activities In and against Nicaragua (Nicaragua* v. *United States)*, 1984 ICJ Reports, p. 392 26 November 1984 at [107].

## Article 103

Article 103 does not create a hierarchy in the same way that domestic constitutional law would, for example, prevail over statutory provisions in many jurisdictions. It only elevates norms arising out of a specific treaty and not specific norms. Chinkin argues that it creates an institutional hierarchy rather than a substantive one.[25] A norm within the scope of Article 103 does not invalidate other norms, but instead suspends the State's duty to abide by them.[26] Article 103 is more akin to a rule of precedence than normative hierarchy because the original conflicting obligation can become good law again once the countervailing UN obligation ceases to apply.

The Court has shown a reluctance to subordinate European Convention provisions to the coercive effect of Article 103. This was clearly evident in *Saramati* v. *France, Germany and Norway* where the Court sought to avoid its coercive effects.[27] In 2001, the applicant was arrested by UN peace keeping forces in Kosovo and subjected to security detention. He was eventually released in 2002. The power to detain the applicant was based on a UNSCR, which authorised 'Member States and relevant international organizations to establish the international security presence in Kosovo [...] with all necessary means to fulfil its responsibilities'.[28] This was deemed to include security detention where necessary. The applicant complained that his detention violated Article 5. His case was addressed to France and Norway because commanders from those States had issued orders to UN peacekeepers to detain him.[29] The Court ruled that the UN had delegated its powers to the security force and retained responsibility for its actions. As a result, the actions of those who detained him were attributable to the UN under international law.[30] The Court therefore dismissed the application *ratione personae*, the complaint did not concern a party bound by the Convention's obligations.

The decision has been criticised by several academics.[31] These criticisms have centred upon the Court's failure to properly address whether the

[25] Christine Chinkin, 'Jus Cogens, Article 103 of the UN Charter and Other Hierarchical Techniques of Conflict Solution' (2008) 17 *Finnish Yearbook of International Law* 63.

[26] Vidmar and De Wet (n. 6) 19.

[27] *Saramati* v. *France and Others* (2007) 45 EHRR SE10.

[28] UNSCR No. 1244 (1999) at [7].

[29] *Saramati* v. *France and Others* (2007) 45 EHRR SE10 at [68].

[30] Ibid at [141].

[31] Marko Milanovic and Tatjana Papic, 'As bad as it gets: The European Court of Human Rights's Behrami and Saramati Decision and General International Law' (2009) 58 ICLQ 267; Aurel Sari, 'Jurisdiction and International Responsibility in Peace Support Operations: The Behrami and Saramati Cases' (2008) 8 HRLR 151; Kjetil Mujezinovic Larsen, 'Attribution of Conduct in Peace Operations: The "Ultimate Authority and Control" Test' (2008) 19 EJIL 509.

applicant came within the jurisdiction of the contracting States,[32] and the failure to properly assess whether the conditions for responsibility of an international organisation were satisfied.[33] However, the Court was obviously also eager to avoid ruling on the norm conflict between the security detention power in the UNSCR and Article 5. Milanovic and Papic ascribe this to the Court's reluctance to accept the subjugation of the Convention's guarantees to the will of the UN Security Council.[34]

The approach of avoiding the coercive power of Article 103 continued in the case of *Al-Jedda* v. *United Kingdom*. In that case, the applicant was held as a security detainee in UK custody in Iraq from October 2004 to December 2007. The UK acquired the power to detain people who posed an imperative risk to security under IHL provisions when they invaded and occupied Iraq in 2003.[35] After the power to govern was transferred to an interim government, UK forces remained in Iraq pursuant to a UNSCR. Through UNSCR 1546, the UK retained the power to detain persons where they posed an imperative risk to security under the same terms as their occupation power.[36] This meant the applicant could be detained for years after the occupation officially ended. His detention was reviewed periodically and his ongoing detention deemed necessary.

The applicant sought judicial review of his detention in the UK courts. His central claim was that his security detention in Iraq was in violation of Article 5. The UK had not derogated from Article 5, but as the power to detain people for security purposes was conferred on the UK by a UNSCR, the UK claimed that this power superseded the obligation under Article 5 by virtue of Article 103 of the UN Charter. The UK argued that the obligation to maintain security in Iraq, which included resort to security detention, took precedence over the UK's obligations under Article 5. The Court again avoided the supremacy issue created by Article 103 stating that:

> in interpreting its resolutions, there must be a presumption that the Security Council does not intend to impose any obligation on Member States to breach fundamental principles of human rights. In the event of any ambiguity in

[32] Sari (n. 31) 159.

[33] Milanovic and Papic (n. 31) 283.

[34] Milanovic and Papic (n. 31) 293; Milanovic (n. 6) 23.

[35] Article 78, Geneva Convention Relative to the Protection of Civilian Persons in Time of War (adopted 12 August 1949, entered into force 21 October 1950) 75 UNTS 287.

[36] Para. 10 of the Resolution gave the military force 'authority to take all necessary measures to contribute to the maintenance of security and stability in Iraq in accordance with the letters annexed to this resolution'. In the annexed letter from Colin Powell he outlined the role the forces would have in Iraq and stated: 'This will include combat operations against members of these groups, internment where this is necessary for imperative reasons of security'.

> the terms of a Security Council Resolution, the Court must therefore choose the interpretation which is most in harmony with the requirements of the Convention and which avoids any conflict of obligations. In the light of the United Nations' important role in promoting and encouraging respect for human rights, it is to be expected that clear and explicit language would be used were the Security Council to intend States to take particular measures which would conflict with their obligations under international human rights law.[37]

Thus even though the letter annexed to the UNSCR specifically mentioned that internment might be used in Iraq, it was one of many options and the resolution did not impose an obligation on the State to intern, it merely gave the State the option to utilise internment. As there was ambiguity over whether the UN had intended States to disregard their human rights obligations in carrying out internment, the Court considered that the Convention obligations continued to apply. This borders on an inversion of the relationship Article 103 sought to create by ensuring the subsistence of Convention rules in spite of contradictory UN rules.

In *Nada* v. *Switzerland*,[38] the applicant was subject to a sanctions regime against suspected members of terrorist organisations, which was imposed by a series of UNSCRs.[39] The sanctions regime, which was overseen by a UN Sanctions Committee and administered by UN member States, froze many of the applicant's assets and imposed restrictions on his ability to travel. The applicant raised a series of objections against the sanctions, arguing that the travel restrictions violated his right to respect for his private and family life and amounted to a deprivation of liberty contrary to Article 5. In evaluating the UNSCR, the Court recalled the presumption it had developed in *Al-Jedda* but noted differences between that case and *Nada*. In *Al-Jedda*, the resolution did not specifically mention internment and the presumption that the UN intended States to maintain their human rights obligations applied. In this case, the first resolution specifically demanded that States adhere strictly to the terms of the UNSCR 'notwithstanding the existence of any rights or obligations conferred or imposed by any international agreement'.[40] Furthermore

37 *Al-Jedda* v. *United Kingdom* (2011) 53 EHRR 23 at [102]; This was suggested as a possible solution to the clash between UNSCRs and the Convention in Cordula Droege and Louise Arimatsu, 'The European Convention on Human Rights and International Humanitarian Law: Conference Report' (2009) 12 *Yearbook of International Humanitarian Law* 435, 447.

38 *Nada* v. *Switzerland* (2013) 56 EHRR 18.

39 Most notably UNSCR No. 1267 (1999) and UNSCR No. 1390 (2002).

40 UNSCR No. 1267 (1999) at [7].

Resolution 1390(2002) expressly required States to prevent the individuals on the UN list from entering or transiting through their territory.[41] The Court stated:

> As a result, the abovementioned presumption is rebutted in the present case, having regard to the clear and explicit language, imposing an obligation to take measures capable of breaching human rights, that was used in that resolution.[42]

The ruling is interesting for a number of reasons. Firstly, it is open to question whether this case is different from *Al-Jedda*, as Hollenberg argues the UNSCR at issue in *Nada* did not explicitly consider how these measures should relate to a State's obligations under international human rights law.[43] Secondly, the finding was largely devoid of consequence as the Court went on to find that the State still had to uphold its Convention obligations under Articles 8 and 13. Switzerland was found to have violated Article 8 because it retained some discretion over how the sanctions were implemented and had not mitigated the effects of the sanctions as best they could. The State could:

> not validly confine itself to relying on the binding nature of Security Council resolutions, but should have persuaded the Court that it had taken – or at least had attempted to take – all possible measures to adapt the sanctions regime to the applicant's individual situation. That finding dispenses the Court from determining the question [...] of the hierarchy between the obligations [...] the respondent Government has failed to show that it attempted, as far as possible, to harmonise the obligations that it regarded as divergent.[44]

By refusing to acknowledge the existence of a norm conflict, ruling that the State could have upheld the sanctions regime and the Convention obligations, the Court once again avoided ruling that the UNSCR provisions were hierarchically superior to the Convention.

The Court took a similar approach in the case of *Al-Dulimi* v. *Switzerland*,[45] another case related to the sanctions regime imposed through UNSCRs. The applicant, who had been head of finance for the Iraqi secret services

41 UNSCR No. 1390 (2002) at [2].

42 *Nada* v. *Switzerland* (2013) 56 EHRR 18 at [172].

43 Stephan Hollenberg, 'The Diverging Approaches of the European Court of Human Rights in the cases of Nada and Al-Dulimi' (2015) 64(2) ICLQ 445, 451.

44 *Nada* v. *Switzerland* (2013) 56 EHRR 18 at [196]–[197].

45 *Al-Dulimi and Montana Management Inc.* v. *Switzerland* App no 5809/08 (ECtHR, 21 June 2016).

under Saddam Hussein, had his assets and those of a company he managed confiscated by the Swiss authorities pursuant to a UNSCR.[46] He claimed the confiscation procedure violated his right of access to a court under Article 6.

In its judgment, the Court again applied the *Al-Jedda* presumption to the UNSCRs at issue. It stated that there was nothing in the UNSCRs imposing the sanctions 'that explicitly prevented the Swiss courts from reviewing, in terms of human rights protection, the measures taken at national level'.[47] The Swiss authorities had a duty to ensure the listing of the applicants by the sanctions committee was not arbitrary and it had not discharged this duty.[48] This judgment seems inconsistent with other rules of international law, for example, it is difficult to see how Switzerland could do what the Court asks without violating the rule that State's cannot rely on their own domestic law to avoid international obligations.[49] It is also difficult to fathom that the UN Security Council would have established the sanctions regime in the manner they did if States were nonetheless capable of modifying its sanctions. The Court appears to be going to great lengths in each of these cases to avoid accepting the supremacy of UN measures over the Convention.

## Peremptory Norms

Peremptory norms also have the capacity to trump other norms under international law, but their capacity to do so is limited because they lack 'both an agreed content and consensus in state practice'.[50] In *Al-Adsani*, discussed above, the Court confronted the issue of whether the peremptory norm prohibiting torture should take precedence over State immunity from civil jurisdiction. The Court recognised the peremptory status of the norm,[51] but declined to rule that it took precedence over the doctrine of State immunity. The Court maintained that the peremptory norm covered cases of individual criminal liability for alleged acts of torture, but did not apply in the context of

[46] UNSCR No. 1483 (2003).

[47] *Al-Dulimi and Montana Management Inc.* v. *Switzerland* App no 5809/08 (ECtHR, 21 June 2016) at [143].

[48] Ibid at [150].

[49] Article 27, Vienna Convention on the Law of Treaties (adopted 23 May 1969, entered into force 27 January 1980) 1155 UNTS 331.

[50] Shelton (n. 12) 291, 297; Vidmar and De Wet (n. 6) 26.

[51] *Al-Adsani* v. *United Kingdom* (2002) 34 EHRR 11 at [61].

civil suits for damages in respect of acts of torture.[52] A number of dissenting judges took issue with the Court's approach noting that:

> It is not the nature of the proceedings which determines the effects that a jus cogens rule has upon another rule of international law, but the character of the rule as a peremptory norm and its interaction with a hierarchically lower rule.[53]

It is difficult to argue with the dissenters' logic, but as Bates points out, the Court faced a very tricky situation in which the weight of State practice was heavily against *Al-Adsani* and ruling in his favour would have represented a very bold shift in judicial policy.[54]

At other times the Court has declined to recognise that certain rights hold the status of peremptory norms. In the case of *Al-Dulimi* v. *Switzerland*, for example, while the applicant claimed that the sanctions regime violated Article 6 and that the right of access to a court was a peremptory norm, the Court noted the importance of the right, but stated 'the Court does not consider these guarantees to be among the norms of jus cogens in the current state of international law'.[55] Thus while peremptory norms may often be invoked by judges and lawyers in a rhetorical fashion to emphasise the importance of particular norms, they are not employed as a means of conflict resolution to declare another norm null and void,[56] and have never to date been employed in that capacity by the Court.

### 5.2.3 *Lex Specialis*

The *lex specialis* principle is both a tool for norm conflict resolution and interpretation. Firstly, it can indicate an order of preference between two rules that regulate the same problem in different ways.[57] Thus one rule may be an

52 Ibid at [61].

53 Ibid, Joint Dissenting Opinion of Judges Rozakis and Caflisch Joined by Judges Wildhaber, Costa, Cabral Barreto and Vajić at [4].

54 Ed Bates, 'The Al-Adsani Case, State Immunity and the International Legal Prohibition on Torture' (2003) 3 HRLR 193, 207–11.

55 *Al-Dulimi and Montana Management Inc.* v. *Switzerland* App no 5809/08 (ECtHR, 21 June 2016) at [136]; The applicant in *Nada* v. *Switzerland* made a similar claim that the sanctions regime violated jus cogens norms before the domestic courts, though the European Court did not address this issue in its judgment – *Nada* v. *Switzerland* (2013) 56 EHRR 18 at [46]–[47].

56 Andrea Bianchi, 'Human Rights and the Magic of Jus Cogens' (2008) 19 EJIL 491, 501–2; Milanovic (n. 6) 466.

57 Koskenniemi (n. 6) at [56]; Laura Olson, 'Practical Challenges of Implementing the Complementarity between International Humanitarian and Human Rights Law – Demonstrated by the Procedural Regulation of Internment in Non-International Armed Conflict' (2009) 40 *Case Western Reserve University's Journal of International Law* 437, 446.

application of a general rule in a specific circumstance and be preferred where those circumstances arise. The Court has invoked the *lex specialis* principle, for example, to prefer the application of one Convention rule over another in given circumstances. Thus, where violations of Articles 10 (freedom of expression) and 11 (freedom of assembly and association) were alleged, Article 11 was preferred over Article 10 for issues related to assemblies.[58] The *lex specialis* rule functions well for such internal precedence issues and within systematised groups of treaties that have a relationship to each other, such as World Trade Organisation treaties. It has been argued that the *lex specialis* principle does not function as well for norm conflicts arising from unrelated norms originating in different legal frameworks, such as IHL and HRL.[59] Secondly, the principle can also be invoked to resolve a norm conflict, with the more specific norm prevailing over the more general norm.[60]

Prud'homme notes that the principle has been used in both ways to determine the relationship between IHL and human rights law. It has been used as an interpretative tool to interpret human rights in light of IHL, but also to promote the primacy of humanitarian law over human rights. This is motivated by the idea that because IHL is better tailored to the specifics of armed conflicts, it should take precedence over human rights law.[61]

As a practical tool for conflict resolution, the *lex specialis* maxim runs into some conceptual difficulties. It is unclear, for example, how one defines which norm is general and which is specific.[62] Many authors point out that it is not axiomatic that the more specific norm is necessarily the better or

[58] *Djavit An* v. *Turkey* (2005) 40 EHRR 45 at [39]; See further examples such as Article 6 taking precedence over Article 13 – *Kudla* v. *Poland* (2002) 35 EHRR 11 at [146] and Article 5(4) taking precedence over Article 13 – *Brannigan and McBride* v. *United Kingdom* (1994) 17 EHRR 539 at [76].

[59] Nancie Prud'homme, 'Lex Specialis: Oversimplifying a More Complex and Multifaceted Relationship?' (2007) 40 *Israel Law Review* 356, 379–80; Olson (n. 57) 447; Iain Scobbie, 'Principle or Pragmatics? The Relationship between Human Rights Law and the Law of Armed Conflict' (2009) 14 *Journal of Conflict and Security Law* 449, 453.

[60] Koskenniemi (n. 6) at [57]; Olson (n. 57) 446.

[61] Prud'homme (n. 59) 369–70. On the issue of IHL superseding human rights law see Natasha Balendra, 'Defining Armed Conflict' (2008) 29 *Cardozo Law Review* 2461, 2482–5; Michael Dennis, 'Application of Human Rights Treaties Extraterritorially to Detention of Combatants and Security Internees: Fuzzy Thinking All Around?' (2006) 12 *ILSA Journal of International & Comparative Law* 459, 474; William Hays Parks, 'Part IX of the ICRC "Direct Participation in Hostilities" Study: No Mandate, No Expertise, and Legally Incorrect' (2010) 42 *International Law and Politics* 769, 797–9; Heike Krieger, 'A Conflict of Norms the Relationship between Humanitarian Law and Human Rights Law in the ICRC Customary Law Study' (2006) 11 *Journal of Conflict and Security Law* 265, 270.

[62] Prud'homme (n. 59) 382; Although Koskenniemi advances a few means of determining this – Koskenniemi (n. 6) at [57].

most protective norm.[63] Academics have also questioned whether IHL should always be considered the *lex specialis* when compared with human rights law.[64] Courts could just as easily analyse the norms in each body of law to determine which norm is the *lex specialis* in the specific context.[65]

As one would expect given the Court's aversion to subordinating Convention norms to other bodies of law, there is scant evidence of the Court taking a so-called 'strong' *lex specialis* approach to IHL, with the IHL superseding human rights law. In *Cyprus* v. *Turkey*, the European Commission was called upon to assess whether the detention of Prisoners of War (POWs) during the Turkish invasion of Cyprus in 1974 was compatible with Article 5. The Commission remarked that given Turkey had expressed its intention to comply with the Geneva Conventions and had allowed the Red Cross access to its POW detention facilities: 'the Commission has not found it necessary to examine the question of a breach of Article 5 [...] with regard to persons accorded the status of prisoners of war'.[66] The Commission's refusal to examine the issue may have been motivated by a belief that IHL, as the *lex specialis*, displaced the Convention obligations under Article 5. However, as Forowicz argues this implicit deference is at best ambiguous.[67]

Returning to the case of *Al-Jedda*, discussed above, after the Court had addressed the issue of whether the UNSCR took precedence over Article 5, it considered whether there was 'any other legal basis for the applicant's detention which could operate *to disapply* the requirements of Article 5 § 1' (emphasis added).[68] It noted that the UNSCR powers were a continuation of occupation powers under IHL. Although the occupation had ended, the Court considered what would happen if the powers continued to apply. It stated: 'the Court does not find it established that international humanitarian law places an obligation on an Occupying Power to use indefinite internment without

63 Noam Lubell, 'Parallel Application of International Humanitarian Law and International Human Rights Law: An Examination of the Debate' (2007) 40 *Israel Law Review* 648, 654; Sandesh Sivakumaran, 'Re-envisaging the International Law of Internal Armed Conflict' (2011) 22 EJIL 219, 240–1; Milanovic (n. 6).

64 Lubell (n. 63) 656; Michael O'Boyle and Jean Paul Costa, 'The ECtHR and IHL' in Christos Rozakis (ed), *The European Convention on Human Rights, a Living Instrument* (Bruylant Press 2011) 123.

65 Louise Doswald-Beck, 'International Humanitarian Law and the International Court of Justice on the Legality of the Threat or Use of Nuclear Weapons' (1997) 37 IRRC 35; Prud'homme (n. 59) 373–4.

66 *Cyprus* v. *Turkey* (1982) 4 EHRR 482 at [313].

67 Magdalena Forowicz, *The Reception of International Law in the European Court of Human Rights* (Oxford University Press 2010) 323–4.

68 *Al-Jedda* v. *United Kingdom* (2011) 53 EHRR 23 at [107].

trial'.[69] It also noted that the ICJ in the *Armed Activities* case had interpreted the obligation to ensure public order and safety during occupations as including an obligation to uphold human rights law.[70] The Court maintained that under the fourth Geneva Convention, security detention was a measure of 'last resort', concluding that these provisions would not operate to disapply the Convention.

This comment has been interpreted in different ways. The first reading is that the Court was considering whether the original provision in IHL granting the power to utilise security detention had any latent effect after the occupation ended. If that were the case, the IHL provision could, in theory at least, provide the obligation necessary for Article 103 to apply and for that detention power to prevail and 'disapply' the Convention norm. This reading could make sense as the entire case revolved around whether UN law superseded Convention law. Although the underlying conflict between IHL and the Convention was relevant, it was a side issue here. The UK was not considered an occupying power when they detained the applicant, therefore IHL did not apply to the applicant's initial detention and the UNSCR provided the legal basis for his detention. Yet, the fact that the Court was prepared to entertain this possibility perhaps illustrates its limited grasp on how international law applied to this scenario.[71] IHL had ceased to apply when the applicant was detained and even if it had not, in order for Article 103 to impart its power for one obligation to supersede another, the prospective superior norm must arise as a result of the State's membership of the UN. As the original IHL norm was not an obligation arising from the UN Charter, it could never have such an effect. While this reading of the Court's statement is most likely correct, the ambiguity and apparent futility of the exercise has prompted alternative views.

Some academics argue that the Court was making a broader statement about the relationship between IHL and the Convention in *Al-Jedda*. They claim the Court was considering whether the IHL norms would 'disapply' the Convention

69 Ibid at [107]; The Court's distinction between obligation and authorisation is arguably overwrought in this judgment. Lord Bingham's judgment on *Al-Jedda* in the House of Lords clearly cautions against reading too much into this apparent distinction, noting the complex language the Security Council uses in UNSCRs and that the terms should not be interpreted too narrowly – *R. (Al-Jedda)* v. *Secretary of State for Defence* [2007] UKHL 58 at [33]–[34]. Pejic rightly notes that IHL alone must provide a sufficient legal basis for detention independently of UN provisions, which again highlights the artificiality of this distinction – Jelena Pejic, 'The European Court of Human Rights' Al-Jedda Judgment: The Oversight of International Humanitarian Law' (2011) 93 IRRC 837, 847–8.

70 *Armed Activities on the Territory of the Congo* (*DRC* v. *Uganda*), 2005 ICJ Reports, p. 168 19 December 2005 at [178].

71 The Court's institutional capacity to deal with IHL is discussed further in Chapter 5.

norms via the *lex specialis* principle, rather than Article 103. Naert contends that *Al-Jedda* clarifies the relationship between IHL and the Convention and the Court's comment limits the degree to which interpretation of the Convention in light of IHL is possible.[72] Krieger considers that the comment concerns how the *lex specialis* principle governs the relationship between IHL and the Convention. She argues that the Court was right to conclude that IHL did not operate to disapply the Convention norms.[73] It is difficult to accept that such a fundamental statement would present itself in this brief, vestigial comment at the end of the Court's main judgment. It would also be at odds with the Court's practice, which has been to avoid addressing conflicts as far as possible and certainly those which may lead to the subordination of Convention law to any other law.

The fact that *Al-Jedda* could be read in these fundamentally different ways shows how confusing and ambiguous the Court's statements on norm conflicts between IHL and HRL have been. It has shown a persistent unwillingness to deal with the practical consequences of applying both the Convention and IHL. While the Court is understandably reluctant to open itself to the influence of IHL, which could potentially undermine the status and protective effect of the Convention, the Court cannot simply bury its head in the sand and pretend it does not have an impact on the applicable norms.[74] The Court may be moving away from this approach as the analysis of *Hassan* v. *United Kingdom* in the next section will demonstrate.

### 5.2.4 *Harmonious Interpretation*

The final approach to norm conflict addressed here is complementarity or harmonious interpretation. There is a general presumption against norm conflict in international law.[75] There is also a presumption that when States adopt new obligations they 'intend something not inconsistent with generally recognised principles of international law, or with previous treaty obligations towards third States'.[76] In other words, they are assumed not to desire the contravention of existing obligations. The general rules on treaty interpretation stipulate that when interpreting treaties one should take into account 'relevant rules of

72 Frederik Naert, 'The European Court of Human Rights' Al-Jedda and Al-Skeini Judgments: An Introduction and Some Reflections' (2011) 50 *Military Law and Law of War Review* 315, 319.

73 Heike Krieger, 'After Al-Jedda: Detention, Derogation, and an Enduring Dilemma' (2011) 50 *Military Law and the Law of War Review* 419, 426–32.

74 O'Boyle and Costa (n. 64) 129.

75 Koskenniemi (n. 6) at [37].

76 Lassa Oppenheim, Robert Jennings and Arthur Desmond Watts, *Oppenheim's International Law Vol. 1, pt. 2–4, Peace* (Longman 1992) 1275; Koskenniemi (n. 6) at [38].

international law applicable in the relations between the parties'.[77] From these principles the notion that IHL and human rights should be applied as far as possible simultaneously to complement one another arises.[78] The idea finds support at the Inter-American Commission on Human Rights,[79] the Human Rights Committee,[80] and the ICJ.[81]

The Court has made positive remarks about applying both bodies of law simultaneously. In *Varnava* v. *Turkey*, it suggested that the Convention articles 'must be interpreted in so far as possible in light of the general principles of international law, including the rules of international humanitarian law'.[82] The Court made similar remarks in its admissibility decision in the case of *Georgia* v. *Russia (II)*, which relates to human rights violations arising during the international armed conflict between Georgia and Russia in 2008. The Court stated that the Convention must be:

> interpreted in so far as possible in the light of the general principles of international law, including the rules of international humanitarian law [...] the Convention should so far as possible be interpreted in harmony with other rules of international law of which it forms part.[83]

77 Article 31, Vienna Convention on the Law of Treaties (adopted 23 May 1969, entered into force 27 January 1980) 1155 UNTS 331.

78 Lubell (n. 63) 654; Matthew Happold, 'International Humanitarian Law and Human Rights Law' in Nigel White and Christian Henderson (eds), *Research Handbook on International Conflict and Security Law* (Edward Elgar Publishing 2013) 16; Damira Kamchibekova, 'State Responsibility for Extraterritorial Human Rights Violations' (2007) 13 *Buffalo Human Rights Law Review* 87, 107–9; Hampson, 'Relationship' (n. 2) 560; Stuart Hendin, 'Detainees in Afghanistan: The Balance Between Human Rights and International Humanitarian Law for Foreign Military Forces' (2008) 14 *Tilburg Law Review* 249, 261–4; *Serdar Mohammed* v. *Ministry of Defence* [2014] EWHC 1369 at [275].

79 In *Coard* v. *United States*, the Inter-American Commission noted that while IHL and HRL had their respective fields of application, there was substantial overlap and 'the potential application of one does not necessarily exclude or displace the other' – *Coard et al.* v. *United States* Report No 109/99 IAComHR 29 September 1999 at [39].

80 In General Comment No.31, the Committee noted: 'While, in respect of certain Covenant rights, more specific rules of international humanitarian law may be specially relevant for the purposes of the interpretation of Covenant rights, both spheres of law are complementary, not mutually exclusive' – UN Human Rights Committee, General Comment No. 31, The Nature of the General Legal Obligation imposed on States Parties to the Covenant, 26 May 2004, CCPR/C/21/Rev.1/Add.13 at [11].

81 In its *Nuclear Weapons Advisory Opinion*, the ICJ considered the simultaneous application of an ICCPR provision guaranteeing the right to life and IHL provisions permitting killings. It concluded that IHL would not function to completely disapply the ICCPR norm. Instead it would affect what would be considered an 'arbitrary' deprivation of life – *Legality of the Threat or Use of Nuclear Weapons*, Advisory Opinion, 1996 ICJ Reports, p. 226 8 July 1996 at [25]; Scobbie (n. 59) 452–4.

82 *Varnava and Others* v. *Turkey* App no 16064/90 (ECtHR, 18 September 2009) at [185].

83 *Georgia* v. *Russia (II)* (2012) 54 EHRR SE10 at [72].

These statements support the view that the Court favours a harmonious interpretation of the Convention and IHL. This approach is also consistent with the Court's general aversion toward subordinating the Convention rules to other rules, discussed above. Notwithstanding these positive statements, the Court's practice on engaging with IHL has not been consistent as the previous chapters have aptly demonstrated. While applicants have regularly explicitly raised conflicts between IHL and human rights law before the Court,[84] the Court has repeatedly avoided dealing with the practical consequences of applying both bodies of law and has often made confusing and ambiguous statements on the subject of norm conflict.[85] As noted in Chapter 3, for example, the application of human rights law to military operations, especially armed conflicts, has led the Court to gloss over fundamental distinctions between human rights law and IHL. It has at times distinguished between the protections accorded to combatants and civilians and accepted the use of force when not absolutely necessary.[86] The Court also appeared to apply IHL standards in its interpretation of Article 2 without acknowledging its influence or clearly assessing whether the threshold for an armed conflict was reached on the facts presented.[87] This led to significant inconsistency in the Court's approach to similar cases, at times applying standards that reflected IHL at other times a standard Convention approach. It also served to undermine the coherency and consistency of Convention standards. If the Court had opted for harmonious interpretation, openly engaging with IHL and interpreting the Convention Articles in light of IHL, much of this confusion and inconsistency could be avoided.

## 5.3 HASSAN V. UNITED KINGDOM

The Court took a very positive step toward harmonious interpretation of IHL and the Convention in the case of *Hassan* v. *United Kingdom*. In that case, the applicant's brother was arrested by UK forces in Iraq on 23 April 2003. At the time of his arrest he was armed with an AK47 and he was arrested on suspicion

[84] Françoise Hampson, 'Is Human Rights Law of any Relevance to Military Operations in Afghanistan?' (2009) 85 *US Naval War College International Law Studies* 485, 495.

[85] Hans-Joachim Heintze, 'On the Relationship between Human Rights Law Protection and International Humanitarian Law' (2004) 86 IRRC 789, 806; Bethlehem also criticises the Court's failure to deal with the consequences of co-application in the context of Article 2 in *Al-Skeini* – Daniel Bethlehem, 'The Relationship between International Humanitarian Law and International Human Rights Law in Situations of Armed Conflict' (2013) 2 *Cambridge Journal of International and Comparative Law* 180, 186–7.

[86] See Chapter 3 – Section 3.3.2.

[87] See Chapter 3 – Section 3.4.

of being a combatant or a civilian posing a threat to security. He was detained at Camp Bucca, interrogated and most probably released in early May 2003. In September 2003, his body was found in Samara, showing signs that he had been tortured and executed.

The applicant alleged that his brother had been arrested and detained by British forces in Iraq and was later found dead in unexplained circumstances. The applicant's claims under Articles 2 and 3 were dismissed as lacking sufficient evidence and manifestly ill-founded. However, the case under Article 5 proceeded. At the time of his arrest, which was during the active phase of hostilities, it was unclear whether the applicant was a combatant or a civilian posing a threat to security. He was registered as a prisoner of war by default,[88] then interviewed to determine his actual status.[89] The UK derived the legal power to subject him to internment from IHL.[90] The UK had not derogated from Article 5 for its operations in Iraq and because the list of grounds of permissible detention in Article 5(1) does not include internment, his detention was *prima facie* a violation of Article 5.[91] Thus, a norm conflict arose between the provisions of IHL, which permitted the UK to detain him, and the Convention.

The Court's resolution of this conflict was consistent with its previous practice in some ways and sharply divergent in others. Perhaps true to form, the Court declined to follow a so-called strong *lex specialis* approach, which would involve the IHL provisions taking precedence over the Convention.[92] Instead, the Court sought a harmonious interpretation of the Convention in light of IHL. The Court observed that States did not derogate from Article 5 to intern people during international armed conflicts.[93] However, it noted:

> the lack of a formal derogation under Article 15 does not prevent the Court from taking account of the context and the provisions of international humanitarian law when interpreting and applying Article 5 in this case.[94]

88 Pursuant to Article 5, Geneva Convention Relative to the Treatment of Prisoners of War (adopted 12 August 1949, entered into force 21 October 1950) 75 UNTS 135.

89 *Hassan* v. *United Kingdom* App no 29750/09 (ECtHR, 16 September 2014) at [21].

90 If the applicant's brother was classified as a prisoner of war, the power would derive from Article 21, Geneva Convention Relative to the Treatment of Prisoners of War (adopted 12 August 1949, entered into force 21 October 1950) 75 UNTS 135. If the applicant's brother was classified as a civilian that posed a threat to security, the power to detain him would derive from Article 42, Geneva Convention Relative to the Protection of Civilian Persons in Time of War (adopted 12 August 1949, entered into force 21 October 1950) 75 UNTS 287.

91 *Hassan* v. *United Kingdom* App no 29750/09 (ECtHR, 16 September 2014) at [97].

92 Claire Landais and Lea Bass, 'Reconciling the Rules of International Humanitarian Law with the Rules of European Human Rights Law' (2015) 97 IRRC 1295, 1307.

93 *Hassan* v. *United Kingdom* App no 29750/09 (ECtHR, 16 September 2014) at [101].

94 Ibid at [103].

The Court maintained that this was the first case in which a State had 'requested the Court to disapply its obligations under Article 5 or in some other way to interpret them' in light of IHL.[95] This was in spite of the comments in *Al-Jedda* noted above. The Court distinguished *Al-Jedda* on the grounds that the UK had not argued that Article 5 was modified or displaced by IHL internment powers in that case.[96] The Court then stated that:

> the grounds of permitted deprivation of liberty [in Article 5] should be accommodated, as far as possible, with the taking of prisoners of war and the detention of civilians who pose a risk to security under the Third and Fourth Geneva Conventions.[97]

It confined this interpretation only to cases of international armed conflict and only when this was specifically pleaded by the State.[98] The Court then offered substantial guidance on how to reconcile the internment provisions of IHL and human rights law. Any detention measures had to comply with IHL and be consistent with the general purpose of human rights law, namely avoiding arbitrariness.[99] The Court recognised that there may be practical problems with upholding procedural elements of Article 5 in conflict zones. It recognised particular problems could arise from Article 5(4), which allows everyone who is deprived of their liberty to take proceedings in a court to determine the lawfulness of their detention. The Court noted that it 'might not be practicable, in the course of an international armed conflict, for the legality of detention to be determined by an independent 'court' in the sense generally required by article 5.4'.[100]

The Court modified the obligations under 5(4) such that the competent body reviewing detention should 'provide sufficient guarantees of impartiality and fair procedure to protect against arbitrariness' and it should review the legality of the detention shortly after a person is placed in detention with subsequent reviews 'at frequent intervals'.[101] Landais and Bass note that this marks an express departure from the Court's previous jurisprudence where it held that the list of permitted grounds for deprivation of liberty contained

95 *Hassan* v. *United Kingdom* App no 29750/09 (ECtHR, 16 September 2014) at [99].

96 The UK instead argued that the obligation to detain in the UNSCR took precedence over its obligations in the Convention and the Court did not endorse that reading.

97 *Hassan* v. *United Kingdom* App no 29750/09 (ECtHR, 16 September 2014) at [104].

98 Ibid at [104]–[107].

99 Ibid at [105].

100 Ibid at [106].

101 Ibid.

in Article 5(1) is exhaustive.[102] Both the judgment itself and the criticisms that have followed it warrant extensive analysis.

### 5.3.1 *Derogation*

The first criticism levelled against the judgment relates to derogation. Stubbins Bates argues that the Court's approach undermines the derogation provision in Article 15, which is already under-used.[103] The dissenting judges in *Hassan* also considered that the Court's approach 'renders Article 15 effectively obsolete within the Convention structure as regards the fundamental right to liberty in times of war'.[104] While Stubbins Bates is correct that Article 15 is already under-utilised and this judgment may obviate the need for derogations, the idea that this judgment renders derogation during international armed conflicts obsolete is an overstatement. The *Al-Jedda* judgment illustrates the benefits that a derogation would have over relying on arguments of precedence based on UNSCRs or IHL to justify internment before the Court. States would be gambling on an uncertain outcome. A derogation would place States on much firmer ground. It could persist through different phases of a conflict or where the exact nature of the conflict is uncertain, thereby making the State less reliant on establishing a specific legal ground for detention, e.g. UNSCR. It is noteworthy that Ukraine derogated from Article 5 in respect of its conflict with Russia even after the *Hassan* judgment was released.[105]

Derogation is clearly the preferred option and this will be discussed extensively in Chapter 7. At this point it is important to view the issue of derogation in context. One can sympathise with the State in this situation. Convention States have used internment during armed conflicts before the Convention was adopted and even after with few legal consequences up to this point. The Court has also been slow to clarify the nature and scope of extra-territorial jurisdiction and has proven reluctant to accept other legal bases for internment or to engage with IHL, leaving States in confusion over the scope of their obligations and with limited scope to justify their actions. The States

[102] Landais and Bass (n. 92) 1308; see *Ireland* v. *United Kingdom* (1979–1980) 2 EHRR 25 at [194] and A *and Others* v. *United Kingdom* (2009) 49 EHRR 29 at [163].

[103] Elizabeth Stubbins Bates, '*Hassan* v. *The United Kingdom*' (2015) 54(1) *International Legal Materials* 83, 85.

[104] *Hassan* v. *United Kingdom* App no 29750/09 (ECtHR, 16 September 2014), Partly Dissenting Opinion of Judge Spano Joined by Judges Nicolaou, Bianku and Kalaydjieva at [16].

[105] Ukraine Government, 'Derogation contained in a Note verbale from the Permanent Representation of Ukraine, dated 5 June 2015, registered at the Secretariat General on 9 June 2015' <www.coe.int/en/web/conventions/full-list/-/conventions/treaty/005/declarations?p_auth=3KfBMbNJ> accessed 16 August 2018.

themselves may have assumed, with some justification, that IHL was the *lex specialis* and took precedence over Convention norms.

A strong *lex specialis* approach would make derogation unnecessary.[106] Indeed Byron argues that Article 15(2) seems to invite the Court to treat IHL as the *lex specialis* in this context by allowing derogations to Article 2 in cases of deaths resulting from lawful acts of war.[107] At the same time, the State's capacity to derogate for extra-territorial military operations has also been openly questioned by several high profile legal minds.[108] It is only relatively recently that States have begun to openly consider the possibility of derogating for extra-territorial military operations,[109] an issue discussed at length in Chapter 7. Thus, while derogation would certainly be the preferred option, there are several extenuating circumstances explaining why derogation was not pursued during previous military operations. The judgment in *Hassan* certainly does not render derogation obsolete and we are likely to see further derogations for international armed conflicts in the future.

### 5.3.2 *Beyond Interpretation*

The second contention is that *Hassan* represents a 'regression in human rights protection in Europe', that the Court has assumed, based on subsequent State practice during international armed conflicts, that all contracting States have implicitly reviewed their Convention obligations and enlarged the exhaustive list of detention grounds in Article 5.[110] Bernard argues that unlike Article 9 of the International Covenant on Civil and Political Rights, which refers to arbitrary deprivation of liberty and can be read in light of IHL,[111] reading the list of grounds of permissible detention in Article 5(1) as including internment

106 Marko Milanovic, 'Extraterritorial Derogations from Human Rights Treaties in Armed Conflict' in Nehal Bhuta (ed), *The Frontiers of Human Rights* (Oxford University Press 2016) 83–4; Dennis makes a similar argument on derogations from the ICCPR – Dennis (n. 61) 136.

107 Christine Byron, 'A Blurring of the Boundaries: The Application of International Humanitarian Law by Human Rights Bodies' (2006–2007) 47 *Virginia Journal of International Law* 839, 865.

108 See Lord Bingham in *R. (Al-Jedda)* v. *Secretary of State for Defence* at [38]; O'Boyle and Costa (n. 64) 116.

109 Ministry of Defence, 'Government to protect Armed Forces from persistent legal claims in future overseas operations' <www.gov.uk/government/news/government-to-protect-armed-forces-from-persistent-legal-claims-in-future-overseas-operations> accessed 15 August 2018.

110 Judge Paulo Pinto de Albuquerque, 'Is the ECHR facing an existential crisis?' (Mansfield College, Oxford, 28 April 2017) 5 <www.law.ox.ac.uk/sites/files/oxlaw/pinto_opening_presentation_2017.pdf> accessed 15 August 2018.

111 See *mutatis mutandis Legality of the Threat or Use of Nuclear Weapons*, Advisory Opinion, 1996 ICJ Reports, p. 226 8 July 1996 at [25]; Scobbie (n. 59) 452–4.

is 'textually excluded' by the wording of Article 5. The suggestion is that the Court has moved beyond interpretation into outright amendment and that the only way to circumvent this 'textual exclusion' is through derogation.[112] Of course, the Court acted in a similar fashion when it ruled that 'Article 2 has been amended so as to prohibit the death penalty in all circumstances'.[113] While this reading of Article 2 was bolstered by the two additional protocols aimed at abolishing the death penalty and thus the situation is not completely analogous,[114] not all State parties had ratified the additional protocols that secured this supposed amendment to Article 2. So what is the difference?

The sense is that *Hassan* curtails human rights protection, which is bad, while the counter-textual reading of Article 2 extended protection, which is good.[115] However, this represents a trite reading of the situation. The Court has deftly threaded a needle in *Hassan*. It avoided a strong *lex specialis* approach wherein the Convention's protection could have been completely overridden. It made allowances for the challenging circumstances presented by an extra-territorial military operation while sustaining the protective thrust of Article 5. As noted above, the judgment is also in line with the practice of other international courts and the approach to interpretation outlined in the Vienna Convention on the Law of Treaties.

Judge Pinto de Albuquerque cautions against the precedent *Hassan* creates stating that IHL will 'weaken IHRL [international human rights law] standards'.[116] Yet such pious lamentations bely the reality that this book lays bare, that Convention standards are already being weakened through their application to military operations. The obligations are being modified in an *ad hoc*, implicit and inconsistent way.[117] The very scope and application of the obligations is unclear in many situations.[118] Surely the Court's approach in *Hassan* is preferable to the current confusion. The Court's approach in *Hassan* is

[112] Frederic Bernard, 'Deprivation of liberty in armed conflicts: the Strasbourg Court's attempt at reconciling human rights law and international humanitarian law in Hassan v. UK' <https://strasbourgobservers.com/2014/10/02/deprivation-of-liberty-in-armed-conflicts-the-strasbourg-courts-attempt-at-reconciling-human-rights-law-and-international-humanitarian-law-in-hassan-v-uk/> accessed 15 August 2018.

[113] *Al-Saadoon and Mufdhi* v. *United Kingdom* (Merits) (2010) 51 EHRR 9 at [120].

[114] See Protocol 6 and Protocol 13 additional to the Convention for the Protection of Human Rights and Fundamental Freedoms 1950.

[115] Judge Paulo Pinto de Albuquerque, 'Is the ECHR facing an existential crisis?' (Mansfield College, Oxford, 28 April 2017) 5 <www.law.ox.ac.uk/sites/files/oxlaw/pinto_opening_presentation_2017.pdf> accessed 15 August 2018.

[116] Ibid.

[117] See Chapter 3.

[118] See Chapters 1 and 2.

overt and it offers a sound justification for modifying the Convention obligations in harmonious interpretation. The Court provides a contextual barrier to the divergent interpretations of the Convention in *Hassan,* it will only adopt such interpretations in the context of international armed conflicts and only when specifically pleaded by the State. This avoids the risk that weaker Convention standards apparently informed by IHL, such as those weakening the protection of the combatant's right to life identified in Chapter 3, establish precedents of weaker standards for other contexts. Furthermore, rather than viewing it as a weakening of human rights standards, it is perhaps more accurately viewed as a strengthening of the procedural protections of IHL. Security detention is so widely utilised in armed conflicts that it is difficult to see how an outright prohibition on it in Article 5 could subsist in the future. It will be derogated from, superseded by a clear UNSCR power or facilitated by harmonious interpretation. As such the 'standard' may not apply in the first place to be weakened, instead we should look, as the Court has in *Hassan,* at how the Convention's protections can inform and enrich the existing IHL paradigms.

### 5.3.3 *Guiding Adaptation*

The preceding chapters have noted a recurring issue with the Court's jurisprudence concerning military operations, specifically that the Court has repeatedly acknowledged that the unusual circumstances of military operations warrant some adaptation of the Convention norms. However, in each of the cases the Court failed to offer any indication of how that would occur. Thus, in Chapter 4, the Court acknowledged that 'Article 2 must be applied realistically, to take account of specific problems faced by investigators',[119] but failed to give any indication of what concessions might be made. While in Chapter 1, the Court noted that where a State had lost de facto control over its own territory the scope of its obligations would be reduced,[120] but declined to offer guidance on what they would be reduced to or how the unusual circumstances would impact on the Convention obligations.

The Court's more detailed guidance in *Hassan* on how the obligations in Article 5 should apply in practice, for example, to ensure the competent body reviewing detention should provide sufficient guarantees of impartiality and fair procedure to protect against arbitrariness, are a welcome development.

119 *Al-Skeini and Others* v. *United Kingdom* (2011) 53 EHRR 18 at [168].
120 *Ilascu and Others* v. *Moldova and Russia* (2005) 40 EHRR 46 at [333].

At the same time, the Court's ruling may draw the Court into some perilous territory. By ruling that in order for an instance of detention to be consistent with Article 5 it must also comply with IHL,[121] the Court potentially draws itself into making pronouncements on whether a State's actions comply with IHL. The Court's capacity to apply IHL will be addressed further in Chapter 6. At this point it suffices to note that while some authors have argued in favour of using human rights courts to directly enforce substantive IHL norms,[122] the Court must be extremely cautious and learn from its Inter-American counterparts. The Inter-American Commission on Human Rights made moves in this direction by finding States responsible for both substantive violations of IHL and human rights law.[123] However, this practice was halted decisively by the Inter-American Court in *Las Palmeras* v. *Colombia* when it held that the Inter-American bodies should stick solely to finding violations of the Inter-American human rights treaties, although it could continue to use IHL as an aid to its interpretation of these where both applied.[124] This is obviously the preferred approach and most consistent with the Court's mandate as noted in the introduction.

## 5.4 CONCLUSION

The International Law Commission's maxims have had little discernible impact on the resolution of norm conflicts at the Court. This chapter has shown that the Court has a very strong aversion to holding any law superior to Convention norms, whether that be through Article 103 of the UN Charter or the application of a strong *lex specialis* approach. The Court has also revealed a tendency to avoid directly addressing the consequences of norm conflicts in its judgments in cases like *Nada* and *Saramati*.

The use of harmonious interpretation in *Hassan* is a welcome development and consistent with the Court's aversion to the supremacy of norms from other bodies of law. The Court has faced some dissension both within the Court and the wider academic community for this move, although the analysis above casts the judgment in a more favourable light. The Court's approach in

[121] *Hassan* v. *United Kingdom* App no 29750/09 (ECtHR, 16 September 2014) at [105].

[122] Françoise Hampson, 'Using International Human Rights Machinery to Enforce the International Law of Armed Conflicts' (1992) 31 *Military Law and Law of War Review* 117; Liesbeth Zegveld, 'The Inter-American Commission on Human Rights and International Humanitarian Law: A Comment on the Tablada Case' (1998) 38 IRRC 505, 506.

[123] See *Arturo Ribón Avilán* v. *Colombia* Report No 26/97 IAComHR 30 September 1997 at [134]; *Hugo Bustios Saavedra* v. *Peru* Report No 38/97 IAComHR 16 October 1997 at [88].

[124] *Las Palmeras* v. *Colombia* Series C No 90 IACtHR 6 December 2001 at [33]–[34].

*Hassan* is commendable and clearly preferable to the inconsistencies in the jurisprudence identified throughout this book. The *Hassan* judgment offers a clear basis for a divergent interpretation of the Convention, clear guidance on how to implement the Court's alternative approach and places strict limitations on that variation. It is hoped that this marks a watershed moment in the interpretation of the Convention with the Court much more open to the influence of IHL. There is still room for derogations in this new paradigm, indeed both derogations and harmonious interpretations should be utilised as Chapter 7 will illustrate. If *Hassan* does mark a change in approach for the Court, we should expect to see explicit references to IHL more regularly in its jurisprudence. The following chapter considers how the Court might fare if called upon to interpret and apply IHL more regularly by examining the Court's track record in doing this under Article 7 of the Convention.

# 6

# Article 7

## 6.1 INTRODUCTION

Article 7 of the Convention sits at a crossroads between the Convention and other bodies of international law. It states:

1. No one shall be held guilty of any criminal offence on account of any act or omission which did not constitute a criminal offence under national or international law at the time when it was committed. Nor shall a heavier penalty be imposed than the one that was applicable at the time the criminal offence was committed.
2. This Article shall not prejudice the trial and punishment of any person for any act or omission which, at the time when it was committed, was criminal according to the general principles of law recognised by civilised nations.

The article provides two basic protections. First, people cannot be tried for criminal offences that were not criminalised at the time they were committed. Second, people should not be subjected to a heavier penalty for a crime than was typically applicable for that crime at the time it was committed. The intersection between the Convention and other bodies of international law occurs because Article 7 relies on external sources, specifically mentioning international law, to provide the content of criminal law. This renvoi in Article 7 acts as a conduit through which international law flows and calls upon the Court to establish whether national or international law provides a sufficient basis for a criminal conviction.[1]

[1] Giulia Pinzauti, 'The European Court of Human Rights' Incidental Application of International Criminal Law and Humanitarian Law: A Critical Discussion of Kononov v. Latvia' (2008) 6 *Journal of International Criminal Justice* 1043, 1046–8.

Article 7 provides insights into the Convention's application to military operations. The principle of legality in Article 7 has historically presented a barrier to criminal prosecutions for international crimes related to military operations and reveals the way in which human rights law is sometimes applied to the aftermath of military operations.[2]

Article 7 also offers an insight into how the Court interprets and applies IHL. The preceding chapters have emphasised the need for the Court to take into account the potential influence IHL can have on the legal paradigm during military operations. In many cases the Court has ignored IHL or failed to explicitly recognise the influence it had on its judgments. In Chapter 3, for example, the Court appears to be influenced by IHL when it interprets Article 2, but it seldom relies explicitly on IHL and certainly does not use it consistently. Notwithstanding the recent *Hassan* case, discussed in Chapter 5, the Court has shown an unwillingness to openly interpret and actively engage with IHL. That trend is completely reversed under Article 7 where the Court is obliged to interpret and apply IHL and international criminal law (ICL). The application of IHL here is ancillary and incidental,[3] it does not foreshadow a wider application of IHL in the Court's normal jurisprudence. Nonetheless, it provides a unique opportunity to evaluate the Court's institutional capacity to interpret and apply this body of law when given a free rein to do so. The analysis below presents a compelling argument for the Court to be more transparent and open about its application of IHL in other areas.

The chapter opens with a brief overview of Article 7 and a broader discussion of cases involving military operations and instances where the Court has applied IHL and its counterpart ICL. It highlights several issues, including apparent errors in interpretation and instances where the Court has retrospectively interpreted the law in light of subsequent developments. This section also highlights instances where the law has arguably been applied to the applicant's detriment and an inconsistent approach toward the

[2] Ward Ferdinandusse, *Direct Application of International Criminal Law in National Courts* (Asser Press 2006) 221. The principle of legality posed such a significant barrier to prosecutions for certain crimes after World War 2 that it was considered necessary to include Article 7(2) in the Convention, which was designed to prevent those convicted by the International Military Tribunals from challenging certain convictions for crimes, such as the crime of aggression, which had a weak basis in international law at the time – William Schabas, 'Synergy or Fragmentation? International Criminal Law and the European Convention on Human Rights' (2011) 9 *Journal of International Criminal Justice* 609, 614.

[3] Rob McLaughlin, 'The Law of Armed Conflict and International Human Rights Law: Some Paradigmatic Differences and Operational Implications' (2010) 13 *Yearbook of International Humanitarian Law* 213, 218.

evaluation of domestic findings of fact and law. The final section attempts to provide explanations for the trends observed in the jurisprudence. It examines whether the complexity of the issues involved, the judges' proficiency in IHL, and perceptions of the Court's role and purpose have influenced the outcomes identified throughout the chapter.

## 6.2 OVERVIEW OF ARTICLE 7

Article 7 demands that people must not be tried under retroactive criminal law or subjected to heavier retroactive penalties for offences. The Article embodies the idea that 'only the law can define a crime and prescribe a penalty'.[4] This term must be given an autonomous meaning within the Court's jurisprudence and the concept of 'the law' here must be understood to encompass all forms of domestic law.[5] Article 7 also opens up broader sources of criminal law than municipal legal systems and clearly envisages criminal liability arising under international law. The Court can look to international law to provide an alternative or sole legal basis for an applicant's conviction.[6] Cassese argues that Article 7(2) must be seen as creating an alternative primary source of criminal law norms in the form of 'general principles of law recognised by civilised nations'. Both the Court and States can rely upon these principles as a basis for criminal liability, even where the impugned conduct is not criminalised under municipal, international treaty or customary rules.[7]

The Court is often called upon to determine the state of the law at a given moment in time and consider whether a specific offence attracted individual criminal liability on the date that it occurred. The Court must evaluate quality of law issues, including whether the law was sufficiently clear and whether it was sufficiently accessible to the applicant. Where the law is less clear, the Court seeks to determine whether it was foreseeable that the applicant could be held criminally liable for the impugned conduct at a later date.[8] These historical assessments of the law, including customary international law, can

4 *Kafkaris* v. *Cyprus* (2009) 49 EHRR 35 at [139].

5 This includes *inter alia* common law (S.W. v. *United Kingdom* (1996) 21 EHRR 363) and custom (*Drozd and Janousek* v. *France and Spain* (1992) 14 EHRR 745 at [110]).

6 Tom Booms and Carrie Van der Kroon, 'Inconsistent Deliberations or Deliberate Inconsistencies? The Consistency of the ECtHR's Assessment of Convictions based on International Norms' (2011) 7 *Utrecht Law Review* 156, 8.

7 Antonio Cassese, 'Balancing the Prosecution of Crimes against Humanity and Non-Retroactivity of Criminal Law' (2006) 4 *Journal of International Criminal Justice* 410, 418.

8 *Streletz, Kessler and Krenz* v. *Germany* (2001) 33 EHRR 31 at [51]; *Veeber* v. *Estonia (No. 2)* (2004) 39 EHRR 6 at [31].

be difficult. The Court often faces a difficult task of interpreting the historical development of unfamiliar law.

Many Article 7 cases are the legacy of totalitarian and unaccountable government regimes in European States. These regimes often failed both in practice and in positive law to censure certain conduct, including war crimes and crimes against humanity. The democratically elected governments that succeeded them have often sought to hold people responsible for these acts.[9] These new governments attempted to redress deficiencies in the national legal systems in two key ways. Firstly, by introducing legal rules prohibiting certain offences and applying them retrospectively and secondly, by changing prosecution policies to enforce laws that were actively ignored in the past. This prompted complaints from those prosecuted that their prosecutions violated Article 7.

These cases often pit ideas of substantive justice against strict legality.[10] A clash between the idea that the principle of legality would not prevent a conviction where an act outrages decency and humanity, but did not reach the level of a concrete 'crime' and the idea that there must be a specific criminal prohibition, in all cases, on the act.[11] An underlying consideration of whether an objective person would consider the conduct for which an individual has been convicted to be right or wrong can have a bearing on the outcome of these cases.[12] The magnitude of a person's perceived wrongdoing may also have a bearing.[13] The Court has been accused of interpreting the law from the time of the impugned events consistently with a normatively desirable human rights regime created *ex post facto*, rather than the one that existed at the time.[14] Sometimes what the Court considers to be a progressive development of the law is to others more akin to a violation of the *nullum crimen sine lege* principle.

9 This is especially true of Eastern European former Soviet States – Triestino Mariniello, 'The "Nuremberg Clause" and Beyond: Legality Principle and Sources of International Criminal Law in the European Court's Jurisprudence' (2008) 82 *Nordic Journal of International Law* 221, 223–4; *Streletz, Kessler and Krenz* v. *Germany* and *Korbely* v. *Hungary* (2010) 50 EHRR 48.

10 Hans Kelsen, 'Will the Judgment in the Nuremberg Trial Constitute a Precedent in International Law?' (1947) 1 *International Law Quarterly* 153, 165.

11 Mohamed Shahabuddeen, 'Does the Principle of Legality Stand in the Way of Progressive Development of Law?' (2004) 2 *Journal of International Criminal Justice* 1007, 1009.

12 Cian Murphy, 'The Principle of Legality in Criminal Law under the European Convention on Human Rights' [2010] EHRLR 192, 206; Mariniello (n. 9) 223.

13 William Schabas, 'Retroactive Application of the Genocide Convention' (2010) 4 *University of St Thomas Journal of Law and Public Policy* 36, 54.

14 Mariniello (n. 9) 246.

## 6.3 THE INTERPRETATION AND APPLICATION OF IHL UNDER ARTICLE 7

The Court has willingly interpreted and applied IHL and ICL in many Article 7 cases. However, a number of faults can be identified in their use of IHL, which cast doubt on the Court's competence in this field. Firstly, the Court has frequently missed obvious violations of IHL and ICL in certain cases. Secondly, when the Court has been asked to evaluate the meaning or substantive content of an IHL or ICL norm at a particular point in time, it has frequently made errors. These have included both overstating the development of the law by imputing later definitions of the law on earlier iterations of it, and understating the development of the law, by holding that a given offence was not criminal at a time when it clearly was. The former errors at times resulted in the law being applied excessively to the applicant's detriment. The Court has also been extremely inconsistent when dealing with domestic applications of IHL and ICL, at times refusing to interfere with the domestic courts' findings, at other times completely revising their decisions.

### 6.3.1 *Omissions*

The Court has failed to identify violations of IHL and ICL in Article 7 cases even when they are clearly presented to the Court in arguments. In the Court's chamber judgment of *Kononov* v. *Latvia*,[15] the Court failed to recognise clear violations of IHL, which could have justified a conviction for war crimes. Although to the Court's credit, many of these errors were recognised in the later Grand Chamber judgment.[16] In that case, the applicant was the commander of a Soviet partisan unit conducting sabotage operations behind enemy lines in German-occupied Latvia during World War 2. The unit conducted an operation in the village of Mazie Bati in May 1944. The villagers were suspected of collaborating with the German army. The applicant and his unit dressed in German army uniforms and entered the village. They carried out a search and discovered German weapons and ammunition in some of the houses. They then attacked the villagers, killing nine of them as they prepared to celebrate a religious festival. They killed six men and three women, including one heavily pregnant woman who was burned alive in her house. The applicant was

[15] *Kononov* v. *Latvia* App no 36376/04 (ECtHR, 24 July 2008).

[16] *Kononov* v. *Latvia (GC)* (2011) 52 EHRR 21.

charged with war crimes and convicted in 2004. He took a case to the Court claiming that his conviction violated Article 7. In its chamber judgment, the Court held that the applicant's conviction amounted to a violation of Article 7.

The key issue was whether the attack was justified because the villagers were suspected of collaborating with the German forces. Pinzauti argues that the Court made numerous errors of law when determining the answer to this question. Firstly, it failed to recognise that the unit's use of German uniforms during the attack was a war crime, which would have sufficed to ground a conviction for war crimes at the time. Under IHL 'it is prohibited to make use of the flags or military emblems, insignia or uniforms of adverse Parties while engaging in attacks or to shield, favour, protect or impede military operations'.[17] This is precisely what the applicant's unit did during its attack on the village. Although a more recent definition of the prohibition is cited above because the language is clearer, the law at the time equally contained prohibitions on 'treacherous wounding or killing', which entailed killing or wounding while unlawfully deceiving the enemy.[18] Trials held soon after World War 2 show that people were tried for precisely such activities. In the trial of *Otto Skorzeny and Others*, for example, German officers were charged with treacherously killing American soldiers while wearing American uniforms, there the court stated:

> [on] the use of the national flag, the military insignia and the uniforms of the enemy, theory and practice are unanimous in prohibiting such use during actual attack and defence since the principle is considered inviolable that during actual fighting belligerent forces ought to be certain of who is friend and who is foe.[19]

The Court failed to recognise this crime in *Kononov*, even though the domestic Latvian courts specifically referred to treacherous wounding as a ground for his criminal liability in their judgments. As the domestic courts did not

[17] Article 39(2), Protocol Additional to the Geneva Conventions of 12 August 1949, and relating to the Protection of Victims of International Armed Conflicts (adopted 8 June 1977, entered into force 7 December 1979) 1125 UNTS 3 (hereinafter Additional Protocol 1).

[18] Article 23, Hague Convention (IV) Respecting the Laws and Customs of War on Land and Its Annex: Regulations concerning the Laws and Customs of War on Land (adopted 18 October 1907, entered into force 26 January 1910) 205 CTS 277 (Hague Regulations).

[19] *The Trial of Otto Skorzeny and Others* Law Reports of Trials of War Criminals United Nations War Crimes Commission, Vol IX, 1949, 92.

elaborate on how the applicant's behaviour was treacherous, the Court complained that:

> the domestic courts failed to explain in what respect the operation was considered to have been performed 'treacherously' within the meaning of Article 23 of the Hague Regulations and not as a legitimate 'ruse of war', as authorised by Article 24.[20]

This excerpt shows a clear lack of understanding of the difference between unlawful behaviour and legitimate ruses. A ruse or stratagem does not infringe IHL and does not invite the enemy's confidence with respect to protection under IHL.[21] The applicant's actions in attacking the village while dressed in German uniforms clearly invited the enemy's confidence and amounted to criminal activity.[22]

Secondly, the Court appeared to accept that killing the villagers was legal as a belligerent reprisal for the villagers' collaboration with the German army. It stated: 'the villagers must have known that by siding with one of the belligerent parties they would be exposing themselves to a risk of reprisals by the other'.[23] The Court again showed a lack of understanding here. A belligerent reprisal entails violating IHL in direct response to another belligerent's violation of IHL. It is aimed at coercing the errant belligerent into compliance with the law in future. Pinzauti points out that as the alleged collaboration was not a violation of IHL, it could not be the subject of a reprisal. Furthermore, reprisals can only be prompted by actions taken on behalf of the other belligerent State and the villagers were not state agents.[24] It is also difficult to see how it could be intended to coerce compliance with IHL, when it was not directed at military forces and not responding to an actual violation of IHL. The Court's ruling clearly shows a lack of understanding of the concept of belligerent reprisals.

The assessment of IHL in the Grand Chamber judgment is more accurate. The Court addressed the central IHL issues arising in the case, in particular, the legal status of the villagers. The Court examined several possible

[20] *Kononov* v. *Latvia* at [134].

[21] Yoram Dinstein, *The Conduct of Hostilities under the Law of International Armed Conflicts* (Cambridge University Press 2004) 206.

[22] Louise Doswald-Beck and Jean-Marie Henckaerts (eds), *Customary International Humanitarian Law*, 2 vols. (Cambridge University Press 2004) vol. I 221–6. Contemporaneous sources also indicate such activity was criminal – Valentine Jobst, 'Is the Wearing of the Enemy's Uniform a Violation of the Laws of War?' (1941) 35 AJIL 435, 441.

[23] *Kononov* v. *Latvia* at [130].

[24] Pinzauti (n. 1) 1058.

characterisations of the villagers' legal status and the unit's acts, while referring extensively to IHL to support its viewpoints. The Court considered, for example, that if the villagers were combatants, they were unarmed and had fallen under the control of the applicant's unit, rendering them *hors de combat* and subject to IHL protections.[25] In the alternative, if the villagers were considered to be civilians who had collaborated, the prevailing law demanded that they be arrested and tried, rather than summarily executed.[26] The Court also addressed the related issues of defining civilians *a contrario* to combatants,[27] issues of command responsibility,[28] perfidious use of uniforms and the protection of women during armed conflict.[29]

Despite its improvements on the chamber judgment, the Grand Chamber judgment is not without its critics. Mariniello argues that by relying solely upon international treaties as the basis for individual criminal responsibility, which created obligations upon States alone, the Court undermined legal certainty.[30] In his view, this created doubts over the foreseeability of such criminal convictions.[31] There are many counter-arguments to this viewpoint. Firstly, the idea that these treaties created obligations on States alone is incorrect as a matter of law. The Hague Regulations were widely regarded, even then, to have provided the content for crimes under international law, which could entail individual criminal responsibility and be tried domestically.[32] Lauterpacht stated as early as 1944 that the Hague Regulations must be binding on individuals because they are declaratory of the fundamental rules of warfare.[33] In his view, the law of nations was binding on all individual members of the armed forces of all belligerents and there is 'no question of any vindictive retroactivity arising out of the creation of crimes of which the accused could not possibly be cognizant'.[34] Further from a legal perspective, the Convention expressly demands that the Court take cognisance of international law as a potential source of individual criminal responsibility and was thus right to do so here.

[25] *Kononov* v. *Latvia (GC)* at [216].

[26] Ibid at [221].

[27] Ibid at [203].

[28] Ibid at [211].

[29] Ibid at [217]–[218].

[30] Mariniello (n. 9) 243–4.

[31] A similar complaint was made by the dissenting judges at the Grand Chamber, see dissenting opinion of Judges Costa, Kalaydjieva and Poalelungi.

[32] Kenneth Gallant, *The Principle of Legality in International and Comparative Criminal Law* (Cambridge University Press 2009) 58 and 70; Kenneth Randall, 'Universal Jurisdiction under International Law' (1988) 66 *Texas Law Review* 785, 795–7.

[33] Hersch Lauterpacht, 'The Law of Nations and the Punishment of War Crimes' (1944) 21 BYIL 58, 65.

[34] Ibid, 67.

Others have criticised the Court for relying on diverse sources of law, such as the Lieber Code, which Latvia could not have been party to at the time.[35] The use of that instrument is not objectionable in my view. The Lieber Code is broadly considered to be the first attempt to codify the laws of war and it clearly illustrates the crystallisation of norms relied on by the Court decades prior to the offences.[36] By referring to such instruments the Court shows the extent of its research and the breadth of the sources consulted in the process of determining the case, which is certainly a positive development.[37] Booms and van der Kroon argue that by retrospectively reading these instruments as part of a linear development of the law, which crystallised during the war, the Court overstated the development of the law to the applicant's detriment.[38] This accusation is certainly apposite in relation to some of the other cases discussed below. However, the Court was not treading new ground here. Its view that the Hague Regulations had crystallised into customary norms is based on contemporaneous judicial and academic views, most notably that of the International Military Tribunal at Nuremburg, which considered the Hague Regulations declaratory of the laws and customs of war by 1939.[39]

[35] Booms and Van der Kroon (n. 6) 166.

[36] Edoardo Greppi, 'The Evolution of Individual Criminal Responsibility under International Law' (1999) 81 IRRC 531, 535; Doswald-Beck and Henckaerts (n. 22) xxxi.

[37] *Kononov* v. *Latvia (GC)* at [207].

[38] Booms and Van der Kroon (n. 6) 13.

[39] In the International Military Tribunal (Nuremberg) Judgment of 1 October 1946 the court stated: 'by 1939 these rules (Hague Regulations) … were recognized by all civilized nations and were regarded as being declaratory of the laws and customs of war' see (1947) 41 AJIL 172, 248–9; Lauterpacht (n. 33) 65. Although Meron has questioned how the Hague Regulations had so quickly metamorphosed into customary norms in the judgment of the Nuremburg trials after World War 2 – Theodor Meron, 'Revival of Customary Humanitarian Law' (2005) 99 AJIL 817, 830. This is another instance of international criminal tribunals being criticised for their loose approach toward interpreting customary international law. The ICTY Appeals Chamber adopted a controversial interpretation of customary international law in its *Tadic* judgment when it held that violations of the laws and customs of war during civil wars attracted criminal liability under customary international law – *Prosecutor* v. *Tadic* (Case no. IT-94-1-AR72) 2 October 1995 at [86]–[137] esp. [134]; Christopher Greenwood, 'International Humanitarian Law and the Tadic Case' (1996) 7 EJIL 265, 276–8. More recently the Appeals Chamber of the Special Tribunal for Lebanon was criticised for ruling that a definition of terrorism under customary international law has emerged despite widespread disagreement among both academics and States over it – *Interlocutory Decision on the Applicable Law: Terrorism, Conspiracy, Homicide, Perpetration, Cumulative Charging* (Case No. STL-11-01/I/AC/R176bis) 16 February 2011 at [85]; Matthew Gillet and Matthias Schuster, 'Fast-track Justice: The Special Tribunal for Lebanon defines Terrorism' (2011) 9 *Journal of International Criminal Justice* 989, 1005–14. Such expansive definitions also create retroactivity problems at the international tribunals.

Ultimately, while the Chamber judgment showed serious flaws in the interpretation of IHL, the Grand Chamber judgment demonstrated a much more considered approach to it, with detailed research and an accurate interpretation and application of the law. This begs the question: how can the same facts and legal history lead to such disparate outcomes? It is difficult to speculate and some suggestions are offered below in Section 6.4. It is worth pointing out a few differences here between the cases at each instance, which may have influenced the outcome. Firstly, there were more third-party interveners before the Grand Chamber, who may have drawn attention to flaws in the Chamber judgment's reasoning. Secondly, Latvia enlisted the assistance of the esteemed international criminal law expert Professor William Schabas to present their case before the Grand Chamber and another international law expert, Professor Alan Vaughan Lowe sat as an *ad hoc* judge to replace the Latvian judge in the Grand Chamber. The expertise of each may have had a bearing on the improved interpretation. Thirdly, the extra resources brought to bear on a Grand Chamber hearing, coupled with the expansion of the pool of judges from seven to seventeen, may also have improved the quality of the judgment. Taking decisions at Grand Chamber level should not, however, be seen as a guarantee that the judgment's assessment of IHL will be correct, as errors can also be made in such cases.

### 6.3.2 *Reinterpreting Historical Law*

A further problem with the Court's application of IHL and ICL through Article 7 is the Court's tendency to misinterpret the law at specific points in time, by either overstating or understating its development. There is a thin line, which is seldom well negotiated by the Court, between examining contemporary sources to clarify law that existed at the time and illegitimate retroactive applications of the law.[40]

The Court supports the gradual clarification of criminal liability, which should be facilitated within any legal system provided that it is consistent with the essence of the offence and reasonably foreseeable.[41] However many cases stray outside the limits of gradual clarification and into the realm of retroactivity. Pinzauti argues that the Court tends to oversimplify the issues when dealing with IHL.[42] In a different context, Meron argues that the Court often fails to engage in a detailed discussion and provide supporting evidence that

40 Pinzauti (n. 1) 1054.
41 *S.W.* v. *United Kingdom* at [34].
42 Pinzauti (n. 1) 1052.

certain substantive law has reached the status of customary law in its judgments.[43] This is a criticism which could also be levied against the Court's judgments under Article 7.

In the *Kononov* chamber judgment, the Court clearly understated the development of the law when it said:

> there is nothing to show that under the *jus in bello* as it existed in 1944 a person who did not satisfy the formal conditions to qualify as a 'combatant' had automatically to be assigned to the category of 'civilians' with all its attendant guarantees.[44]

The Grand Chamber completely overruled the chamber on this issue noting: 'earlier treaty provisions and declarations would indicate that by 1944 "civilians" were defined *a contrario* to the definition of combatants' and cited a number of contemporaneous sources in support of that view.[45]

The opposite problem of the Court overstating the development of IHL and ICL is evident in other cases related to the definition of crimes against humanity. In particular, the Court has struggled with the issue of whether a nexus to an armed conflict was required for a crime against humanity to exist. In *Kolk & Kislyiy* v. *Estonia*,[46] the applicants were officials in the Soviet Union's administration in Estonia who prepared and executed a series of mass deportations from Estonia to remote parts of the Soviet Union in March 1949.[47] The applicants were tried and convicted of crimes against humanity in 2003 for their involvement in the deportations. The applicants alleged a violation of Article 7 on multiple grounds. The most pertinent aspect of the case was their argument that the deportations did not occur before or during a war. As a result, they claimed their actions did not satisfy the definition of a crime against humanity prevailing at that time, which required a nexus between the crime and an armed conflict.[48] Malksoo notes that the commission investigating these crimes derived their definitions of crimes against humanity from the Rome Statute in violation of the principle of non-retroactivity.[49]

43 Meron (n. 39) 819.
44 *Kononov* v. *Latvia* at [131].
45 *Kononov* v. *Latvia (GC)* at [203]; Pinzauti (n. 1) 1053–4; Sonja Grover, *The European Court of Human Rights as a Pathway to Impunity for International Crimes* (Springer 2010) 267–8.
46 *Kolk & Kislyiy* v. *Estonia* App no 23052/04 (ECtHR, 17 January 2006).
47 Malksoo provides a detailed discussion of mass deportations from Eastern European States between 1939 and 1991 – Lauri Malksoo, 'Soviet Genocide? Communist Mass Deportations in the Baltic States and International Law' (2001) 14 *Leiden Journal of International Law* 757.
48 Article 6(c), Charter of the International Military Tribunal 1945.
49 Malksoo (n. 47) 770.

The Court avoided the issue by stating that the deportation of a civilian population was expressly recognised as a crime against humanity in the International Military Tribunal Charter 1945, which established the court responsible for the Nuremburg trials after World War 2 and predated the applicants' acts. According to the Court, even if the applicants' actions were lawful under Soviet law, they were criminal under international law. As Estonia had ratified the Convention on the Non-Applicability of Statutory Limitations to War Crimes and Crimes against Humanity 1968, the applicant's crimes were not subject to any statutory limitation periods. Finally, as the Soviet Union was a party to the International Military Tribunal Charter and a member of the UN, it could not deny that the principles under which crimes against humanity were outlawed were unknown to them. As a result, the Court dismissed the applicants' claims as manifestly ill-founded.

Some academics have criticised the Court's failure to deal with the applicants' arguments on the nexus issue.[50] The Court avoided the issue under the pretence that it was not its role to assess the classification of the applicants' conduct under domestic law or the grounds for prosecution relied on domestically.[51] However, this pretext has been readily cast aside in other cases and the Court has been more than willing to re-evaluate the assessments of domestic courts under Article 7 as Section 6.3.4 below illustrates. Cassese argues that the Court should have addressed this issue head on by determining that the relevant nexus to an armed conflict existed. He claims the deportations were closely related to the original acts of aggression perpetrated by the Soviet Union on Estonia.[52] This error by omission can perhaps be put down to a lack of familiarity with the historical development of the law on crimes against humanity. Further, as a Chamber admissibility decision it may not have received the same attention to detail as a Grand Chamber decision might.

However, the Court made a similar error in the Grand Chamber judgment of *Korbely* v. *Hungary*.[53] There the applicant was a captain in the Hungarian military during the Hungarian Revolution in 1956. When insurgents took control of a police station in Tata, the applicant and a group of soldiers were dispatched to regain control of it. The insurgents were believed to be armed, but were not visibly armed when the applicant reached the station. During heated negotiations with the insurgents, their leader reached into his coat pocket and the applicant ordered his men to open fire on him. Two insurgents, including

[50] Mariniello (n. 9) 232; Cassese (n. 7) 413.

[51] The Court reached an identical conclusion in *Penart* v. *Estonia* App no 14685/04 (ECtHR, 24 January 2006).

[52] Cassese (n. 7) 418.

[53] *Korbely* v. *Hungary* (2010) 50 EHRR 48.

the leader were killed in the incident and others were injured. In 1994, the applicant was charged with having committed a crime against humanity for his actions at the police station. He was eventually convicted in 2001 and following unsuccessful appeals, brought his case to the Court alleging a violation of Article 7.

In its judgment, the Court examined whether the applicant's actions were capable of amounting to a crime against humanity as that concept was understood in 1956 it stated: 'in the Court's view, one of these criteria – a link or nexus with an armed conflict – may no longer have been relevant by 1956'.[54] The Court cited a number of sources in support of this view, yet it appears that many of the sources cited do not support the position that a crime against humanity could have been committed in the absence of a nexus to an armed conflict at that time. Egon Schwelb's article, which was cited as supporting the idea that a nexus to an armed conflict was not necessary at the time, expressly endorses the contrary position. Schwelb states that a crime against humanity is a 'by-product of war, applicable only in time of war or in connexion with war'.[55]

The Court also referred to the Draft Code of Offences against the Peace and Security of Mankind as supporting its view, yet there was significant debate and disagreement over the nexus to armed conflict during the drafting of that document and no definitive conclusion was reached on the issue.[56] The most accurate reflection of customary law from that era was arguably the Nuremburg Principles from 1950, which expressly demand that crimes against humanity have a link to any crime against peace or any war crime.[57]

The literature on this subject reveals a gradual abandonment of the requirement for a nexus to an armed conflict. Yet, this abandonment only began in the late 60s.[58] It commenced with a modification of the definition of crimes against humanity in the Convention on the Non-Applicability of Statutory Limitations to War Crimes and Crimes against Humanity

[54] Ibid at [82]. In support the Court cited Egon Schwelb, 'Crimes Against Humanity' (1946) 23 BYIL 178, 211; Jean Graven, 'Les Crimes Contre l'Humanité' (1950) 76 *Recueil des Cours de l'Académie de Droit International de La Haye* 427, 467 and the Draft Code of Offences against the Peace and Security of Mankind 1954.

[55] Schwelb (n. 54) 206.

[56] Stuart Ford, 'Crimes against Humanity at the Extraordinary Chambers in the Courts of Cambodia: Is a Connection with Armed Conflict Required?' (2007) 24 *University of California Los Angeles Pacific Basin Law Journal* 125, 153–8.

[57] Ibid, 151; Principle 6(c), Principles of International Law Recognised in the Charter of the Nuremberg Tribunal and in the Judgment of the Tribunal (adopted 29 July) International Law Commission Document A/1316; The Court has stated that these principles were recognised as universally valid at the time in *Kolk & Kislyiy* v. *Estonia*.

[58] Cassese (n. 7) 413; Ford (n. 56) 183.

1968,[59] which was still opposed by a number of States at the time. Doubts over the nexus issue were still evident even up until the adoption of the original International Criminal Tribunal for Yugoslavia (ICTY) Statute in 1993, which still required that there be a nexus to an armed conflict in its definition of crimes against humanity.[60] While the exact point at which the nexus was abandoned is debatable,[61] it was certainly abandoned from the mid-90s with the International Criminal Tribunal for Rwanda Statute,[62] the Rome Statute,[63] and in judicial opinion.[64] Thus for the Court to claim as it did explicitly in *Korbely* that the nexus may no longer have been relevant by 1956 is incorrect and shows the Court superimposing later developments in the law on earlier ones.

In *Jorgic* v. *Germany*,[65] the applicant was arrested in Germany in 1995 on suspicion of having committed genocide and ethnic cleansing in Bosnia between May 1992 and September 1992. It was alleged that he had created a paramilitary group, which was responsible for various abuses against Muslim men including unlawful detention, ill-treatment and murder. He was convicted in September 1997 on eleven counts of genocide, murder, assault and unlawful detention and sentenced to life in prison. The applicant brought a claim under Article 7 alleging that the German courts had interpreted the crime of genocide too widely. The case centred upon the so-called *dolus specialis*, the specific intent to destroy the group necessitated by the crime of genocide. The German courts had held that physical destruction of the group was not necessary for genocide to be proven. The applicant argued that this was not a foreseeable interpretation of the offence and the prevailing definition of genocide at the time required intent to physically or biologically destroy a group. He claimed the intent behind the ethnic cleansing in Serbia was not the physical destruction of Muslims, but rather their expulsion by force from

59 Article 1(b), Convention on the Non-Applicability of Statutory Limitations to War Crimes and Crimes against Humanity (adopted 26 November 1968, entered into force 11 November 1970) 754 UNTS 73.

60 Article 5, Statute of the International Criminal Tribunal for the Former Yugoslavia (adopted 3 May 1993) UN doc. S/25704.

61 William Schabas, 'Problems of International Codification – Were the Atrocities in Cambodia and Kosovo Genocide?' (2001) 35 *New England Law Review* 287, 292.

62 Article 3, Statute of the International Criminal Tribunal for Rwanda (adopted 12 January 1995) UN doc. SC/5974.

63 Article 7, Rome Statute of the International Criminal Court (adopted 17 July 1998, entered into force 1 July 2002) 2187 UNTS 3 (Rome Statute).

64 *Prosecutor* v. *Tadic* (Case no. IT-94-1-AR72) 2 October 1995 at [140]–[141].

65 *Jorgic* v. *Germany* (2008) 47 EHRR 6.

the territory. In essence, while ethnic cleansing tolerates the existence of the group elsewhere, genocide does not.[66]

The Court had to decide whether it was reasonably foreseeable that the applicant's actions would amount to genocide at the time they were committed. The Court held that the domestic courts' interpretation did not appear unreasonable,[67] stating that it was up to the German courts to decide which interpretation they wished to use and concluded that:

> the national courts' interpretation of the crime of genocide could reasonably be regarded as consistent with the essence of that offence and could reasonably be foreseen by the applicant at the material time.[68]

Van der Wilt and Vervliet criticised the Court's failure to explain what it considered to be the 'essence of the offence'.[69] The Court also focused on whether the domestic court's interpretation was 'reasonable', rather than engaging in its own interpretation. Other academics accused the Court of cherry-picking sources that supported its view, while dismissing sources that contradicted its position.[70] The Court cited a UN General Assembly Resolution as support for its view on the definition of genocide. The resolution stated that ethnic cleansing such as occurred in Serbia was a form of genocide. However, this resolution was passed in December 1992, after the actions of the applicant had taken place.[71] At the same time, the Court refused to consider judgments from both the ICTY and the ICJ, which supported the applicant's interpretation, because they 'were delivered subsequent to the commission of his offences'.[72]

The majority of scholarly opinion at the time also supported the applicant's interpretation of the Genocide Convention and the Court itself admitted this.[73] Equally, many judges evaluating events from the era have refused to characterise ethnic cleansing as genocide. In the 2007 *Bosnian Genocide* case, for example, the ICJ had to determine whether Serbia bore State responsibility for acts of genocide committed against Bosnian Muslims. The ICJ stated: 'neither the intent, as a matter of policy, to render an area 'ethnically homogeneous', nor

[66] William Schabas, *Genocide in International Law: The Crime of Crimes* (2nd edn, Cambridge University Press 2009) 234.

[67] *Jorgic* v. *Germany* at [105].

[68] Ibid at [114].

[69] Harmen van der Wilt and Jeroen Vervliet, *The Genocide Convention: The Legacy of 60 Years* (Brill 2012) 57.

[70] Booms and Van der Kroon (n. 6) 16.

[71] UN General Assembly Resolution on the situation in Bosnia and Herzegovina, 18 December 1992, UN Doc. AG/Res./47/121.

[72] *Jorgic* v. *Germany* at [112].

[73] Ibid at [47].

the operations that may be carried out to implement such policy, can *as such* be designated as genocide'.[74] Similarly, the ICTY's judgment in the trial of Radislav Krstic, who was charged with command responsibility for the Srebrenica massacre, was critical of the German court's interpretation of genocide, which it considered violated the principle of *nullum crimen sine lege*. It stated:

> despite recent developments, customary international law limits the definition of genocide to those acts seeking the physical or biological destruction of all or part of the group.[75]

The misinterpretation of the law here is admittedly less clear cut than it was in the *Korbely* judgment, because there can be an overlap between ethnic cleansing and genocide. One could also argue this interpretation is closer to a progressive development of the law than the interpretations the Court endorsed above.

The Court's approach in the case of *Vasiliauskas* v. *Lithuania* was arguably better.[76] In that case, the applicant was convicted of genocide of a political group under the Lithuanian Criminal Code and sentenced to six years in prison. The acts grounding his conviction took place in 1953 while Lithuania was under Soviet rule and the applicant worked as an agent for the State security ministry. The ministry ordered 'the extermination of nationalist elements in Šakiai district' where the applicant worked.[77] He was involved in a successful operation to track down and kill two Lithuanian partisans in 1953.

The case centred on the definition of groups for the purposes of the crime of genocide. The crime of genocide requires that certain acts be committed against a group with intent to destroy the group 'in whole or in part'. The problem with this case was that while the protected groups under international law were limited to 'national, ethnical, racial or religious' groups,[78] the definition in Lithuanian law extended also to political groups.[79]

The Court ruled, by 9 votes to 8, that the applicant's conviction for genocide could not have been foreseen at the time the partisans were killed.[80]

74 *Case concerning Application of the Convention on the Prevention and Punishment of the Crime of Genocide* (*Bosnia-Herzegovina* v. *Yugoslavia*), 2007 ICJ Reports, p. 43 26 February 2007 at [190].

75 *Prosecutor* v. *Radislav Krstic* (Case no. IT-98-33-T) 2 August 2001 at [580].

76 *Vasiliauskas* v. *Lithuania* (2016) 62 EHRR 31. See commentary Kai Ambos, 'The Crime of Genocide and the Principle of Legality under Article 7 of the European Convention on Human Rights' (2017) 17(1) HRLR 175.

77 *Vasiliauskas* v. *Lithuania* (2016) 62 EHRR 31 at [18].

78 Article 2, Convention on the Prevention and Punishment of the Crime of Genocide (adopted 9 December 1948, entered into force 12 January 1951) 78 UNTS 277.

79 Article 99, Lithuanian Criminal Code of 1 May 2003.

80 *Vasiliauskas* v. *Lithuania* (2016) 62 EHRR 31 at [186].

While the crime of genocide was clearly recognised under international law by 1953 and the law was sufficiently accessible, the definition of groups did not refer to social or political groups and this was specifically excluded by the drafters.[81] Equally the requirement that the group be destroyed 'in part' at the time should have been understood to relate to a substantial part of the group.[82]

The Court resisted the temptation to opt for a broader reading, but the situation is different from *Korbely* and *Jorgic*. The definition of crimes against humanity, for example, has shifted over time to no longer require a nexus with an armed conflict, whereas the definition of genocide in subsequent international instruments has not moved away from the definition of groups given in the Genocide Convention. As the Court expressly noted these instruments 'describe that crime in similar, if not identical, terms' to the Genocide Convention.[83]

### 6.3.3 *Construing Law to the Applicant's Detriment*

In principle, Article 7 is meant to protect applicants against the retroactive application of criminal law to their detriment.[84] Yet, in many of the cases examined thus far, the Court has arguably applied the law to the applicant's disadvantage. Murphy has criticised the Court for endorsing the domestic court's approach in *KHW* v. *Germany*, wherein the domestic court applied East German law to try the applicant, but would not allow the applicant to rely on defences available in East German law at the time.[85] Focusing specifically on IHL and ICL, the Court allowed domestic courts to apply the law to the applicants' disadvantage in the cases of *Kolk and Kislyiy* and *Jorgic*. By endorsing the domestic court's interpretation of crimes against humanity in *Kolk and Kislyiy*, which allowed conviction despite the absence of a link to an armed conflict, the Court arguably allowed the law to be interpreted and applied excessively to the applicant's detriment. Equally, in *Jorgic* the Court endorsed the domestic court's interpretation of genocide, which did not require intent to physically destroy the group, thereby allowing the law to be applied to the applicant's detriment.

The Court has not always allowed this to happen though. In *Maktouf and Damjanovic*, for example, when a new law was promulgated, which

[81] Ibid at [170].
[82] Ibid at [176].
[83] Ibid at [170]; see, for example, Article 6, Rome Statute.
[84] *Del Rio Prada* v. *Spain* (2014) 58 EHRR 37 at [78]; *Kokkinakis* v. *Greece* (1994) 17 EHRR 397 at [52].
[85] Murphy (n. 12) 196.

imposed heavier sentences for the applicants' crimes, the Court insisted that the domestic courts sentence the applicants under the older more liberal regime.[86] In *Vasiliauskas*, the Court rejected the domestic court's finding that the nationalists killed by the applicant were 'representatives of the Lithuanian nation' and as a result could be classed as members of a 'national or ethnic' group rather than a political group.[87] The Court expressly rejected this finding because it thought that this was an interpretation by analogy that would be to the applicant's detriment.[88] Nevertheless, the outcomes in *Jorgic* and *Kolk* seem to confound the central purpose of Article 7. These judgments prompt questions over whether it is fair for the Court to endorse minority interpretations of ICL or re-interpretations of past law in light of future developments, when the outcome leads to the applicant's conviction, rather than acquittal.

### 6.3.4 *Interference with Domestic Rulings*

The Court has a subsidiary role to the domestic courts, which are charged with the initial responsibility to guarantee Convention rights. The subsidiary role of the Court is manifested through the Court's refusal to act as a court of 'fourth instance', as it stated in *Kemmache* v. *France (No.3)*:

> It is not the Court's role to assess itself the facts which have led a national court to adopt one decision rather than another. If it were otherwise, the Court would be acting as a court of third or fourth instance, which would be to disregard the limits imposed on its action.[89]

The practical consequence of this doctrine is that the Court will generally avoid calling into question domestic determinations on the establishment of facts, interpretation and application of domestic law, admissibility and assessment of evidence or the guilt or innocence of an accused person.[90] As a general rule, the Court will only intervene where domestic errors of fact or law have led to an infringement of the applicant's rights or freedoms under the Convention and/or where there is evidence of arbitrariness in the decisions of the domestic courts.[91] The Court should be consistent in the exercise of its

86 *Maktouf and Damjanovic* v. *Bosnia and Herzegovina* (2014) 58 EHRR 11 at [70].
87 *Vasiliauskas* v. *Lithuania* (2016) 62 EHRR 31 at [36].
88 Ibid at [183].
89 *Kemmache* v. *France (No.3)* App no 17621/91 (ECtHR, 24 November 1994) at [44].
90 Laurence Helfer, 'Redesigning the European Court of Human Rights: Embeddedness as a Deep Structural Principle of the European Human Rights Regime' (2008) 19 EJIL 125, 142.
91 *Streletz, Kessler and Krenz* v. *Germany* at [49]; *Sisojeva and Others* v. *Latvia* (2007) 45 EHRR 33 at [89].

discretion on whether or not to interfere with domestic findings and when it does decide to interfere, it must do so to correct errors, rather than making errors of its own.

A prime example of this problem can be seen if we compare the Court's intervention in the *Kononov* chamber case, with the lack of intervention in the cases of *Kolk and Kislyiy* and *Penart* v. *Estonia*. In the latter cases, even though the domestic courts had made a clear error of law by holding that crimes against humanity did not require a specific nexus to an armed conflict when the alleged crime was committed in 1949, the Court found 'no reason to call into question the Estonian courts' interpretation and application of domestic law made in the light of the relevant international law'.[92]

In the *Kononov* chamber judgment, by contrast, when the domestic court correctly held that civilians could be defined *a contrario* to combatants and that the villagers killed by the applicant's unit should be classed as civilians, the Court overturned the domestic court's finding. It was 'not satisfied' that the six men killed by the applicant's unit could reasonably be regarded as civilians under the law and disputed that the definition of civilians *a contrario* was part of customary law at the time.[93] As noted above, this was clearly part of customary law at that time.[94] The central issue here is not the interference *per se*, but rather that the Court has interfered with a correct finding of a domestic court in one case, while relying on the fourth instance doctrine to refuse to interfere to correct a mistake in the other case.

## 6.4 ANALYSIS

The preceding sections show the Court has had issues interpreting IHL and ICL in the context of Article 7. It failed to recognise clear violations of IHL and ICL in some cases and made significant errors in its interpretation and application of those bodies of law, but what do these apparent mistakes and omissions reveal about the Court's institutional capacity to interpret and apply IHL? Is it simply that retrospectively evaluating the law is difficult and often gives rise to mistakes? This section attempts to explain the issues identified in this chapter. There seem to be a number of factors at play influencing the outcome in these cases.

[92] *Kolk & Kislyiy* v. *Estonia* App no 23052/04 (ECtHR, 17 January 2006); see also *Penart* v. *Estonia* App no 14685/04 (ECtHR, 24 January 2006).

[93] *Kononov* v. *Latvia* at [131].

[94] Pinzauti (n. 1) 1052fn.

### 6.4.1 Genuine Error

In the first place, the Court faces an inherently difficult task. IHL and ICL are bodies of law characterised by progressive, incremental development. While the same could be said about any body of law, the assessment of international law is complicated by several factors – the absence of a centralised legislator, the presence of treaties with varying parties and scope, a multiplicity of sources dealing with the same subject matter and the inherent fluidity of customary law, which demands the assessment of multifarious State practice and *opinio juris*.[95] This can be further complicated by a paucity of contemporaneous sources. International law has a tendency to develop in fits and starts with consensus built gradually over time.[96] This can make determining the point when a given norm or interpretation 'crystallises' particularly difficult. The retrospective assessment of historical developments within a body of law characterised by progressive, incremental development is inherently difficult and any court could genuinely struggle with it.[97]

The errors identified above could simply be put down to genuine mistakes in the process of assessing these complex developments. However, genuine error cannot explain the instances where the Court expressly recognises that it is following a minority interpretation of the law at the specific time, as the Court did in *Jorgic*. While genuine mistakes can be excused and even expected, at times the Court rushes to conclusions about the status of law at a given time while offering little if any concrete support for the views it expounds. The apparent failure to appreciate some of the subtleties and finer details of the law is perhaps the most worrying feature of this jurisprudence.[98] This is why the Court should stop implicitly applying IHL.[99] This practice shields the Court from scrutiny, preventing people from determining whether the Court has correctly applied IHL and has not missed some of the finer points.

Mariniello argues that prior to the chamber case in *Kononov*, the Court and European Commission on Human Rights regularly relied on Article 7(2) to dismiss cases where the crimes at issue were punishable pursuant to the general

95 On the fluidity of customary law – James Crawford and Thomas Viles, 'International Law on a Given Day' in James Crawford (ed), *International Law as an Open System* (Cameron May 2002).

96 Dinstein (n. 21) 4–12.

97 O'Boyle and Costa note that such cases take the Court 'outside its comfort zone' – Michael O'Boyle and Jean Paul Costa, 'The ECtHR and IHL' in Christos Rozakis (ed), *The European Convention on Human Rights, a Living Instrument* (Bruylant Press 2011), 127–8.

98 Pinzauti (n. 1) 1052.

99 See discussion in Chapters 2 and 3.

principles of law recognised by civilised nations.[100] This shielded these cases from scrutiny of whether they complied with the principle of legality. Interestingly, the Court decided to stop applying Article 7(2) and in cases like *Kononov* and *Korbely*, the Court instead opted to evaluate whether there was a clear basis in international law at the time for the applicants' convictions.[101] Thus while the Court could have avoided such assessments by applying Article 7(2), it instead voluntarily assumed a greater responsibility to interpret and evaluate IHL and ICL than it needed to. It is difficult to draw concrete conclusions from this change in policy. It could indicate that the Court does not have any reservations about its ability to correctly apply and interpret IHL. If the Court had such reservations, it would arguably have avoided applying IHL as much as possible. Alternatively, the Court may have considered that interpreting and applying IHL was central to resolving the specific case before it and while evaluating IHL was avoidable in principle, it was not avoidable in practice.

The Court may feel emboldened to freely interpret ICL and IHL in these cases given that its interpretations will have little impact on its own jurisprudence. The Court's pronouncement on whether the nexus between armed conflict and crimes against humanity was a necessary element of the crime in the 1950s will have little if any bearing on how the Court interprets the right to life in the Convention today. By contrast, when the sanctity of its substantive law is on the line, notwithstanding the *Hassan* case, the Court seems markedly slower to explicitly refer to IHL. While errors in interpretations of IHL may have little impact on the Court's substantive jurisprudence, they are not without consequence. They clearly undermine jurists' faith in the Court's ability to correctly interpret and apply IHL in other circumstances. Ultimately, while genuine error could explain some of the issues with interpretation identified above, it clearly cannot explain all of them.

### 6.4.2 *Deliberate Error*

The possibility that the Court deliberately misinterpreted the law in these cases may seem fanciful, but it should not be dismissed. It is possible that the Court upheld an incorrect interpretation of IHL because it could not stomach

[100] Mariniello (n. 9) 229 citing *Papon* v. *France (no. 2)* App no 54210/00 (ECtHR, 15 November 2001); *Touvier* v. *France* App no 29420/95 (EComHR, 13 January 1997); *Kolk & Kislyiy* v. *Estonia* and *Penart* v. *Estonia*.

[101] This shift in practice is reminiscent of the Court's change of approach toward evaluating offensive forms of speech under the Convention, with the Court moving away from rejecting cases at the admissibility stage under Article 17 toward analysing whether the speech fell within the limits of Article 10 – see Antoine Buyse, 'Dangerous expressions: The ECHR, violence and free speech' (2014) 63(2) ICLQ 491, 496.

the consequences of the correct interpretation when that would result in finding a violation of Article 7. Finding a violation of Article 7 in some of these cases could be seen as tacitly endorsing impunity for reprehensible acts and could inflict lasting damage on the Court's reputation and role as defender of human rights in Europe.

Forowicz argues that the political climate can be a key factor in determining the result in some cases. Forowicz cites the cases *Streletz, Kessler and Krenz* v. *Germany* and *KHW* v. *Germany* as examples. There former East Germans citizens were tried for their role in implementing border controls between East Germany and West Germany prior to the collapse of the Soviet Union and the fall of the Berlin wall. Under this border control regime, armed guards, landmines and automatic firing systems were deployed to prevent people fleeing East Germany. In *KHW*, the applicant was an individual border guard who had shot a person attempting to flee, while the applicants in *Streletz* were higher ranking officials responsible for developing and implementing the border control policy. When these cases were decided by the Court, a number of East German officials had previously avoided responsibility for their actions. As a result, Forowicz claims that the Court was willing to uphold the findings of the German courts at all costs, which she claims was reflected in artificial and strained legal arguments advanced by the Court in its judgments.[102]

There is undoubtedly also a sense that the Convention is being misused in some cases by offering a means for war criminals and genocidaires, who readily disregard human rights in their actions, to rely on the Convention to avoid or mitigate criminal sanctions.[103] The principle expressed in Article 17 of the Convention, that it should not be used as a means of destroying the rights of others, certainly has a latent influence on the Court's judgments here. The idea that the perpetrators of despicable acts could avoid punishment because of what many would consider technicalities may have had a powerful influence on the outcome of cases.

This clearly splits the Court in *Vasiliauskas*. In the main dissenting opinion, the judges criticised the majority's 'excessively formalistic' interpretation of the genocide Convention.[104] They expressly referred to the Court's role as the

102 Magdalena Forowicz, *The Reception of International Law in the European Court of Human Rights* (Oxford University Press 2010) 179; O'Boyle and Costa note that these cases risk involving the Court in political controversies and undermining the confidence States have in the Court's independence – O'Boyle and Costa (n. 97) 128.

103 Murphy (n. 12) 206.

104 *Vasiliauskas* v. *Lithuania* (2016) 62 EHRR 31, dissenting opinion of Judges Villiger, Power-Forde, Pinto de Albuquerque and Kūris at [11].

'conscience' of Europe.[105] The dissenting Judge Ziemele went further arguing that the Court should be guided in its application of Article 7 by 'broader principles regarding the right to truth and prohibition of impunity'.[106] Ambos rightly describes this as reflecting an anti-impunity, *effet utile* approach.[107] It is open to question whether a court charged with human rights protection should side with a person who denied the human rights of hundreds, if not thousands, of people simply because their crimes were not related to an armed conflict or give a free pass to an applicant who intended to cause grievous harm to a specific group of people, but did not specifically intend to completely destroy them.

The actions of an alleged victim can certainly influence how the Court handles a case. The Court has been keen to avoid the perception that it condones or endorses illegal behaviour in any way, especially when the behaviour is anathema to the Convention's ideals. This is perhaps most evident in the Court's refusal to award just satisfaction to the relatives of Irish Republican Army members killed while trying to carry out a terrorist attack in Gibraltar. There the Court stated: 'having regard to the fact that the three terrorist suspects who were killed had been intending to plant a bomb in Gibraltar, the Court does not consider it appropriate to make an award [for just satisfaction]'.[108]

Thus, the Court may have recognised that it was getting the law wrong in some of the cases above, but it may have considered it was doing so for the right reasons. This underlying sensitivity to the Court's perceived role and purpose could offer some insight into the Court's reluctance to use IHL in the context of its substantive law. The Court's sensitivity to its mandate and role to uphold human rights and protect victims of rights abuses could inhibit it from utilising IHL. The Court's judges may consider that IHL creates a more permissive environment and tolerates certain human rights abuses as it tries to make the best of a bad situation. It reveals that the Court is prepared to sacrifice veracity for political expediency when it interprets IHL.

### 6.4.3 *Institutional Capacity*

The aforementioned approaches arguably indicate a different underlying problem, namely a lack of IHL and ICL expertise at the Court. The reality is that the Court never faced a binary choice between misinterpreting IHL

105 Ibid at [18].

106 *Vasiliauskas* v. *Lithuania* (2016) 62 EHRR 31, dissenting opinion of Judge Ziemele at [27].

107 Ambos (n. 76) 185.

108 *McCann and Others* v. *United Kingdom* (1996) 21 EHRR 97 at [219]; The Court has similarly refused or curtailed awards in other contexts – Philip Leach, *Taking a Case to the European Court of Human Rights* (Oxford University Press 2005) 470.

and ICL in order to uphold the values of the Convention or interpreting IHL and ICL correctly and compromising its values in these cases. IHL and ICL provided alternatives for the Court, which would have meant that they did not have to find a violation of Article 7. The Court could have made technically correct pronouncements on IHL and ICL while avoiding the unpalatable consequences.

The Court has been hamstrung in some cases by errors made by domestic prosecutors and judges, which are difficult to remedy after a final criminal judgment. However, the Court often searches for alternative bases for the applicant's conviction under international law where the reasoning of the domestic court is deficient in some way.[109] While the applicants may not have satisfied the specific conditions of the crime they were convicted of domestically in some cases, there may have been alternative bases for their convictions under international law had the Court examined the facts in more detail. In *Jorgic*, for example, the Court could have ruled that the applicant's actions had not satisfied the legal definition of genocide, but that he was still liable because his acts were sufficient to meet the threshold for other offences, such as persecution as a crime against humanity.[110] In the *KHW* and *Streletz* cases, the applicants' actions arguably met the criteria for an alternative charge of murder as a crime against humanity, rather than the charges for intentional homicide which were originally brought against them.

Forowicz claims that the Court judges' lack of experience with IHL and the fact that they find themselves 'incompetent in this field' is the underlying reason behind their reluctance to apply IHL.[111] A review of the CVs of the 47 judges sitting at the Court in 2018 reveals a great deal about the Court's proficiency in IHL.[112] While some judges at the Court had abundant experience

109 See, for example, the *Kononov* (GC) case.

110 The ICC has stated: 'ethnic cleansing usually amounts to the crime against humanity of persecution' – *Prosecutor* v. *Omar Hassan Ahmad Al Bashir* (ICC-02/05-01/09) 4 March 2009 at [145]; Fausto Pocar, 'Persecution as a Crime Under International Criminal Law' (2008) 2 *Journal of National Security Law and Policy* 355, 358.

111 Forowicz (n. 102) 348. Other academics have noted the lack of expertise in IHL at the Court: Christine Byron, 'A Blurring of the Boundaries: The Application of International Humanitarian Law by Human Rights Bodies' (2006–2007) 47 *Virginia Journal of International Law* 839, 882–3; Theodor Meron, 'The Humanization of Humanitarian Law' (2000) 94 AJIL 239, 247.

112 As at 20/08/2018 the CVs of judges P. Koskelo; G. Kucsko-Stadlmayer; P. Vilanova; S. O'Leary; C. Ranzoni; S. Mourou-Vikström; G. Ravarani; M. Mits; A. Harutyunyan; A. Poláčková; G. Serghides; M. Bošnjak; T. Eicke; L. Hüseynov; J. Ilievski; J. Schukking; P. Paczolay; L. Chanturia; M. Elósegui Ichaso; I. Jelic; G. Felici; B. Lubarda; J. F. Kjolbro; Y. Grozev; J. Laffranque; L.-A. Sicilianos; K. Turković; D. Dedov; G. Raimondi; I. Karakaş P. Pinto de Albuquerque; H. Keller; E. Kūris; K. Pardalos; V. Griţco; L. Bianku; V. De Gaetano; K. Wojtyczek; F. Vehabović; R. Spano; A. Nußberger; G. Yudkivska; A. Potocki; P. Lemmens; H. Jäderblom; A. Pejchal; I. Motoc were all reviewed.

in the field of public international law,[113] there were very few with extensive experience directly in the field of IHL or ICL.[114] If we examine specific Chambers that decided cases above, such as the *Kolk* case, none of the judges that decided that case had significant expertise in IHL and only one, Martii Pellonpää, had extensive experience in public international law.[115] The lack of experience among judges of the Court in public international law more generally has been a persistent problem. It was highlighted in both the Interlaken declaration and guidelines on the selection of judges for the Court.[116]

There are clearly instances where this lack of familiarity plays a role in the outcome of the cases, particularly in the judges' misunderstanding of treacherous wounding and belligerent reprisals in the *Kononov* chamber case. The general lack of familiarity with IHL among the judges may also explain the failure to identify alternative legal bases for the applicants' criminal liability in some cases. Conversely, where the Court has experts in IHL at its disposal and extensive research support, as in the *Kononov* Grand Chamber case, there is a marked improvement in the handling of IHL.[117] While the Court has modest research support given the size of its case load, the assistance of the Court's internal research division may also provide important assistance when examining IHL and ICL issues.[118] The foregoing analysis is not a scientific measure by any means, but it does reflect the general institutional capacity of the Court. It illustrates a lack of familiarity with IHL and ICL among judges and offers a possible explanation for the Court's apparent reluctance to consider how IHL can impact upon the legal paradigm in specific cases.

The apparent lack of institutional expertise in this field should militate against any implicit applications of IHL in the Court's jurisprudence. Close

[113] Most notably Judges Mits, Hüseynov, Keller, Eicke and Nußberger.

[114] Specifically Judges Turković, Jelic and Motoc.

[115] Judge Bratza's areas of expertise lay in commercial, public law and human rights law; Judge Casadevall's expertise is in Roman law, criminal law and human rights law; Judge Maruste specialises in human rights law and EU law; Judge Pavlovschi was a former public prosecutor with expertise in anti-corruption cases; Judge Borrego Borrego was also a public prosecutor with expertise in minority rights and EU law; Judge Sikuta specialised in civil law, administrative law and refugee law.

[116] Interlaken Declaration, 19 December 2010; Guidelines of the Committee of Ministers on the Selection of Candidates for the Post of Judge at the European Court of Human Rights, 29 March 2012, CM(2012)40 final.

[117] A single judge with expertise in IHL can have a significant impact. Cerna attributes the extensive use of IHL at the Inter-American Commission to one member to the Commission with extensive IHL experience, Robert K Goldman – Christina Cerna, 'The History of the Inter-American System's Jurisprudence as Regards Situations of Armed Conflict' (2011) 2 *International Humanitarian Legal Studies* 3, 31fn.

[118] O'Boyle and Costa (n. 97) 128.

public scrutiny of the interpretations and sources relied upon by the Court is required when it is acting outside its main area of expertise. Of course, the Court's focus is on human rights issues that are germane to national legal systems and it is not suggested that each needs to be an expert in IHL. There may however be a correlation between the absence of expertise in IHL and the problems with interpreting and applying IHL identified above and indeed the broader failure to engage with IHL in its other jurisprudence. While a lack of familiarity and expertise in IHL cannot excuse the Court from failing or refusing to consider the implications of all pertinent international law in its judgments, it may go some way toward explaining it.

## 6.5 CONCLUSION

The Court's jurisprudence on Article 7 offers insights into the Court's application of IHL and its institutional capacity to correctly interpret IHL. The analysis uncovered some shortcomings in the Court's application of IHL, including errors in interpretation, failures to recognise obvious violations of IHL along with overstatements or understatements of the development of the law at particular times. The Court appeared acutely conscious of its role as a supra-national defender of human rights when assessing many cases under Article 7. The Court wrestled with the conflicting motivations of substantive justice and strict legality, at times sacrificing technical accuracy in favour of an ahistorical, normatively desirable human rights regime.

While the tension between substantive justice and strict legality could explain some missteps in interpretation, the Court's lack of expertise in IHL was also readily apparent in several cases. Indeed, there appears to be a wider lack of expertise in public international law among the Court's judges. This is a cause for concern as the Court is increasingly being called upon to adjudicate matters related to military operations in which IHL is applicable. Its current practice of implicitly applying IHL in some of its judgments is problematic because it shields the Court from scrutiny of its interpretation and application of the law. This is precisely why the Court needs to be more open and transparent in its application of IHL. The Court should also hear cases under Article 7 that engage issues of IHL in the Grand Chamber and utilise the capacity of its research division to assist its evaluations. It is hoped that the Court's engagement with IHL in these cases and wider exposure to its terms in other cases will improve its familiarity with IHL leading to better judgments and better concurrent application of both bodies of law in the future.

# 7

# Derogation

## 7.1 INTRODUCTION

The preceding chapters have presented the challenge that States face in upholding human rights obligations during military operations. States need institutions and administrative control to uphold human rights obligations and these obligations become extremely difficult to enforce when those institutions are absent.[1] Positive obligations were identified as being particularly problematic to maintain. Once the State's jurisdiction is called into question, the nature and scope of the State's Convention obligations become very uncertain.

States have not been able to reliably invoke IHL to justify activities that comply with IHL, but that violate human rights law before the Court. The Court's references to and use of IHL have been sporadic, from totally ignoring its relevance, to implicitly applying it in some cases, to harmoniously applying the Convention in light of IHL. In sum, the State can face a very uncertain situation in which they have limited capacity to uphold Convention rights. The solution of derogating from the Convention during military operations seems obvious. Derogation could shield States from many of the issues identified in the preceding chapters.

The Convention's derogation provisions are outlined in Article 15 of the Convention, which states that:

> In time of war or other public emergency threatening the life of the nation any High Contracting Party may take measures derogating from its obligations under this Convention to the extent strictly required by the exigencies

[1] Secretary of State for Defence, 'Letter to the Chair of the Joint Committee on Human Rights' (28 February 2017) <www.parliament.uk/documents/joint-committees/human-rights/correspondence/2016-17/170301_SoS_to_Chair_re_Derogation.pdf> accessed 23 August 2018 at [2].

of the situation, provided that such measures are not inconsistent with its other obligations under international law.

No derogation from Article 2, except in respect of deaths resulting from lawful acts of war, or from Articles 3, 4 § 1 and 7 shall be made under this provision.

Article 15 demands that certain conditions are met before a legitimate derogation can be made. First, there must be a war or other public emergency. Second, the war or public emergency must threaten the life of the nation as a whole. Third, the measures taken in response to the situation must be strictly required by the exigencies of the situation. Fourth, these measures must be consistent with the State's other international law obligations. Finally, the Council of Europe must be notified of the derogating measures. The Court has, however, been flexible when interpreting and applying Article 15 and these strictures are not rigidly enforced.[2]

In principle, Article 15 provides States with much needed flexibility to alter their human rights obligations during military operations. However, derogations are not a panacea. As El-Zeidy notes, some of the gravest human rights violations occur in the context of emergencies.[3] States of emergency are often used as a pretext for State repression and thus utilising derogations carries with it a greater risk of human rights abuses.[4] Furthermore, some Convention rights, such as Article 3, are non-derogable meaning Article 15 cannot shield States from their effects. Derogating from the Convention can also present significant legal, practical and political obstacles to States, especially in the extra-territorial context. This chapter explores the potential benefits that derogation offers States in respect of military operations, while also examining some of the problems presented by derogations and how they can be addressed in practice.

## 7.2 BENEFITS OF DEROGATION

Derogating from the Convention, in particular from Articles 2 and 5, could offer significant benefits to both the Court and the State. First, derogating could mitigate some of the more onerous burdens States face in upholding

[2] Scott Sheeran, 'Reconceptualizing States of Emergency under International Human Rights Law: Theory, Legal Doctrine, and Politics' (2012–2013) 34 *Michigan Journal of International Law* 491, 537.

[3] Mohamed El Zeidy, 'The ECHR and States of Emergency: Article 15 – A Domestic Power of Derogation from Human Rights Obligations' (2003) 4 *San Diego International Law Journal* 277, 282–3.

[4] Sheeran (n. 2) 492–4; Christina Cerna, 'The History of the Inter-American System's Jurisprudence as Regards Situations of Armed Conflict' (2011) 2 *International Humanitarian Legal Studies* 3, 15.

human rights obligations during military operations. As noted previously, any deprivation of life resulting from a use of force that was not absolutely necessary within the terms of Article 2 could *prima facie* be a violation of Article 2.[5] However, there is an exception to the general non-derogability of Article 2 for lawful acts of war. A deprivation of life which is a consequence of a lawful act of war may be the subject of a derogation,[6] meaning that if the State derogated from Article 2 it would not face responsibility for such an act. As noted in Chapter 4, this could also serve to limit the procedural obligation to the investigation of suspected unlawful acts of war.

This would not amount to a *carte blanche* for States to act with impunity. Any measures taken by the State in response to the war or public emergency must be strictly required by the exigencies of the situation. This may lead to a less permissive normative environment governing the use of force than IHL.[7] The Court would likely still demand that the State adopt strict rules of engagement and ensure compliance with IHL and ICL.

Secondly, derogation would compel the Court to engage directly with IHL.[8] While a derogation is not required for either the State or the Court to apply IHL, because IHL applies automatically once the threshold for its application is reached,[9] the Court has nonetheless often appeared reluctant to openly and directly apply and interpret IHL in its jurisprudence.[10] It has been argued throughout the preceding chapters that the Court needs to actively engage with IHL. If the State derogated from Article 2 for lawful acts of war, for example, the Court would be compelled to assess whether the State's actions in killing or inflicting life-threatening injuries, were consistent with the State's other obligations under international law, which would include

5 See Chapter 3.

6 Elizabeth Wicks, *The Right to Life and Conflicting Interests* (Oxford University Press 2010) 82.

7 Ibid.

8 Christine Byron, 'A Blurring of the Boundaries: The Application of International Humanitarian Law by Human Rights Bodies' (2006–2007) 47 *Virginia Journal of International Law* 839; Noam Lubell, 'Challenges in Applying Human Rights Law to Armed Conflict' (2005) 87 IRRC 737, 742–4.

9 David Kretzmer, 'Rethinking the Application of IHL in Non-International Armed Conflicts' (2009) 42 *Israel Law Review* 8, 15.

10 Eriko Tamura, 'The Isayeva Cases of the European Court of Human Rights: The Application of International Humanitarian Law and Human Rights Law in Non-International Armed Conflicts' (2011) 10 *Chinese Journal of International Law* 129, 137; *Isayeva* v. *Russia* (2005) 41 EHRR 38 at [191].

ICL and IHL.[11] It could also serve to dispel any lingering doubts about the Court's mandate to apply and interpret IHL,[12] although doubts about its competence to apply IHL may remain.[13]

Thirdly, if States derogated from the Convention, they would implicitly accept that they were exercising jurisdiction during military operations.[14] States have consistently tried, with varying degrees of success, to deny jurisdiction during military operations or limit its scope,[15] and recent UK practice illustrates this trend well. In four different cases, the UK has presented an array of arguments denying jurisdiction. In *Al-Saadoon* v. *United Kingdom*, the UK denied that it was exercising jurisdiction over people detained on a British military base in Iraq because they were held under the legal authority of Iraq.[16] In *Al-Skeini* v. *UK*, the UK contradicted its argument in *Al-Saadoon* claiming that it only exercised jurisdiction within military bases abroad, but not outside them in areas under occupation by British forces.[17] The UK intervened in *Jaloud* v. *Netherlands* to claim that jurisdiction only arises when a State is an occupying power or is exercising governmental powers over the territory.[18] While in *Hassan* v. *United Kingdom*, it argued that detainees held in its custody, but on a US base in Iraq, fell outside its jurisdiction.[19] As contradictory and convoluted as these arguments may seem, they illustrate the spirited

[11] William Abresch, 'A Human Rights Law of Internal Armed Conflict: the European Court of Human Rights in Chechnya' (2005) 16 EJIL 741, 746; Michael O'Boyle and Jean Paul Costa, 'The ECtHR and IHL' in Christos Rozakis (ed), *The European Convention on Human Rights, a Living Instrument* (Bruylant Press 2011) 117–18; See by analogy Article 5 detention measures also Douglass Cassel, 'Pretrial and Preventive Detention of Suspected Terrorists: Options and Constraints under International Law' (2008) 98 *The Journal of Criminal Law and Criminology* 811, 821; *Serdar Mohammed* v. *Ministry of Defence* [2014] EWHC 1369 at [284].

[12] Giulia Pinzauti, 'The European Court of Human Rights' Incidental Application of International Criminal Law and Humanitarian Law: A Critical Discussion of Kononov v. Latvia' (2008) 6 *Journal of International Criminal Justice* 1043, 1044; O'Boyle and Costa (n. 11) 107.

[13] See Chapter 5; Magdalena Forowicz, *The Reception of International Law in the European Court of Human Rights* (Oxford University Press 2010) 348.

[14] Heike Krieger, 'After Al-Jedda: Detention, Derogation, and an Enduring Dilemma' (2011) 50 *Military Law and the Law of War Review* 419, 437; Marko Milanovic, 'Extraterritorial Derogations from Human Rights Treaties in Armed Conflict' in Nehal Bhuta (ed), *The Frontiers of Human Rights* (Oxford University Press 2016) 56.

[15] See Chapters 1 and 2.

[16] *Al-Saadoon and Mufdhi* v. *United Kingdom (Admissibility)* (2009) 49 EHRR SE11 at [79].

[17] *Al-Skeini and Others* v. *United Kingdom* (2011) 53 EHRR 18 at [109]–[119].

[18] *Jaloud* v. *Netherlands* (2015) 60 EHRR 29 at [121]–[126].

[19] *Hassan* v. *United Kingdom* App no 29750/09 (ECtHR, 16 September 2014) at [72].

rear-guard defence mounted by the UK against any expansion in the scope of extra-territorial jurisdiction. It is time States moved away from debating these issues and spent their time pragmatically discussing what a regulatory environment governed by both IHL and human rights law looks like. It is time to 'stop debating the theory and start defining the pragmatic',[20] derogations may help to facilitate that discussion.

A derogation could also offer a sounder basis for detention operations during different military operations. If a State derogated from Article 5 to permit security detention during a military operation, its right to engage in security detention would be respected. As noted in Chapter 5, the State would not have to rely on arguments that IHL displaced the Convention via the *lex specialis* principle, or that a UNSCR superseded the Convention via Article 103 of the UN Charter to justify security detention.[21]

It is uncertain at this point whether the Court's reasoning in *Hassan* would extend to other sources of international law (e.g. UNSCRs) or to NIACs. According to the UK government, the desire for States to make operational and strategic decisions against a 'clear legal framework' acts as an incentive to derogate.[22] Derogation represents a safer bet for States than these other approaches.

The failure to derogate could also expose the State to significant economic penalties. While the Court's awards tend to be modest, the scale of violations arising from security detention coupled with domestic legal cases, public inquiries etc. could be substantial.[23] The UK has settled hundreds of claims alleging violations of Article 5 following the *Al-Jedda* judgment where the acts of detention were compliant with IHL, but did not accord with the finite list

[20] Geoffrey Corn, 'Mixing Apples and Hand Grenades: The Logical Limits of Applying Human Rights Norms to Armed Conflict' (2010) 1 *International Humanitarian Legal Studies* 52, 90.

[21] This would also benefit the UN, which has expressed disquiet about using Article 103 to override human rights law and dispel doubts over whether the UN organs are legally permitted to override human rights law when they act – *Al-Jedda* v. *United Kingdom* (2011) 53 EHRR 23 at [82]; Terry Gill, 'Legal and Some Political Limitations on the Power of the UN Security Council to Exercise its Enforcement Powers under Chapter VII of the Charter' (1995) 26 *Netherlands Yearbook of International Law* 33, 77–9; Dapo Akande, 'The International Court of Justice and the Security Council: Is there Room for Judicial Control of Decisions of the Political Organs of the United Nations?' (1997) 46 ICLQ 309, 323–5.

[22] Secretary of State for Defence (n. 1) at [17].

[23] Thomas Tugendhat and Laura Croft, *The Fog of Law: An Introduction to the Legal Erosion of British Fighting Power* (Policy Exchange 2013) 35; *R. (Long)* v. *Secretary of State for Defence* [2014] EWHC 2391 (Admin) at [79]. The Baha Mousa inquiry into human rights abuses carried out by British soldiers against one man was reported to have cost almost £13 million – 'Q&A: Baha Mousa inquiry' (*BBC News*, 8 September 2011) <www.bbc.co.uk/news/uk-14698722> accessed 12 September 2018.

of grounds for detention under Article 5. The UK government has suggested that following the reinterpretation of Article 5 in *Hassan*,[24] there would have been no need to settle these claims.[25] Had the UK derogated in the first place it would not have faced these financial and legal costs.

Of course, States should still be held accountable for violations of the Convention outside the scope of their derogations. We must be careful to distinguish between violations arising from activities that accord with IHL and other bodies of law and those that do not, equally if States continually fail to derogate, whether it is the result of political calculation or negligence, they should be made to suffer the consequences.[26]

Derogation would also provide a contextual barrier for some of the unusual interpretations of the Convention identified in the preceding chapters. In Chapter 3, for example, the Court's act of distinguishing between the right to life of combatants and civilians negated a basic tenet of human rights law.[27] Such interpretations undermine the unity and coherence of Article 2 standards. A derogation could provide a clear contextual barrier between such interpretations and the Court's normal jurisprudence. It could avoid the risk that divergent interpretations of the law, which aim to account for the unusual circumstances of military operations, do not contaminate the Court's normal jurisprudence. Given the clear benefits of derogation for military operations, it is open to question why State practice on derogations for military operations is so sporadic.

## 7.3 DEROGATION PRACTICE

Since the creation of the Convention, States have tended to derogate from the Convention in response to domestic threats, for example, the PKK in Turkey,[28] the IRA in the Republic of Ireland and United Kingdom.[29] Convention States have not derogated for the many extra-territorial military operations in which

[24] See discussion in Chapter 5.

[25] Secretary of State for Defence (n. 1) at [15]–[16]; Elizabeth Chadwick and Katja Samuel, 'In Faint Praise of the Derogating Will' (2017) 26 *Nottingham Law Journal* 87, 96–7.

[26] Milanovic (n. 14) 84.

[27] See Chapter 3; Noelle Quenivet, 'The Right to Life in International Humanitarian Law and Human Rights Law' in Roberta Arnold and Noelle Quenivet (eds), *International Humanitarian Law and Human Rights Law: Towards a New Merger in International Law* (Brill 2008) 343.

[28] PKK terrorism has prompted derogation by Turkey – *Aksoy* v. *Turkey* (1997) 23 EHRR 553.

[29] Terrorist offences perpetrated by the IRA have prompted derogations by both Ireland and the UK – *Lawless* v. *Ireland* (1979–1980) 1 EHRR 15; *Brannigan and McBride* v. *United Kingdom* (1994) 17 EHRR 539.

they have acted, such as the NATO-led intervention in Kosovo,[30] and the war in Iraq.[31] Some have interpreted this absence of State practice to mean that States lack the capacity to derogate during extra-territorial military operations.[32] However, Milanovic and Sari have argued that the failure to derogate does not prove that the State considered itself unable as a matter of law to derogate for these operations. Such a view must be positively proven and cannot be assumed, especially when there are alternative explanations for the failure to derogate.[33] As Da Costa and Loucaides point out in a different context, just because a State does not derogate does not mean that a derogation is not necessary or possible.[34] A failure to derogate may, for example, be motivated by a broader lack of respect for the rule of law and human rights within a State.[35]

As noted in the previous section, States may not have thought it necessary to derogate for extra-territorial military operations in the past because they did not believe that they were exercising jurisdiction.[36] States have repeatedly argued that they were not exercising jurisdiction extra-territorially in several cases before the Court, derogating would have conceded the point. Alternatively, States may have legitimately believed that the *lex specialis* principle would displace their Convention obligations.[37] While relatively recent jurisprudence from the Court has made these positions vis-à-vis *lex specialis* and extra-territorial jurisdiction increasingly untenable, it is entirely

30 *Bankovic and Others* v. *Belgium and Others* (2007) 44 EHRR SE5 at [37].

31 *Al-Skeini and Others* v. *United Kingdom* (2011) 53 EHRR 18 and *Jaloud* v. *Netherlands* (2015) 60 EHRR 29.

32 *R. (Al-Jedda)* v. *Secretary of State for Defence* [2007] UKHL 58 at [38]; *Smith and Others* v. *Ministry of Defence* [2013] UKSC 41 at [60]; O'Boyle and Costa (n. 11) 116.

33 House of Commons Defence Committee, *UK Armed Forces Personnel and the Legal Framework for Future Operations: Twelfth Report of Session 2013–14* (The Stationery Office 2014) Evidence 55; Milanovic (n. 14) 57. Interestingly in *Hassan* v. *United Kingdom*, the Court expressly referred to the right of States to derogate from Convention rights before noting the UK had not derogated from the Convention while in occupation of Iraq. At no point did the Court say it was not possible for a State to derogate extra-territorially *Hassan* v. *United Kingdom* App no 29750/09 (ECtHR, 16 September 2014) at [98].

34 Karen da Costa, *The Extraterritorial Application of Selected Human Rights Treaties* (Brill 2012) 133 and Loukis Loucaides, 'Determining the Extra-Territorial Effect of the European Convention: Facts, Jurisprudence and the Bankovic case' [2006] EHRLR 391, 396.

35 In a study on State practice on derogations, Helfer and others noted that States which had more developed democracies and a stronger adherence to the rule of law were more likely to derogate than those which did not – Laurence Helfer, Emilie Hafner-Burton and Christopher Fariss, 'Emergency and Escape: Explaining Derogations from Human Rights Treaties' (2011) 65 *International Organization* 673, 675.

36 Secretary of State for Defence (n. 1) at [3].

37 Milanovic (n. 14) 86–7; Secretary of State for Defence (n. 1) at [4].

conceivable that they motivated the failure to derogate in the past.[38] Following the extension of extra-territorial jurisdiction and the failure of the strong *lex specialis* approach, States appear to be more open to derogation. Ukraine has derogated in respect of its international armed conflict with Russia and the UK has announced 'a presumption to derogate' from the Convention in its future overseas conflicts.[39]

The political cost of derogation could also have acted as a significant deterrent in the past. When considering domestic military operations, the government may consider that derogating would legitimise opposition forces within the State, conceding that they are succeeding in undermining the foundations of the State.[40] Foreign military operations are largely elective in many contracting States and may need to be sanctioned by their national parliaments. National politicians may balk at the idea of removing human rights protection for their own troops or the citizens of the State they are supposedly assisting.[41] As the cost-benefit equation shifts economically (with increasing legal claims and compensation), militarily (with human rights obligations compromising operational effectiveness) and politically, derogation may be considered a political price worth paying.

There are multiple potential explanations for the limited State practice in respect of derogations, none of which stem from a perceived lack of legal capacity on the part of States to derogate from the Convention. Although there are many clear benefits to derogation, the prospect of derogation both for military operations within the State's territory and extra-territorially presents significant difficulties, which are addressed in the following sections.

[38] Milanovic (n. 14) 57.

[39] Ukrainian Government, *Resolution of the Verkhovna Rada of Ukraine on Declaration on Derogation from Certain Obligations under the International Covenant on Civil and Political Rights and the Convention for the Protection of Human Rights and Fundamental Freedoms* (21 May 2015) <https://rm.coe.int/CoERMPublicCommonSearchServices/DisplayDCTMContent?documentId=0900001680304c47#search=ukraine%20derogate> accessed 23 August 2018; UK Ministry of Defence, 'Government to protect Armed Forces from persistent legal claims in future overseas operations' (4 October 2016) <www.gov.uk/government/news/government-to-protect-armed-forces-from-persistent-legal-claims-in-future-overseas-operations>.

[40] O'Boyle and Costa (n. 11) 117–18. This desire to avoid legitimating opposition groups permeates other aspects of human rights law too – Cerna (n. 4) 13; Abresch (n. 11) 756; Elspeth Guild, 'Inside Out or Outside In? Examining Human Rights in Situations of Armed Conflict' (2007) 9 *International Community Law Review* 33, 37.

[41] Krieger (n. 14) 438.

## 7.4 KEY ISSUES WITH DEROGATION DURING MILITARY OPERATIONS

As noted above, for a derogation to be legitimate it must conform to a number of conditions:

1. There must be a war or other public emergency;
2. The war or public emergency must threaten the life of the nation as a whole;
3. The measures taken in response to the situation must be strictly required by the exigencies of the situation;
4. These measures must be consistent with the State's other international law obligations;
5. The Council of Europe must be notified of the derogating measures;

These conditions can present difficulties for States attempting to derogate for military operations, particularly extra-territorial military operations.

### 7.4.1 *War or Other Public Emergency*

The first threshold criterion to satisfy is that there must be a 'war or other public emergency', Article 15 also refers to 'lawful acts of war', which prompts the question, what does the Convention mean when it says war? The answer is unclear,[42] in particular, it is questionable whether the provision encompasses both IACs and NIACs.[43] When the Convention was drafted, regulation of NIACs at the international level was sparse,[44] and war was distinctly associated with IACs. The drafters may have only meant for States to be able to derogate for acts that were lawful under rules governing IACs and the Court could follow this interpretation.[45]

[42] Ronald MacDonald, 'Derogations under Article 15 of the European Convention on Human Rights' (1998) 36 *Columbia Journal of Transnational Law* 225, 235; El Zeidy (n. 3) 283.

[43] Joan Fitzpatrick, *Human Rights in Crisis: The International System for Protecting Human Rights During States of Emergency* (University of Pennsylvania Press 1994) 57; Louise Doswald-Beck, 'The Right to Life in Armed Conflict: Does International Humanitarian Law Provide all the Answers?' (2006) 88 IRRC 881, 882. For a similar discussion in the context of the American Convention on Human Rights see Robert Norris and Paula Reiton, 'The Suspension of Guarantees: A Comparative Analysis of the American Convention on Human Rights and the Constitutions of the States Parties' (1980) 30 *American University Law Review* 189, 195.

[44] The Geneva Conventions, drafted in 1949 one year before the Convention, only included a single article, common Article 3, to regulate armed conflicts 'not of an international character'.

[45] Louise Doswald-Beck, *Human Rights in Times of Conflict and Terrorism* (Oxford University Press 2011) 192–3; O'Boyle and Costa (n. 11) 115.

There have, however, been many developments in international law since the Convention was drafted. There is some State practice on interpreting 'war' to include both NIACs and IACs.[46] The Additional Protocols to the Geneva Conventions, especially the second protocol, have developed international rules governing NIACs. Equally, many IHL provisions governing IACs have been applied by analogy to NIACs. Customary rules of IHL governing both NIACs and IACs have also filled the gaps in the international regulation of NIACs with international criminal tribunals playing a significant role in this process.[47] The differences in the legal regulation of IACs and NIACs have thus been gradually eroded. The Court could simply follow this trend and interpret the terms of this Article to encompass both war in the sense of IACs and NIACs.[48] At the same time, the State could simply issue a derogation that is ambiguous as to its coverage, covering both IAC and NIAC as the Ukraine has done in respect of its conflict with Russia and other armed groups in the East of Ukraine.

The drafters of the Convention also clearly envisaged that Article 2 would continue to apply in the context of insurrections, which can be considered synonymous with NIACs.[49] Under Article 2, the use of force is permitted when absolutely necessary and lawfully taken for the purpose of quelling an insurrection.[50] Thus even assuming a derogation from Article 2 for a NIAC was possible, the State would have to demonstrate that the exigencies of the situation meant that they needed to use more force than was absolutely necessary. States would have to justify a shift toward more permissive assessments of the use of force under IHL, which would only look at whether the use of force was proportional and pursued a military objective.

As a matter of policy, it seems unlikely that the Court would encourage more permissive rules on the use of force. The more important the right is, the

46 See the interpretation of the term 'war' in the 1925 Geneva Gas Protocol – Sandesh Sivakumaran, *The Law of Non-International Armed Conflict* (Oxford University Press 2012) 394–5.

47 Louise Doswald-Beck and Jean-Marie Henckaerts, *Customary International Humanitarian Law* (International Committee of the Red Cross 2005); Sivakumaran (n. 46) 54–84; Theodor Meron, 'The Humanization of Humanitarian Law' (2000) 94 AJIL 239, 243–5.

48 Milanovic argues general rules of treaty interpretation facilitate each of the possible interpretations postulated in this section, although he seems to favour the more expansive interpretation including IACs and NIACs – Milanovic (n. 14) 66–8.

49 Doswald-Beck (n. 45) 193; *Serdar Mohammed* v. *Ministry of Defence* [2014] EWHC 1369 at [279]; Admas Habteslasie, 'Derogation in Time of War: The Application of Article 15 of the ECHR in Extraterritorial Armed Conflicts' (2016) 21(4) *Judicial Review* 302, 305.

50 Article 2(2)(c), European Convention on Human Rights.

more closely the Court scrutinises restrictions upon it and the Court clearly considers the right to life to be extremely important.[51] At the same time, the Court has generally been extremely deferential to States, allowing them to determine how they wish to respond to emergency situations, giving them the benefit of the doubt more often than not.[52] The Court would likely allow States to derogate from Article 2 for NIACs, but demand that specific safeguards be put in place as it has in other cases.[53] This could include strict rules of engagement, strong legal oversight of targeting and planning as well as assiduous enforcement of applicable IHL.

On the subject of deference, the Court has faced criticism over the level of scrutiny it applies to the question of whether a public emergency exists.[54] The Court grants States a margin of appreciation to determine whether an emergency exists. In *Marshall* v. *United Kingdom*, for example, the Court considered whether the derogation the UK made from Article 5 in Northern Ireland was still necessary given the improvements in the security situation there. A ceasefire between the main parties was in place and holding and the Good Friday agreement, which secured peace in Northern Ireland, was close to completion. Despite the stabilisation of the situation, the Court considered that the State should be given a margin of appreciation and that the national authorities were 'better placed than the international judge to decide both on the presence of such an emergency and on the nature and scope of the derogation necessary to avoid it'.[55]

The *Marshall* judgment is problematic given the wider practice of States when they derogate from the Convention. Derogations are supposed to respond to temporary problems, but States have used them predominantly in situations like Northern Ireland and South-East Turkey to respond to

[51] *Brannigan and McBride* v. *United Kingdom* at [43]; Jean Allain, 'Derogation from the European Convention of Human Rights in the Light of "Other Obligations under International Law"' [2005] EHRLR 480, 482; MacDonald (n. 42) 244.

[52] MacDonald (n. 42) 245.

[53] The Court's focus on safeguards is evident in the cases on administrative detention – see *Aksoy* v. *Turkey* at [82]–[83]; *Brannigan and McBride* v. *United Kingdom* at [64]–[65]; *Lawless* v. *Ireland* at [37].

[54] Fionnuala Ní Aoláin and Oren Gross, 'From Discretion to Scrutiny: Revisiting the Application of the Margin of Appreciation Doctrine in the Context of Article 15 of the European Convention on Human Rights' (2001) 23 *Human Rights Quarterly* 625, 638–9; Ed Bates, 'A "Public Emergency Threatening the Life of the Nation"? The United Kingdom's Derogation from the European Convention on Human Rights of 18 December 2001 and the "A" case' (2005) 76 BYIL 245, 291; Sheeran (n. 2) 493.

[55] *Marshall* v. *United Kingdom* App no 41571/98 (ECtHR, 10 July 2001).

long-term threats and 'entrenched emergencies'.[56] Ní Aoláin and Gross criticise the Court's approach of granting States a margin of appreciation here, which they feel acts as a substitute for coherent legal analysis and is an abdication of the Court's duty to adjudicate complex and sensitive cases.[57] As the state of emergency continues over time, the Court should provide greater scrutiny of whether the derogation remains necessary.

### 7.4.2 *'Threaten the Life of the Nation as a Whole'*

One of the pre-conditions for a valid derogation is that the war or public emergency must threaten the life of the nation. In principle, to reach the requisite threshold for derogation there must be a threat to the State's physical population, its territorial integrity or the functioning of the State's organs.[58] The situation must be actual or imminent and normal measures must be plainly inadequate for dealing with it.[59] Yet, as with the issue of the existence of an emergency, the Court has been deferential on the scale of the threat necessary to justify derogation.[60] Bates highlights the example of *Lawless* v. *Ireland*, where Ireland derogated from Articles 5 and 6 following relatively low levels of terrorist violence. At the time, terrorist attacks in Ireland had resulted in approximately six deaths over the space of six years.[61] This low level of violence led some to question whether the life of

56 Terrorist offences perpetrated by the IRA have prompted derogations by both Ireland and the UK – *Lawless* v. *Ireland* (1979–1980) 1 EHRR 15; *Brannigan and McBride* v. *United Kingdom* (1994) 17 EHRR 539. Meanwhile, PKK terrorism has prompted derogation by Turkey – *Aksoy* v. *Turkey* (1997) 23 EHRR 553. On the subject of entrenched emergencies see Oren Gross, '"Once More unto the Breach": The Systemic Failure of Applying the European Convention on Human Rights to Entrenched Emergencies' (1998) 23 *Yale Journal of International Law* 437 and Sheeran (n. 2) 512–17.

57 Ní Aoláin and Gross (n. 54) 628; Bates (n. 54) 315–19.

58 Dominic McGoldrick, 'The Interface Between Public Emergency Powers and International Law' (2004) 2 *International Journal of Constitutional Law* 380, 393–4; The American Convention on Human Rights by contrast arguably has a lower threshold demanding a 'public danger, or other emergency that threatens the independence or security' of the State – See Article 27(1), American Convention on Human Rights (adopted 22 November 1969, entered into force 18 July 1978) 1144 UNTS 144.

59 *A and Others* v. *United Kingdom* (2009) 49 EHRR 29 at [176].

60 Alan Greene, 'Separating Normalcy from Emergency: The Jurisprudence of Article 15 of the European Convention on Human Rights' (2011) 12 *German Law Journal* 1764, 1781.

61 Bates (n. 54) 298–9.

the nation was truly threatened.[62] The Court ruled that the derogation was justified because there was:

> a secret army engaged in unconstitutional activities and using violence to attain its purposes both within and outside its territory and to the steady and alarming increase in terrorist activities between autumn 1956 and the middle of 1957.[63]

Similar doubts were raised about the scale of the threat justifying the UK's derogation from Article 5 following the terrorist attacks in the US on 11 September 2001. The UK's derogation was challenged in *A and Others* v. *United Kingdom*. In the House of Lords, Lord Hoffman argued against the majority, that the threat posed by international terrorism was insufficient to threaten the existence of the State's institutions or the UK as a civil community.[64] The applicants raised a similar argument before the Court, but the Court granted the State a wide margin of appreciation to determine the scale of the threat. The Court stated that it considered:

> a much broader range of factors in determining the nature and degree of the actual or imminent threat to the 'nation' and has in the past concluded that emergency situations have existed even though the institutions of the State did not appear to be imperilled to the extent envisaged by Lord Hoffman.[65]

Doubts have also been raised over whether it is possible for this threat pre-condition to be satisfied in an extra-territorial context.[66] Lord Bingham raised this specific issue in *Al-Jedda* when examining the UK's deployment in Iraq stating that the power to derogate:

> may only be exercised in time of war or other public emergency threatening the life of the nation seeking to derogate [...] It is hard to think that these conditions could ever be met when a state had chosen to conduct an overseas peacekeeping operation, however dangerous the conditions, from which it could withdraw.[67]

62 Brian Doolan, *Lawless* v. *Ireland (1957–1961): The First Case before the European Court of Human Rights: An International Miscarriage of Justice?* (Ashgate 2001) 38; Sheeran (n. 2) 532.

63 *Lawless* v. *Ireland* at [28]; Bates argues that the Court was concerned that these attacks could lead to a civil war or international conflict between the UK and Ireland – Bates (n. 54) 304.

64 *A and Others* v. *Secretary of State for the Home Department* [2004] UKHL 56 at [96]–[97]; Sheeran and Bates are similarly critical – Bates (n. 54) 280 and Sheeran (n. 2) 536.

65 *A and Others* v. *United Kingdom* at [179].

66 Krieger (n. 14) 435; *Smith and Others* v. *Ministry of Defence* [2013] UKSC 41 at [60]; Milanovic (n. 14) 57; O'Boyle and Costa (n. 11) 116; Michael Dennis, 'Application of Human Rights Treaties Extraterritorially in Times of Armed Conflict and Military Occupation' (2005) 99 AJIL 119, 125–6.

67 *R. (Al-Jedda)* v. *Secretary of State for Defence* [2007] UKHL 58 at [38].

This element of threat has been interpreted liberally by the Court.[68] The extra-territorial threat could, for example, be considered in more abstract terms. In *Lawless*, a minimal level of threat to the State was sufficient to justify the derogation, while in A *and Others* v. *United Kingdom*, the Court allowed the prospective threat to the nation of international terrorism to justify the derogation. A public emergency need not engulf an entire nation before it can be said to 'threaten the life of the nation'.[69] When the Court considered the *Al-Jedda* case, they seemed open to the possibility of extra-territorial derogations, noting that: 'the Government do not contend that the detention was justified under [...] Article 5 s 1, nor did they purport to derogate under Article 15'.[70] There is arguably an implicit acceptance of the possibility here.[71]

It seems unjust to deny States the possibility to derogate on the grounds advanced by Lord Bingham. As jurisdiction extends extra-territorially, so too should the option of derogation. As Sassoli argues 'one cannot simultaneously hold a State accountable because it has a certain level of control abroad and deny it the possibility to derogate because there is no emergency on that State's own territory. An emergency on the territory where the State has a certain limited control must be sufficient'.[72] This position is also supported by many others.[73]

The extra-territorial threat could also be interpreted so that a threat to the life of a non-contracting State was deemed sufficient to justify a derogation while a contracting State undertakes military action there to assist it.[74] The Court could also consider threats to the life of the nation in more collective terms. Thus when the United Nations recognises a threat to international peace and security and sanctions military action in response,[75] this could be

68 El Zeidy (n. 3) 284–5.

69 Thomas Buergenthal, 'To Respect and to Ensure, State Obligations and Permissible Derogations' in Louis Henkin (ed), *The International Bill of Human Rights: The Covenant on Civil and Political Rights* (Columbia University Press 1981) 80; El Zeidy (n. 3) 285.

70 *Al-Jedda* v. *United Kingdom* at [100].

71 Krieger (n. 14) 436.

72 Marco Sassoli, 'The International Legal Framework for Stability Operations: When May International Forces Attack or Detain Someone in Afghanistan?' (2009) 85 *US Naval War College International Law Studies* 431, 438.

73 Dennis (n. 66) 476; Milanovic (n. 14) 71; *Serdar Mohammed* v. *Ministry of Defence* at [155]. The European Commission on Human Rights seemed to consider that once jurisdiction was made out, it was open to the State to derogate – *Cyprus* v. *Turkey* (1982) 4 EHRR 482 at [525]–[528].

74 Krieger (n. 14) 436; House of Commons Defence Committee (n. 33) Evidence 54; *Serdar Mohammed* v. *Ministry of Defence* at [156].

75 Chapter VII, UN Charter 1945.

considered a sufficient threat to justify derogation where contracting States assist in the military action.[76] It has also been suggested that the Court could read Article 15 so that the threat to the life of the nation condition only applies to emergencies and not to wars, which could go some way toward alleviating the problem.[77]

### 7.4.3 *Proportionality and Necessity*

The third criterion, that the measure must be strictly required by the exigencies of the situation, is typically the main focus of the Court's attention.[78] It involves a multifaceted assessment examining the necessity, proportionality and duration of measures adopted.[79] As noted above, the Court offered limited scrutiny of duration above in *Marshall*.

On the necessity of measures, the Court's approach has been problematic if we examine the UK's derogation in Northern Ireland. The UK decided to withdraw its derogation from Article 5 in Northern Ireland in August 1984. This derogation allowed the UK, *inter alia*, to detain people for extended periods of time without bringing them before a judicial authority. In 1988, the Court decided *Brogan* v. *United Kingdom* where four applicants, who had been detained under normal Article 5 rules, successfully challenged their detention for between four and six days without being brought before a judicial authority. The Court held that this conduct amounted to a violation of Article 5(3).[80] This decision prompted the UK to derogate from Article 5 again in December 1988. However, by withdrawing the derogation in the first place, the UK had implicitly conceded that the conditions justifying the derogation no longer existed.[81]

When the later derogation was challenged in *Brannigan and McBride* v. *United Kingdom*, the Court should have scrutinised why the derogation was withdrawn and then reinstated, as there was no significant deterioration in the situation in Northern Ireland between its withdrawal and reinstatement.[82]

76 Ralph Wilde, 'The Extraterritorial Application of International Human Rights Law on Civil and Political Rights' in Scott Sheeran and Nigel Rodley (eds), *Routledge Handbook of International Human Rights Law* (Routledge 2013), 652–5.

77 Habteslasie (n. 49) 312–14.

78 Bates (n. 54) 297.

79 El Zeidy (n. 3) 286.

80 *Brogan* v. *United Kingdom* (1989) 11 EHRR 117.

81 El Zeidy (n. 3) 311–13.

82 Brice Dickson, *The European Convention on Human Rights and the Conflict in Northern Ireland* (Oxford University Press 2010) 125.

Instead the Court decided that the derogation was a 'genuine response' to a 'persistent emergency' and offered little scrutiny of the UK's justifications for the derogation.[83] It is open to question whether this derogation was 'strictly required by the exigencies of the situation' or simply a knee-jerk response to the adverse judgment in *Brogan*.[84]

On the question of proportionality, there are two potential approaches to assessment: a strict approach, which means the State must show there is no other alternative way to deal with the emergency, or a lax approach, which offers the State some discretion or a margin of appreciation. The Court follows the latter approach giving States a wide margin of appreciation as in *Marshall* and other cases. The Court is usually more willing to strike down measures on proportionality grounds.[85] However, the Court's consistency in scrutinising proportionality has been questioned, as the Court offers limited scrutiny of some derogations, e.g. in Northern Ireland above, and much closer scrutiny of others, e.g. Turkish derogations.[86]

In Northern Ireland, seven days detention without charge was deemed acceptable in *Brannigan*, while longer periods of detention without charge in Turkey of fourteen days or more were deemed disproportionate.[87] The Court emphasised objective differences between these cases and claimed that the duration of detention in Turkey was longer and the UK provided more safeguards.[88] However, the justification for differentiating between the Northern Irish and Turkish derogations is difficult to fathom. The Court ruled that the Turkish derogation was disproportionate because it: 'left the applicant vulnerable not only to arbitrary interference with his right to liberty but also to torture'.[89] Clearly long periods of detention without judicial supervision create environments conducive to ill-treatment,[90] but this risk arises whether the person is detained for seven days or fourteen days. If detention for fourteen days

83 *Brannigan and McBride* v. *United Kingdom* at [51].

84 Gross (n. 56) 480–2; Ed Bates, 'Avoiding Legal Obligations Created by Human Rights Treaties' (2008) 57 ICLQ 751, 753–4.

85 The Court, for example, dismissed the UK's derogation because it was discriminatory in *A and Others* v. *United Kingdom*.

86 Allain (n. 51) 489; Frederick Cowell, 'Sovereignty and the Question of Derogation: An Analysis of Article 15 of the ECHR and the Absence of a Derogation Clause in the ACHPR' (2013) 1 *Birkbeck Law Review* 135, 147; Marie-Bénédicte Dembour, *Who Believes in Human Right: Reflections on the European Convention* (Cambridge University Press 2006) 49–53.

87 See *inter alia Aksoy* v. *Turkey* (1997) 23 EHRR 553 and *Demir* v. *Turkey* (2001) 33 EHRR 43.

88 *Aksoy* v. *Turkey* (1997) 23 EHRR 553 at [82]–[83].

89 Ibid at [78].

90 El Zeidy (n. 3) 314.

without judicial supervision is disproportionate because of the risk of torture, then detention for seven days should also be disproportionate.[91]

### 7.4.4 *Interaction of Derogations with IHL*

The interactions between derogations and other bodies of law could impact the scope of the derogation and limit the State's capacity to truly alter the legal paradigm governing a military operation. While the list of specifically enumerated non-derogable rights is reasonably small, other rights may be considered non-derogable informally or rendered non-derogable in practice because of their relationship to other provisions.

Where a provision already has a generous limitation clause, such as freedom of assembly and freedom of movement, this may be considered to offer sufficient flexibility in all cases to obviate the need for derogations.[92] Although some rights, such as the right to non-discrimination, are not listed among the non-derogable rights, there are elements of that right that cannot be derogated from under any circumstances.[93] Some rights can attain non-derogable status through their relationship to other rights.[94] Thus while Article 5 is derogable in principle, the right to resort to a competent court or tribunal within it can be considered non-derogable because of its centrality to ensuring other non-derogable rights, such as the prohibition on torture, inhuman and degrading treatment or punishment.[95] Similarly, elements of the right to a fair trial, which are simultaneously reflected in other international law, such as IHL, become non-derogable once that law is applicable.[96]

Martin has argued, for example, that the combined effect of several factors means that even if a State did derogate from Article 2, it would still have to use force only when absolutely necessary. He contends that the condition that derogations be strictly required by the exigencies of a situation is 'identical to the absolute necessity test'. Further, the right to humane treatment under human rights law is non-derogable and creates an obligation to cause the least amount of suffering. Thus, unless the taking of a life occurs without any suffering, it

91 Kathleen Kavanaugh, 'Policing the Margins: Rights Protection and the European Court of Human Rights' [2006] EHRLR 422, 441.

92 UN Human Rights Committee, General Comment No. 29, Article 4: Derogations during a State of Emergency, 31 August 2001, CCPR/C/21/Rev.1/Add.11 at [5]; McGoldrick (n. 58) 384.

93 UN Human Rights Committee (n. 92) at [8]; McGoldrick (n. 58) 412–14.

94 McGoldrick (n. 58) 416–19.

95 Inter-American Commission on Human Rights, *Report on Terrorism and Human Rights* (OEA/SerL/V/II116 Doc 5 rev 1 corr, 2002) at [126].

96 UN Human Rights Committee (n. 92) at [16].

violates this right. As derogations must be consistent with other obligations under international law, any derogation from Article 2 would have to comply with this measure also.[97]

While this theory is plausible, the Court is unlikely to follow it and it ignores key practical factors.[98] The Court has bent the rules on absolute necessity in the past.[99] The Court does not engage in particularly close scrutiny of proportionality, especially if the State puts in place safeguards along with its derogation to avoid excessive effects. In the context of Article 2 this could include strict rules of engagement and enforcement of IHL and ICL.

While the right to humane treatment is non-derogable, Martin neglects the fact that whether or not something amounts to inhumane treatment is often context specific and inhumane treatment can be justified in certain circumstances.[100] Thus treatment such as strip-searching may be justified if the applicant represents a security risk,[101] or force feeding a person may be justified for medical reasons.[102] In the context of the military, the Court accepts that military work is inherently dangerous,[103] and it has been willing to adjust the limits of Article 3 accordingly.[104] The Court would likely take a similar approach to lawful deprivations of life during an armed conflict.

Martin's interpretation of Article 15(2) would also effectively deprive it of any meaningful effect. The object of Article 15(2) is to alter the standard against which the legality of deaths are judged from a Convention standard, to a standard based on legality under IHL. Demanding that the absolute necessity test continue to apply would frustrate that outcome, as IHL does not apply an absolute necessity test. Any derogation from Article 2 contains an implicit

97 Francisco Martin, 'Using International Human Rights Law for Establishing a Unified Use of Force Rule in the Law of Armed Conflict' (2001) 64 *Saskatchewan Law Review* 347, 367.

98 Hampson discusses some practicalities of implementing such an approach – Francoise Hampson, 'Direct Participation in Hostilities and the Interoperability of the Law of Armed Conflict and Human Rights Law' (2011) 87 *US Naval War College International Law Studies* 187, 192–3.

99 See discussion in Chapter 3; Jordan Paust, 'The Right to Life in Human Rights Law and the Law of War' (2002) 65 *Saskatchewan Law Review* 411, 418.

100 Steven Greer, *The European Convention on Human Rights: Achievements, Problems, Prospects* (Cambridge University Press 2006) 236; Antonio Cassese, 'Prohibition of Torture and Inhuman or Degrading Treatment or Punishment' in Ronald Macdonald, Franz Matscher, and Herbert Petzold (eds), *The European System for the Protection of Human Rights* (Martinus Nijhoff 1993) 248.

101 *Frerot* v. *France* App no 70204/01 (ECtHR, 12 June 2007).

102 *Nevmerzhitsky* v. *Ukraine* (2006) 43 EHRR 32.

103 *Stoyanovi* v. *Bulgaria* App no 42980/04 (ECtHR, 9 November 2010) at [61].

104 *Chember* v. *Russia* App no 7188/03 (ECtHR, 3 July 2008) at [49]–[50].

assumption that the exigencies of the situation meant that the full force of Article 2, including the absolute necessity test, could not be applied satisfactorily by the State.

### 7.4.5 *Tailoring Extra-Territorial Derogations*

The extent to which derogations can be adapted to the specific requirements of extra-territorial military operations is also problematic. One central problem is the connection between derogations and territory. Derogations are typically issued over the entire home territory of a State or parts thereof, such as Northern Ireland.[105] Given that the Court has accepted such geographically limited derogations in the past, it may accept localised derogations for emergencies outside the State where the treaties apply.[106] The real problem is that extra-territorial jurisdiction arises not only through geographical links, but also through the actions of State agents anywhere in the world.[107] Adapting the territory-centric derogation scheme in the Convention to cover the acts of individuals could present a particularly insidious problem if States pursued it. Block derogations governing all State agents abroad are likely to fail the necessity test in Article 15. By contrast, more limited individualised derogations for specific State agents would give the distasteful impression that some State agents are above and beyond the law.

The issue of impunity is perhaps wider and more problematic than this though. Rooney suggests that we should also consider the symbolic significance of derogation and that derogation may have a wider chilling effect on legitimate human rights litigation.[108] The UK government, for example, has sought to justify derogation not simply on the basis of technical issues surrounding the relationship between IHL and the Convention or the Court's jurisprudence on jurisdiction, but on the grounds that the British armed forces have been subject to vexatious and unsubstantiated litigation presented by unscrupulous lawyers.[109] This is part of a wider narrative that the UK's armed forces have acted impeccably during extra-territorial

[105] *Ireland* v. *United Kingdom* (1979–80) 2 EHRR 25; El Zeidy (n. 3) 284.
[106] Milanovic (n. 14) 71–2.
[107] See Chapter 2.
[108] Jane Rooney, 'Extraterritorial Derogation from the European Convention on Human Rights in the UK' [2016] EHRLR 656, 662.
[109] Secretary of State for Defence (n. 1) at [11]–[14].

military operations and that human rights lawyers are engaged in a witch hunt against innocent members of the British armed forces.[110]

While some claims brought against the armed forces lacked merit, others clearly warranted investigation and sanction. The Al-Sweady inquiry, for example, looked into events in 2004 in Iraq that gave rise to allegations against British troops of murder, torture, mutilation and inhuman and degrading treatment. The inquiry largely exonerated the troops concluding that the vast majority of allegations made against the British military that the inquiry investigated 'were wholly and entirely without merit or justification'.[111] However, the inquiry also concluded that some of the soldiers' conduct and military procedures fell well below the standards expected and that the treatment of nine detainees during that incident amounted to ill-treatment.[112]

The application of human rights law has also been responsible for other important investigations into clear wrongdoing by British soldiers, most notably in the Baha Mousa inquiry.[113] The Convention has given rise to some vexatious claims and some meritorious claims, just as some soldiers deployed to Iraq and elsewhere carried out their work impeccably, while others acted unlawfully and violated rules of human rights law and IHL. The concern is that in future where a State has derogated claims will be dismissed automatically on the grounds that the State has derogated and that this will foster impunity and stifle legitimate human rights claims.

The challenge here is to realise the benefits of derogation, while avoiding the pitfalls of impunity and entrenched emergencies. The problem is that the Court has historically been extremely deferential to States in respect of their derogation practices. As noted above, the Court has given States a wide margin of appreciation as regards the existence of emergencies and threats, the scale of the threat required to necessitate derogation and even the duration and necessity of derogating measures. Gross argues that some derogations, in particular those arising from entrenched emergencies, clearly run 'against the theoretical underpinnings of the derogation system' as a whole.[114]

110 See Chapter 4 and Ryan Sabey, 'Legal witch-hunt of British Army veterans set to be over in MONTHS after it sparked outrage', *The Sun* (London, 14 July 2018); Nicholas Soames, 'Mr Cameron MUST stop these vile witch-hunts against our brave troops: From a former Armed Forces minister who's Winston Churchill's grandson, a blistering call to arms...', *The Daily Mail* (London, 20 January 2016); Robert Mendick, 'Senior police repeatedly warned bosses about Iraq inquiry witch hunt... but were ignored for years', *The Telegraph* (London, 4 March 2018).

111 Thayne Forbes, *The Report of the Al Sweady Inquiry* (2014) HC 818-I at [5.198].

112 Ibid at [5.196].

113 William Gage, *The Report of the Baha Mousa Inquiry* (The Stationery Office 2011).

114 Gross (n. 56) 473.

The Court needs to be more rigorous in evaluating each aspect of derogations and in the particular context of derogations for military operations, evaluating whether the derogations are consistent with other measures of international law. The margin of appreciation should not continue, as it currently does, to function as a means of avoiding scrutiny of difficult issues. If the Court continues to grant a margin of appreciation for derogations, it should at least create a procedural requirement that these issues are subject to effective domestic scrutiny and supervise the domestic authorities on this.[115]

## 7.5 CONCLUSION

Derogations are not a panacea, nor are they an ideal solution to the problems identified throughout this book. Ideally States would not engage in military operations and the security detention and loss of life that accompanies them would not occur. In reality, applying the Convention to military operations presents significant challenges to the Court, contracting States and applicants.

The Convention has an increasingly broad sphere of influence, encompassing military operations at home and abroad. The application of the Convention to military operations is having adverse effects on the consistency of the Court's jurisprudence and the Convention's standards. Academics and practitioners are starting to realise the potential impact it will have on the ability of States to carry out military operations and positive obligations represent a particularly challenging obstacle. Derogations offer States a means of avoiding some of these issues, particularly in relation to Article 2 and 5, by explicitly altering the legal paradigm in which the actions of its State agents are assessed. This is not an abdication of responsibility for protecting human rights, but rather a frank recognition of the State's limited ability to uphold unmodified human rights obligations during military operations.

A number of latent safeguards remain in place to ensure human rights continue to be protected even in the context of a derogation. The fact that each derogation must be consistent with other provisions of international law acts as a safeguard. The non-derogable core of human rights, customary international law, IHL and other bodies of law will provide a safety net against derogating measures which could go too far. Equally, when the Court and domestic courts evaluate whether a measure is consistent with Article 15, they can rule that a derogating measure is inconsistent with the Convention and demand that the State adjust the derogating measures accordingly to ensure that only measures strictly required by the exigencies of the situation pass muster.

[115] Bates (n. 54) 332.

It is clear from the foregoing analysis that a change in policy and practice is required on the part of States and the domestic and international courts before Article 15 can be utilised effectively to cover military operations.

States need to change their attitudes toward derogation. Despite a number of contracting States engaging in military operations in many countries, such as Syria Afghanistan and Georgia, none of these States have derogated from the Convention in respect of these operations. Arguments that the State is not exercising jurisdiction during foreign or domestic military operations, or that IHL completely displaces human rights law, are becoming increasingly untenable before the Court. Derogation represents a viable strategy for States to ensure co-application of IHL and to limit their liability for actions which are consistent with IHL, but may be inconsistent with the Convention. States cannot guarantee human rights in all situations and when derogations are subject to adequate and appropriate supervision, they offer a pragmatic solution during emergency situations. Indeed, by openly disclosing repressive policies and subjecting them to monitoring procedures, States recognise the limits of their ability to guarantee human rights and thereby demonstrate their commitment to them.[116]

The courts, both at the domestic level and at the European Court's level, need to change their approach to Article 15. They will need to interpret Article 15 more flexibly to accommodate different types of military operations, for example, by interpreting war to encompass both IACs and NIACs and conceiving of threats in more abstract or collective terms to facilitate different derogations. This increased flexibility in interpretation must be accompanied by increased scrutiny of the necessity, proportionality and duration of derogating measures to safeguard against impunity and entrenched emergencies that undermine human rights protection.

[116] Helfer, Hafner-Burton and Fariss (n. 35) 680.

# Conclusion

For many years the focus of academic attention has been upon theoretical questions related to the application of the Convention to military operations: whether jurisdiction arises during military operations, whether IHL supersedes human rights law etc. This book has shown that the currency of these debates is waning. Chapter 2 showed that outright denials of jurisdiction by States are becoming increasingly untenable. The principle that the State is obliged to uphold human rights obligations during military operations foreign and domestic is becoming incontrovertible. Chapter 5 showed that international courts are moving toward a position where IHL and human rights are applied simultaneously and away from notions of one body of law superseding the other. As a result, both the Court and States need to consider the practicalities of applying every aspect of the Convention during every kind of military operation, including extra-territorial conflict situations and this book looked squarely at these practicalities.

At the outset two hypotheses were put forward. First, that applying the Convention to military operations would lead the Court to compromise the integrity, coherency and universality of the Convention's guarantees. Second, that applying the Convention to military operations would result in States being held to standards that are extremely difficult, if not impossible, to achieve during many military operations. The book sought evidence of these phenomena in the Court's jurisprudence and by looking at prospective issues arising in this area of law. A number of conclusions can be drawn.

1. **The application of the Convention to all types of military operations, especially extra-territorial military operations, has introduced a great deal of uncertainty into the law.**

The Convention has come to permeate almost every conceivable field of State action, applying to domestic and foreign military operations ranging from internal disturbances through to full blown international armed conflicts. This unprecedented development has left the law in a state of flux. The unity and coherency of the Convention's obligations has been undermined by their application to military operations. As the State's control has receded, the Court has held States to uncertain obligations, compromising both the integrity of the Convention and holding States to impossible obligations. States that have lost de facto control over their territory have been held to unfathomable positive obligations. States operating extra-territorially have been obliged to uphold all of the Convention's guarantees in some instances and only 'relevant' obligations in others, with no clear division between when the State is expected to uphold one or the other. There may be further challenges to the integrity of the obligations in the future as the Court 'divides and tailors' the rights to specific situations. Despite efforts to rationalise the Court's jurisprudence *ex post facto,* it is clear that the jurisprudence has developed in an unprincipled and extemporaneous manner. The sophistries supposedly differentiating the models of jurisdiction from one another belie what is in effect a casuistic approach toward determining State jurisdiction. In many cases there is enduring uncertainty over the scope and content of the State's obligations during military operations, which the Court has done little to dispel.

The Court has been placed in an unenviable position by applicants demanding that it apply the Convention to military operations at home and abroad. Adhering to strict Convention standards for military operations could risk imposing obligations upon States that are impossible to achieve. At the same time, if the Court attenuates the Convention's standards to 'fit' military operations, it risks compromising the comprehensive protection it has painstakingly created over decades. The Court has clearly struggled to reconcile these contradictory impulses and this book has catalogued this struggle, providing a clear insight into the problems presented.

2. **States are being held to, and will continue to be held to, standards that are difficult, if not impossible, to achieve in the context of many military operations.**

The book presented extensive evidence that States were currently being held to standards that were impossible to achieve and likely future problems with applying the Convention to military operations. As Chapter 1 showed, where States had lost de facto control over their own territory, there was a severe disparity between the obligations the Court expected the State to uphold and what the State could realistically achieve. In Chapter 3, the problems upholding the State's positive obligation to protect its soldiers against foreseeable threats to their lives were presented. There were obvious problems with establishing when liability should arise in such cases and figuring out how the modified expectations of protection in the military could be accommodated within the Convention. Chapter 4 noted that the procedural obligation to investigate suspicious deaths or threats to life would be extremely difficult, if not impossible, to uphold during many military operations. The expectation that deployed forces should investigate deaths caused by third parties seemed implausible, while the standards of independence, transparency and quality in investigations demanded by the Convention were virtually impossible for a military force to achieve in many cases. Thus while it may be possible for States to satisfy elements of the multi-faceted protections during some military operations, it would be virtually impossible to satisfy these provisions in their entirety.

### 3. The application of the Convention to military operations has led to compromises in the standards of protection demanded by the Court.

The book also identified many compromises in the standards of protection demanded by the Court for military operations. Chapter 1 showed that once a State's control was undermined, its Convention obligations became uncertain. This led to compromises in both the integrity and coherency of its rules. Domestically, a loss of de facto control resulted in States being held to unspecified positive obligations, which were difficult to infer from the Convention. In the extra-territorial sphere discussed in Chapter 2, the scope of the State's obligations varied depending on the type of extra-territorial jurisdiction it was exercising, whether spatial, personal or personal plus. The absence of clear divisions between these types of jurisdiction meant that it was unclear what obligations the State was obliged to uphold in different circumstances. Indeed, the Court openly accepted the division and tailoring of rights in extra-territorial situations, thereby compromising the integrity and coherency of the Convention's protection.

The book also identified specific examples where substantial changes were made to the Convention rules. In Chapter 3, the rule that force should only be used where absolutely necessary was significantly undermined in many judgments. The Court also condoned attacks in the absence of immediate threats. There is a creeping relativism in the standards accepted by the Court exemplified by the use of ideologically loaded terms from IHL like 'civilian' in their judgments.

These developments pose a significant challenge to the Convention's integrity. By demanding standards that cannot possibly be achieved, the Court encourages disobedience among States. It also undermines the utility of the law and creates expectations of protection among applicants that can never be met in practice. Equally, when the Court does alter the standards to 'fit' military operations, it does not acknowledge that they are making special dispensations specifically for military operations. This makes the adjustments appear arbitrary. It also risks establishing precedents of lower protection, which could be invoked by States outside of the context of military operations.

These issues are a natural by-product of applying HRL to the unusual circumstances of military operations and there is no panacea to resolve them. Although these problems are, to an extent, inevitable, there are ways of mitigating them and better ways of handling the application of the Convention to military operations. Firstly, the Court needs to interpret the provisions of the Convention holistically, consistently and transparently, especially by openly acknowledging the influence of IHL where it is relevant. Secondly, when States recognise that they cannot uphold the obligations in the Convention, they need to derogate from their obligations.

4. **The Court needs to interpret the Convention more consistently, holistically and transparently, especially when it comes to the use of IHL.**

The Court always aspires to provide protection that is practical and effective rather than theoretical and illusory. To achieve this, the Court must look at applying the Convention in its totality. If the Court wants to protect the right to life, it cannot focus exclusively on the absolute necessity test in Article 2 while ignoring other parts of Article 2. By consistently applying the articles in their entirety, the Court will minimise future violations, reduce its case load and offer meaningful protection to individual applicants.

At present the application of IHL in the Court's jurisprudence is far from consistent. The book showed that it was used selectively. In Chapter 3, IHL seemed to have a big influence on some cases concerning indiscriminate attacks and none in other cases. It also influenced decisions even though the Court did not examine whether the threshold for its application had been reached. If the Court is going to rely on IHL, it needs to do so consistently.

Otherwise arbitrary distinctions in the way the Court handles similar cases will continue to arise.

The book also highlighted the Court's implicit application of IHL in many cases. It needs to be more transparent and open about when it is applying IHL because if it does not draw a clear distinction between military operations and other contexts, it risks compromising the integrity of the Convention's peacetime norms. A number of obvious errors in the Court's interpretation and application of IHL were explored in Chapter 6 when the Court openly applied IHL in Article 7 cases. The Court cherry-picked sources that supported its viewpoint, while discounting other views that contradicted it, even when these were in the majority. The Court's judges also seemed to lack expertise in IHL. It is only when IHL is openly applied that these issues become apparent, by implicitly applying IHL, the Court shields itself from much needed scrutiny over how it applies and interprets IHL. Yet, some of the Court's more recent engagements with IHL have been more promising. The interpretation of the Convention in light of IHL in *Hassan* and the more accurate interpretation of IHL evident in *Vasiliauskas* are welcome developments.

**5. States need to derogate from the Convention where possible during military operations.**

States are being, and will continue to be, held to standards that are difficult, if not impossible, to achieve during military operations. If States are concerned about how the Convention will impact upon their ability to carry out military operations, they need to do everything available to them to limit its impact, including using derogations. Chapter 7 made a strong case for utilising derogations where they were available. Chapter 4 demonstrated that derogations can help to reduce the scope of the procedural obligation to a more manageable level so that the State would only be obliged to investigate a death or life-threatening injury where a violation of IHL was suspected. Chapter 5 illustrated that derogations could also help to limit the norm conflicts arising between Article 5 and measures which sanction security detention in IHL and UNSCRs.

Overall, Chapter 7 showed that the true benefit of utilising Article 15 lay in its ability to strike a balance and limit the extent of any modifications to Convention standards. The proportionality requirements of Article 15 would provide States with much needed flexibility during military operations. It would also ensure some oversight of States' actions to guarantee that they do not go beyond what is necessary. Derogations would also offer a natural contextual barrier to any modifications of obligations that the Court undertook.

It would limit their scope to the specific context of the derogation and limit wider impacts on the Court's jurisprudence.

This book has also identified a number of pressing issues for the future. States are likely to change their legal defence strategy in extra-territorial military operations cases in the near future. There will be a shift away from outright denials that the State is exercising jurisdiction, toward arguments over the type of State jurisdiction at issue and the scope and content of their obligations. This will emphasise how the obligations vary depending on the type of jurisdiction exercised and force the Court to confront and rationalise the distinctions between them.

Determining the limits of positive obligations during military operations was a recurring theme throughout this book and it is an area ripe for further study. As the status of many territories like the MRT, TRNC, and Nagorno-Karabakh remain unresolved, more cases invoking the States' positive obligations when they have lost de facto control of territory are likely to come before the Court. It also seems likely that the Court will be confronted with cases invoking positive obligations during extra-territorial military operations. This could take the form of a soldier or his relatives claiming a substantive breach of the soldier's right to life. This could create an existential crisis for positive obligations in the extra-territorial field. The Court will likely apply positive obligations extra-territorially, but in doing so it will curtail their scope and potency, thereby undermining some of their functional benefits.

The high standards that States are held to during military operations will likely fuel the criticism that the Court is exceeding its mandate and that the Convention was never meant to apply in that context. There will likely be a growing trend toward more open and transparent references to IHL in the Court's jurisprudence, especially as the Court is called upon to adjudicate issues arising in the context of IACs. Hopefully the *Varnava* and *Hassan* cases foreshadow a wider and more open reliance on IHL at the Court in the future. The case of *Georgia* v. *Russia (II)* will be a significant bellwether in this process. However, the Court is likely to only explicitly refer to IHL when there is absolutely no doubt that the threshold for its application has been met and it has been invoked by parties to the case in their arguments.

The aim of this book was to examine the practicalities of applying the Convention to military operations. It sought to determine whether States were being held to impossible standards by the Court and whether the Convention's norms were compromised in their application to military operations. We can safely conclude that both of these phenomena are evident in the Court's jurisprudence and that they represent a threat to the Convention system. The analysis indicated changes that could be made to mitigate these phenomena. If the Court interpreted the Convention consistently, openly and transparently engaging with IHL where relevant, it would limit the impact upon its normal peacetime jurisprudence. If States derogated from the Convention obligations in the context of military operations, it would limit their exposure to impossible standards while retaining the Court's oversight of the necessity and proportionality of their actions.

# Bibliography

## A. BOOKS


Arnold R and Quenivet N, *International Humanitarian Law and Human Rights Law: Towards a New Merger in International Law* (Brill 2008).

Bantekas I and Oette L, *International Human Rights Law and Practice* (Cambridge University Press 2013).

Brownlie I, *Principles of Public International Law* (Cambridge University Press 2008).

Carcano A, *The Transformation of Occupied Territory in International Law* (Brill 2015).

Cassese A, *International Law* (Oxford University Press 2005).

Cullen A, *The Concept of Non-international Armed Conflict in International Humanitarian Law* (Cambridge University Press 2010).

da Costa K, *The Extraterritorial Application of Selected Human Rights Treaties* (Brill 2012).

Dembour M-B, *Who Believes in Human Right: Reflections on the European Convention* (Cambridge University Press 2006).

Dickson B, *The European Convention on Human Rights and the Conflict in Northern Ireland* (Oxford University Press 2010).

Dinstein Y, *The Conduct of Hostilities under the Law of International Armed Conflicts* (Cambridge University Press 2004).

Doolan B, *Lawless v. Ireland (1957–1961): The First Case before the European Court of Human Rights: An International Miscarriage of Justice?* (Ashgate 2001).

Doswald-Beck L, *Human Rights in Times of Conflict and Terrorism* (Oxford University Press 2011).

Doswald-Beck L and Henckaerts J-M, *Customary International Humanitarian Law* 2 vols. (Cambridge University Press 2004).

Ferdinandusse W, *Direct Application of International Criminal Law in National Courts* (Asser Press 2006).

Fitzpatrick J, *Human Rights in Crisis: The International System for Protecting Human Rights during States of Emergency* (University of Pennsylvania Press 1994).

Forowicz M, *The Reception of International Law in the European Court of Human Rights* (Oxford University Press 2010).

Gallant K, *The Principle of Legality in International and Comparative Criminal Law* (Cambridge University Press 2009).

Giacca G, *Economic, Social and Cultural Rights in Armed Conflict* (Oxford University Press 2014).

Greer S, *The European Convention on Human Rights: Achievements, Problems, Prospects* (Cambridge University Press 2006).

Grover S, *The European Court of Human Rights as a Pathway to Impunity for International Crimes* (Springer 2010).

Harris D, O'Boyle M, Bates E, Buckley C and Warbrick C, *Law of the European Convention on Human Rights* (3rd edn, Oxford University Press 2014).

Kohen MG, *Secession: International Law Perspectives* (Cambridge University Press 2006).

Koskenniemi M, *Fragmentation of International Law: Difficulties Arising from the Diversification and Expansion of International Law* (International Law Commission 2006).

Leach P, *Taking a Case to the European Court of Human Rights* (Oxford University Press 2005).

Malanczuk P, *Akehurst's Modern Introduction to International Law* (7th edn, Routledge 1997).

Melzer N, *Interpretive Guidance on the Notion of Direct Participation in Hostilities under International Humanitarian Law* (International Committee of the Red Cross 2009).

*Targeted Killing in International Law* (Oxford University Press 2009).

Milano E, *Unlawful Territorial Situations in International Law – Reconciling Effectiveness, Legality and Legitimacy* (Martinus Nijhoff 2006).

Milanovic M, *Extraterritorial Application of Human Rights Treaties: Law, Principles, and Policy* (Oxford University Press 2011).

Mowbray A, *The Development of Positive Obligations under the European Convention on Human Rights by the European Court of Human Rights* (Hart 2004).

Oppenheim L, Jennings R and Watts A, *Oppenheim's International Law Vol. 1, pt. 2–4, Peace* (Longman 1992).

Pictet J, *Development and Principles of International Humanitarian Law* (Martinus Nijhoff 1985).

Rainey B, Wicks E and Ovey C, *Jacobs, White and Ovey: The European Convention on Human Rights* (7th edn, Oxford University Press 2017).

Schabas W, *Genocide in International Law: The Crime of Crimes* (2nd edn, Cambridge University Press 2009).

Shaw M, *International Law* (Cambridge University Press 2008).

Sivakumaran S, *The Law of Non-International Armed Conflict* (Oxford University Press 2012).

Tomuschat C, Lagrange E and Oeter S, *The Right to Life* (Martinus Nijhoff Publishers 2010).

Van Der Wilt H and Vervliet J, *The Genocide Convention: The Legacy of 60 Years* (Brill 2012).

Wicks E, *The Right to Life and Conflicting Interests* (Oxford University Press 2010).

Xenos D, *The Positive Obligations of the State under the European Convention of Human Rights* (Routledge 2012).

## B. EDITED BOOKS


Ben-Naftali O (ed) *International Humanitarian Law and International Human Rights Law* (Oxford University Press 2012).

Buyse A (ed) *Margins of Conflict: The ECHR and Transitions to and from Armed Conflict* (Intersentia 2011).

Kolb R and Gaggioli G (eds), *Research Handbook on Human Rights and Humanitarian Law* (Elgar 2013).

Vidmar J and De Wet E (eds), *Hierarchy in International Law: The Place of Human Rights* (Oxford University Press 2012).

Zwaak L and others (eds), *Theory and Practice of the European Convention on Human Rights* (5th edn, Intersentia 2018).


## C. JOURNAL ARTICLES


Abdel-Monem T, 'Precedent of the European Convention on Human Rights to the CIA's High Value Detainees Program in and through Europe' (2008) 31 *Suffolk Transnational Law Review* 45–73.

Abresch W, 'A Human Rights Law of Internal Armed Conflict: The European Court of Human Rights in Chechnya' (2005) 16 *European Journal of International Law* 741–67.

Acevedo JPP-L, 'The Role of the Inter-American Court of Human Rights in dealing with Armed Conflicts and Post-Conflict Reconstruction: Jurisprudential Analysis and Some Comparative Considerations' (2009) 7 *International Journal of Civil Society Law* 7–21.

Akande D, 'The International Court of Justice and the Security Council: Is there Room for Judicial Control of Decisions of the Political Organs of the United Nations?' (1997) 46 *International & Comparative Law Quarterly* 309–43.

Allain J, 'Derogation from the European Convention of Human Rights in the Light of "Other Obligations under International Law"' [2005] *European Human Rights Law Review* 480–98.

Altiparmak K, 'Bankovic: An Obstacle to the Application of the European Convention on Human Rights in Iraq?' (2004) 9 *Journal of Conflict & Security Law* 213–51.

Ambos K, 'The Crime of Genocide and the Principle of Legality under Article 7 of the European Convention on Human Rights' (2017) 17(1) *Human Rights Law Review* 175–86.

Andenas M and Bjorge E, 'Human Rights and Acts by Troops Abroad: Rights and Jurisdictional Restrictions' (2012) 18 *European Public Law* 473–92.

Balendra N, 'Defining Armed Conflict' (2008) 29 *Cardozo Law Review* 2461–516.

Basch FF, 'The Doctrine of the Inter-American Court of Human Rights Regarding States' Duty to Punish Human Rights Violations and its Dangers' (2007) 23 *American University International Law Review* 195–229.

Bassiouni MC, 'Unlawful Seizures and Irregular Rendition Devices as Alternatives to Extradition' (1974) 7 *Vanderbilt Journal of Transnational Law* 25–70.

'Searching for Peace and Achieving Justice: The Need for Accountability' (1996) 59 *Law & Contemporary Problems* 9–28.

Bates E, 'The Al-Adsani Case, State Immunity and the International Legal Prohibition on Torture' (2003) 3 *Human Rights Law Review* 193–224.

'A 'Public Emergency Threatening the Life of the Nation'? The United Kingdom's Derogation from the European Convention on Human Rights of 18 December 2001 and the 'A' case' (2005) 76 *British Yearbook of International Law* 245–335.

'Avoiding Legal Obligations Created by Human Rights Treaties' (2008) 57 *International & Comparative Law Quarterly* 751–88.

Benison A, 'War Crimes: A Human Rights Approach to a Humanitarian Law Problem at the International Criminal Court' (2000) 88 *Georgetown Law Journal* 141–75.

Bennoune K, 'Toward a Human Rights Approach to Armed Conflict: Iraq 2003' (2004) 11 *UC Davis Journal of International Law and Policy* 171–228.

Besson S, 'The Extraterritoriality of the European Convention on Human Rights: Why Human Rights Depend on Jurisdiction and What Jurisdiction Amounts to' (2012) 25 *Leiden Journal of International Law* 857–84.

Bethlehem D, 'The Relationship between International Humanitarian Law and International Human Rights Law in Situations of Armed Conflict' (2013) 2 *Cambridge Journal of International and Comparative Law* 180–95.

Bhuta N, 'Conflicting International Obligations and the Risk of Torture and Unfair Trial: Critical Comments on R. (Al-Saadoon and Mufdhi) v Secretary of State for Defence and Al-Saadoon and Mufdhi v United Kingdom' (2009) 7 *Journal of International Criminal Justice* 1133–47.

Bianchi A, 'Human Rights and the Magic of Jus Cogens' (2008) 19 *European Journal of International Law* 491–508.

Booms T and Van der Kroon C, 'Inconsistent Deliberations or Deliberate Inconsistencies? The Consistency of the ECtHR's Assessment of Convictions based on International Norms' (2011) 7 *Utrecht Law Review* 156–79.

Bowring B, 'Fragmentation, Lex Specialis and the Tensions in the Jurisprudence of the European Court of Human Rights' (2009) 14 *Journal of Conflict & Security Law* 485–98.

Burgorgue-Larsen L and Úbeda de Torres A, '"War" in the Jurisprudence of the Inter-American Court of Human Rights' (2011) 33 *Human Rights Quarterly* 148–74.

Buyse A, 'Dangerous Expressions: The ECHR, Violence and Free Speech' (2014) 63(2) *International & Comparative Law Quarterly* 491–503.

Byron C, 'A Blurring of the Boundaries: The Application of International Humanitarian Law by Human Rights Bodies' (2006–2007) 47 *Virginia Journal of International Law* 839–96.

Cassel D, 'Pretrial and Preventive Detention of Suspected Terrorists: Options and Constraints under International Law' (2008) 98 *The Journal of Criminal Law and Criminology* 811–52.

Cassese A, 'Balancing the Prosecution of Crimes against Humanity and Non-retroactivity of Criminal Law' (2006) 4 *Journal of International Criminal Justice* 410–18.

Cassimatis A, 'International Humanitarian Law, International Human Rights Law, and Fragmentation of International Law' (2007) 56 *International & Comparative Law Quarterly* 623–39.

Cerna C, 'Out of Bounds? The Approach of the Inter-American System for the Promotion and Protection of Human Rights to the Extraterritorial Application of Human Rights Law' [2006] 6/2006 Center for Human Rights and Global Justice Working Papers 1.

'The History of the Inter-American System's Jurisprudence as Regards Situations of Armed Conflict' (2011) 2 *International Humanitarian Legal Studies* 3–52.

Cerone J, 'Human Dignity in the Line of Fire: The Application of International Human Rights Law During Armed Conflict, Occupation, and Peace Operations' (2006) 39 *Vanderbilt Journal of Transnational Law* 1447–510.

'Jurisdiction and Power: The Intersection of Human Rights Law and the Law of Non-International Armed Conflict in an Extraterritorial Context' (2007) 40 *Israel Law Review* 396–452.

Chadwick E and Samuel K, 'In Faint Praise of the Derogating Will' (2017) 26 *Nottingham Law Journal* 87–102.

Chevalier-Watts J, 'Effective Investigations under Article 2 of the European Convention on Human Rights: Securing the Right to Life or an Onerous Burden on a State?' (2010) 21 *European Journal of International Law* 701–21.

'Military Operations and the Right to Life: The Uneasy Bedfellows' (2011) 5 *Human Rights and International Legal Discourse* 207–32.

Chinkin C, 'Jus Cogens, Article 103 of the UN Charter and Other Hierarchical Techniques of Conflict Solution' (2008) 17 *Finnish Yearbook of International Law* 63–82.

Clarke A, 'Rendition to Torture: A Critical Legal History' (2009–2010) 62 *Rutgers Law Review* 1–74.

Claude O, 'A Comparative Approach to Enforced Disappearances in the Inter-American Court of Human Rights and the European Court of Human Rights Jurisprudence' (2010) 5 *Intercultural Human Rights Law Review* 407–62.

Cleveland SH, 'Embedded International Law and the Constitution Abroad' (2010) 110 *Columbia Law Review* 225–87.

Corn G, 'Mixing Apples and Hand Grenades: The Logical Limits of Applying Human Rights Norms to Armed Conflict' (2010) 1 *International Humanitarian Legal Studies* 52–94.

Corn G and Corn G, 'The Law of Operational Targeting: Viewing the LOAC through an Operational Lens' (2012) 47 *Texas International Law Journal* 337–80.

Cowan A, 'A New Watershed? Re-evaluating Bankovic in Light of Al-Skeini' (2012) 1 *Cambridge Journal of International and Comparative Law* 213–27.

Cowell F, 'Sovereignty and the Question of Derogation: An Analysis of Article 15 of the ECHR and the Absence of a Derogation Clause in the ACHPR' (2013) 1 *Birkbeck Law Review* 135–62.

Crawford J, 'Draft Articles on Responsibility of States for Internationally Wrongful Acts, with commentaries' (2001) 2 *Yearbook of the International Law Commission*.

Cullen A and Wheatley S, 'The Human Rights of Individuals in De Facto Regimes under the European Convention on Human Rights' (2013) 13 *Human Rights Law Review* 691–728.

Cusack C, 'We've Talked the Talk, Time to Walk the Walk: Meeting International Human Rights Law Standards for U.S. Military Investigations' (2013) 217 *Military Law Review* 48–90.

de Sanctis F, 'The Practice of National and International Court on Transnational Seizure: Is a Fair Balance between Human Rights and Accountability Possible?' (2004) 22 *Netherlands Quarterly of Human Rights* 529–57.

'What Duties Do States have with Regards to the Rules of Engagement and the Training of Security Forces under Article 2 of the European Convention on Human Rights?' (2006) 10 *International Journal of Human Rights* 31–44.

de Zayas A, 'Human Rights and Indefinite Detention' (2005) 87 *International Review of the Red Cross* 15–38.

Dennis M, 'Application of Human Rights Treaties Extraterritorially in Times of Armed Conflict and Military Occupation' (2005) 99 *American Journal of International Law* 119–41.

'Application of Human Rights Treaties Extraterritorially to Detention of Combatants and Security Internees: Fuzzy Thinking All Around?' (2006) 12 *ILSA Journal of International & Comparative Law* 459–80.

Doswald-Beck L, 'International Humanitarian Law and the International Court of Justice on the Legality of the Threat or Use of Nuclear Weapons' (1997) 37 *International Review of the Red Cross* 35–55.

'The Right to Life in Armed Conflict: Does International Humanitarian Law Provide All the Answers?' (2006) 88 *International Review of the Red Cross* 881–904.

Draper G, 'Human Rights and the Law of War' (1971–1972) 12 *Virginia Journal of International Law* 326–42.

Droege C, 'The Interplay between International Humanitarian Law and International Human Rights Law in Situations of Armed Conflict' (2007) 40 *Israel Law Review* 310–55.

'Elective Affinities? Human Rights and Humanitarian Law' (2008) 90 *International Review of the Red Cross* 501–48.

'Transfers of Detainees: Legal Framework, Non-refoulement and Contemporary Challenges' (2008) 90 *International Review of the Red Cross* 669–701.

Droege C and Arimatsu L, 'The European Convention on Human Rights and International Humanitarian Law: Conference Report' (2009) 12 *Yearbook of International Humanitarian Law* 435–49.

Duttwiler M, 'Authority, Control and Jurisdiction in the Extraterritorial Application of the European Convention on Human Rights' (2012) 30 *Netherlands Quarterly of Human Rights* 137–62.

El Zeidy M, 'The ECHR and States of Emergency: Article 15 – A Domestic Power of Derogation from Human Rights Obligations' (2003) 4 *San Diego International Law Journal* 277–318.

Erdal U, 'Burden and Standard of Proof in Proceedings under the European Convention' (2001) 26 *European Law Review* 68–85.

Fabbrini F, 'The European Court of Human Rights, Extraordinary Renditions and the Right to the Truth: Ensuring Accountability for Gross Human Rights Violations Committed in the Fight against Terrorism' (2014) 14 *Human Rights Law Review* 85–106.

Farrior S, 'State Responsibility for Human Rights Abuses by Non-State Actors' (1998) 92 *American Society of International Law Proceedings* 299–303.

Feinrider M, 'Extraterritorial Abductions: A Newly Developing International Standard' (1980–1981) 14 *Akron Law Review* 27–47.

Feinstein B, 'The Applicability of the Regime of Human Rights in Times of Armed Conflict and Particularly to Occupied Territories: The Case of Israel's Security Barrier' (2005–2006) 4 *Northwestern University Journal of International Human Rights* 238–302.

Ford S, 'Crimes against Humanity at the Extraordinary Chambers in the Courts of Cambodia: Is a Connection with Armed Conflict Required?' (2007) 24 *University of California Los Angeles Pacific Basin Law Journal* 125–200.

Forster A, 'British Judicial Engagement and the Juridification of the Armed Forces' (2012) 88 *International Affairs* 283–300.

Garraway C, '"To Kill or Not to Kill?' – Dilemmas on the Use of Force' (2010) 14 *Journal of Conflict and Security Law* 499–510.

Gibney M, Tomagevski K and Vedsted-Hansen J, 'Transnational State Responsibility for Violations of Human Rights' (1999) 12 *Harvard Human Rights Journal* 267–95.

Gill T, 'Legal and Some Political Limitations on the Power of the UN Security Council to Exercise its Enforcement Powers under Chapter VII of the Charter' (1995) 26 *Netherlands Yearbook of International Law* 33–138.

Gillard E-C, 'Reparation for Violations of International Humanitarian Law' (2003) 85 *International Review of the Red Cross* 529–53.

'There's No Place Like Home: States' Obligations in Relation to Transfers of Persons' (2008) 90 *International Review of the Red Cross* 703–50.

Gillet M and Schuster M, 'Fast-track Justice: The Special Tribunal for Lebanon Defines Terrorism' (2011) 9 *Journal of International Criminal Justice* 989–1020.

Gondek M, 'Extraterritorial Application of the European Convention on Human Rights: Territorial Focus in the Age of Globalization?' (2005) 52 *Netherlands International Law Review* 347–87.

Graven J, 'Les Crimes Contre l'Humanité' (1950) 76 *Recueil des Cours de l'Académie de Droit International de La Haye* 427–607.

Green L, 'The Unified Use of Force Rule and the Law of Armed Conflict: A Reply to Professor Martin' (2002) 65 *Saskatchewan Law Review* 427–50.

Greene A, 'Separating Normalcy from Emergency: The Jurisprudence of Article 15 of the European Convention on Human Rights' (2011) 12 *German Law Journal* 1764–85.

Greenwood C, 'International Humanitarian Law and the Tadic Case' (1996) 7 *European Journal of International Law* 265–83.

Greppi E, 'The Evolution of Individual Criminal Responsibility under International Law' (1999) 81 *International Review of the Red Cross* 531–53.

Gross A, 'Human Proportions: Are Human Rights the Emperor's New Clothes of the International Law of Occupation?' (2007) 18 *European Journal of International Law* 1–35.

Gross O, '"Once More unto the Breach": The Systemic Failure of Applying the European Convention on Human Rights to Entrenched Emergencies' (1998) 23 *Yale Journal of International Law* 437–501.

Guild E, 'Inside Out or Outside In? Examining Human Rights in Situations of Armed Conflict' (2007) 9 *International Community Law Review* 33–58.

Habteslasie A, 'Derogation in Time of War: The Application of Article 15 of the ECHR in Extraterritorial Armed Conflicts' (2016) 21(4) *Judicial Review* 302–16.

Haijer F, Ryngaert C, 'Reflections on Jaloud v. the Netherlands Jurisdictional Consequences and Resonance in Dutch Society' (2015) 19 *Journal of International Peacekeeping* 174–89.

Hakimi M, 'State Bystander Responsibility' (2010) 21 *European Journal of International Law* 341–85.

'A Functional Approach to Targeting and Detention' (2012) 110 *Michigan Law Review* 1365–420.

Hampson F, 'Using International Human Rights Machinery to Enforce the International Law of Armed Conflicts' (1992) 31 *Military Law and Law of War Review* 117–47.

'The Relationship between International Humanitarian Law and Human Rights Law from the Perspective of a Human Rights Treaty Body' (2008) 90 *International Review of the Red Cross* 549–72.

'Is Human Rights Law of Any Relevance to Military Operations in Afghanistan?' (2009) 85 *US Naval War College International Law Studies* 485–524.

'Direct Participation in Hostilities and the Interoperability of the Law of Armed Conflict and Human Rights Law' (2011) 87 *US Naval War College International Law Studies* 187–213.

Hansen M, 'Preventing the Emasculation of Warfare: Halting the Expansion of Human Rights into Armed Conflict' (2007) 194 *Military Law Review* 1–65.

Happold M, 'Bankovic v Belgium and the Territorial Scope of the European Convention on Human Rights' (2003) 3 *Human Rights Law Review* 77–90.

Hathaway OA and Others, 'Human Rights Abroad: When Do Human Rights Treaty Obligations Apply Extraterritorially?' (2011) 43 *Arizona State Law Journal* 389–426.

Hays Parks W, 'Part IX of the ICRC "Direct Participation in Hostilities" Study: No Mandate, No Expertise, and Legally Incorrect' (2010) 42 *International Law and Politics* 769–830.

Heintze H-J, 'On the Relationship between Human Rights Law Protection and International Humanitarian Law' (2004) 86 *International Review of the Red Cross* 789–814.

Helfer L, 'Redesigning the European Court of Human Rights: Embeddedness as a Deep Structural Principle of the European Human Rights Regime' (2008) 19 *European Journal of International Law* 125–59.

Helfer L, Hafner-Burton E and Fariss C, 'Emergency and Escape: Explaining Derogations from Human Rights Treaties' (2011) 65 *International Organization* 673–707.

Hendin S, 'Detainees in Afghanistan: The Balance between Human Rights and International Humanitarian Law for Foreign Military Forces' (2008) 14(3) *Tilburg Law Review* 249–71.

Hollenberg S, 'The Diverging Approaches of the European Court of Human Rights in the cases of Nada and Al-Dulimi' (2015) 64(2) *International & Comparative Law Quarterly* 445–60.

Horowitz J, 'Transferring Wartime Detainees and a State's Responsibility to Prevent Torture' (2012) 2 *National Security Law Brief* 43–66.

Jobst V, 'Is the Wearing of the Enemy's Uniform a Violation of the Laws of War?' (1941) 35 *American Journal of International Law* 435–43.

Junor G, 'A Soldier's (Human) Rights When Fighting Abroad: The Supreme Court Decides' (2013) 37 *Scots Law Times* 251–6.

Kamchibekova D, 'State Responsibility for Extraterritorial Human Rights Violations' (2007) 13 *Buffalo Human Rights Law Review* 87–150.

Kamminga M, 'Is the European Convention on Human Rights Sufficiently Equipped to Cope with Gross and Systematic Violations?' (1994) 12 *Netherlands Quarterly of Human Rights* 153–64.

Kavanaugh K, 'Policing the Margins: Rights Protection and the European Court of Human Rights' [2006] *European Human Rights Law Review* 422–44.

Kelsen H, 'Will the Judgment in the Nuremberg Trial Constitute a Precedent in International Law?' (1947) 1 *International Law Quarterly* 153–71.

King H, 'The Extraterritorial Human Rights Obligations of States' (2009) 9 *Human Rights Law Review* 521–56.

Koroteev K, 'Legal Remedies for Human Rights Violations in the Armed Conflict in Chechnya: The Approach of the European Court of Human Rights in Context' (2010) 1 *International Humanitarian Legal Studies* 275–303.

Kretzmer D, 'Rethinking the Application of IHL in Non-International Armed Conflicts' (2009) 42 *Israel Law Review* 8–45.

Krieger H, 'A Conflict of Norms the Relationship between Humanitarian Law and Human Rights Law in the ICRC Customary Law Study' (2006) 11 *Journal of Conflict & Security Law* 265–92.

'After Al-Jedda: Detention, Derogation, and an Enduring Dilemma' (2011) 50 *Military Law and the Law of War Review* 419–45.

Lamp N, 'Conceptions of War and Paradigms of Compliance: The 'New War' Challenge to International Humanitarian Law' (2011) 16 *Journal of Conflict & Security Law* 225–62.

Landais C and Bass L, 'Reconciling the Rules of International Humanitarian Law with the Rules of European Human Rights Law' (2015) 97 *International Review of the Red Cross* 1295–311.

Larsen KM, 'Attribution of Conduct in Peace Operations: The "Ultimate Authority and Control" Test' (2008) 19 *European Journal of International Law* 509–31.

'Territorial Non-application of the European Convention on Human Rights' (2009) 78 *Nordic Journal of International Law* 73–94.

Lauterpacht H, 'The Law of Nations and the Punishment of War Crimes' (1944) 21 *British Yearbook of International Law* 58–95.

Leach P, 'The British Military in Iraq – The Applicability of the Espace Juridique Doctrine under the European Convention on Human Rights' [2005] *Public Law* 448–58.

'The Chechen Conflict: Analysing the Oversight of the European Court of Human Rights' [2008] *European Human Rights Law Review* 732–61.

Lester A and Beattie K, 'Risking Torture' [2005] *European Human Rights Law Review* 565–71.

Loucaides L, 'Determining the Extra-territorial Effect of the European Convention: Facts, Jurisprudence and the Bankovic case' [2006] *European Human Rights Law Review* 391–407.

Lubell N, 'Challenges in Applying Human Rights Law to Armed Conflict' (2005) 87 *International Review of the Red Cross* 737–54.

'Parallel Application of International Humanitarian Law and International Human Rights Law: An Examination of the Debate' (2007) 40 *Israel Law Review* 648–60.

'Human Rights Obligations in Military Occupation' (2012) 94 *International Review of the Red Cross* 317–37.

MacDonald R, 'Derogations under Article 15 of the European Convention on Human Rights' (1998) 36 *Columbia Journal of Transnational Law* 225–67.

Malksoo L, 'Soviet Genocide? Communist Mass Deportations in the Baltic States and International Law' (2001) 14 *Leiden Journal of International Law* 757–87.

Mallory C, 'European Court of Human Rights Al-Skeini and Others v United Kingdom (Application No 55721/07) Judgment of 7 July 2011' (2012) 61 *International & Comparative Law Quarterly* 301–12.

Mariniello T, 'The 'Nuremberg Clause' and Beyond: Legality Principle and Sources of International Criminal Law in the European Court's Jurisprudence' (2008) 82 *Nordic Journal of International Law* 221–48.

Martin F, 'Using International Human Rights Law for Establishing a Unified Use of Force Rule in the Law of Armed Conflict' (2001) 64 *Saskatchewan Law Review* 347–96.

Mastorodimos K, 'The Utility and Limits of International Human Rights Law and International Humanitarian Law's Parallel Applicability' (2009) 5 *Review of International Law and Politics* 129–52.

Mavronicola N, 'Taking Life and Liberty Seriously: Reconsidering Criminal Liability Under Article 2 of the ECHR' (2017) 80(6) *Modern Law Review* 1026–51.

McGoldrick D, 'The Interface between Public Emergency Powers and International Law' (2004) 2 *International Journal of Constitutional Law* 380–430.

'The Boundaries of Justiciability' (2010) 59 *International & Comparative Law Quarterly* 981–1020.

McLaughlin R, 'The Law of Armed Conflict and International Human Rights Law: Some Paradigmatic Differences and Operational Implications' (2010) 13 *Yearbook of International Humanitarian Law* 213–43.

Meron T, 'On the Inadequate Reach of Humanitarian and Human Rights Law and the Need for a New Instrument' (1983) 77 *American Journal of International Law* 589–606.

'The Humanization of Humanitarian Law' (2000) 94 *American Journal of International Law* 239–78.

'Revival of Customary Humanitarian Law' (2005) 99 *American Journal of International Law* 817–34.

Michaelsen C, 'The Renaissance of Non-refoulement? The Othman (Abu Qatada) Decision of the European Court of Human Rights' (2012) 61 *International & Comparative Law Quarterly* 750–65.

Milanovic M, 'From Compromise to Principle: Clarifying the Concept of State Jurisdiction in Human Rights Treaties' (2008) 8 *Human Rights Law Review* 411–48.

'Norm Conflict in International Law: Whither Human Rights?' (2009a) 20 *Duke Journal of Comparative & International Law* 69–132.

'A Norm Conflict Perspective on the Relationship between International Humanitarian Law and Human Rights Law' (2009b) 14 *Journal of Conflict & Security Law* 459–84.

'Al-Skeini and Al-Jedda in Strasbourg' (2012) 23 *European Journal of International Law* 121–40.

Milanovic M and Papic T, 'As Bad as It Gets: The European Court of Human Rights's Behrami and Saramati Decision and General International Law' (2009) 58 *International & Comparative Law Quarterly* 267–96.

Miller S, 'Revisiting Extraterritorial Jurisdiction: A Territorial Justification for Extraterritorial Jurisdiction under the European Convention' (2009) 20 *European Journal of International Law* 1223–46.

Miltner B, 'Broadening the Scope of Extraterritorial Application of the European Convention on Human Rights?' [2007] *European Human Rights Law Review* 172–82.

'Revisiting Extraterritoriality after Al-Skeini: The ECHR and Its Lessons' (2012) 33 *Michigan Journal of International Law* 693–748.

Modirzadeh N, 'The Dark Sides of Convergence: A Pro-civilian Critique of the Extraterritorial Application of Human Rights Law in Armed Conflict' (2010) 86 *US Naval War College International Law Studies* 349–410.

Mole N, 'Issa v Turkey: Delineating the Extra Territorial Effect of the European Convention on Human Rights?' [2005] *European Human Rights Law Review* 86–91.

Moor L and Simpson B, 'Ghosts of Colonialism in the European Convention on Human Rights' (2005) 76 *British Yearbook of International Law* 121–93.

Mowbray A, 'Duties of Investigation under the European Convention on Human Rights' (2002) 51 *International & Comparative Law Quarterly* 437–48.

Mullender R, 'Military Operations, Fairness and the British State' (2014) 130 *Law Quarterly Review* 28–33.

Murphy C, 'The Principle of Legality in Criminal Law under the European Convention on Human Rights' [2010] *European Human Rights Law Review* 192–207.

Mus J, 'Conflicts between Treaties in International Law' (1998) 45 *Netherlands International Law Review* 208–32.

Naert F, 'The European Court of Human Rights' Al-Jedda and Al-Skeini Judgments: An Introduction and Some Reflections' (2011) 50 *Military Law and Law of War Review* 315–20.

Ni Aolain F, 'The No-Gaps Approach to Parallel Application in the Context of the War on Terror' (2007) 40 *Israel Law Review* 563–91.

Ní Aoláin F and Gross O, 'From Discretion to Scrutiny: Revisiting the Application of the Margin of Appreciation Doctrine in the Context of Article 15 of the European Convention on Human Rights' (2001) 23 *Human Rights Quarterly* 625–49.

Noll G, 'Diplomatic Assurances and the Silence of Human Rights Law' (2006) 7 *Melbourne Journal of International Law* 104–26.

Norris R and Reiton P, 'The Suspension of Guarantees: A Comparative Analysis of the American Convention on Human Rights and the Constitutions of the States Parties' (1980) 30 *American University Law Review* 189–224.

Nzelibe J, 'The Uniqueness of Foreign Affairs' (2004) 89 *Iowa Law Review* 941–1010.

Olson L, 'Practical Challenges of Implementing the Complementarity between International Humanitarian and Human Rights Law – Demonstrated by the Procedural Regulation of Internment in Non-international Armed Conflict' (2009) 40 *Case Western Reserve University's Journal of International Law* 437–62.

Orakhelashvili A, 'Restrictive Interpretation of Human Rights Treaties in the Recent Jurisprudence of the European Court of Human Rights' (2003) 14 *European Journal of International Law* 529–68.

'The Interaction between Human Rights and Humanitarian Law: Fragmentation, Conflict, Parallelism, or Convergence?' (2008) 19 *European Journal of International Law* 161–82.

Papastavradis E, 'European Court of Human Rights: Medvedyev *et al* v France (Grand Chamber, application no.3394/03) Judgment of 29 March 2010' (2010) 59 *International & Comparative Law Quarterly* 867–82.

Paust J, 'The Right to Life in Human Rights Law and the Law of War' (2002) 65 *Saskatchewan Law Review* 411–26.

Pejic J, 'Procedural Principles and Safeguards for Internment/Administrative Detention in Armed Conflict and Other Situations of Violence' (2005) 87 *International Review of the Red Cross* 375–92.

'The European Court of Human Rights' Al-Jedda Judgment: The Oversight of International Humanitarian Law' (2011) 93 *International Review of the Red Cross* 837–51.

Phillips G, 'Rules of Engagement: A Primer' [1993] *The Army Lawyer* 4–27.

Pinzauti G, 'The European Court of Human Rights' Incidental Application of International Criminal Law and Humanitarian Law: A Critical Discussion of Kononov v. Latvia' (2008) 6 *Journal of International Criminal Justice* 1043–60.

Pocar F, 'Persecution as a Crime under International Criminal Law' (2008) 2 *Journal of National Security Law and Policy* 355–66.

Prud'homme N, 'Lex Specialis: Oversimplifying a More Complex and Multifaceted Relationship?' (2007) 40 *Israel Law Review* 356–95.

Raible L, 'The Extraterritoriality of the ECHR: Why Jaloud and Pisari Should be Read as Game Changers' [2016] *European Human Rights Law Review* 161–8.

Randall K, 'Universal Jurisdiction under International Law' (1988) 66 *Texas Law Review* 785–841.

Reidy A, 'The Approach of the European Commission and Court of Human Rights to International Humanitarian Law' (1998) 38 *International Review of the Red Cross* 513–29.

Reidy A, Hampson F and Boyle K, 'Gross Violations of Human Rights: Invoking the European Convention on Human Rights in the Case of Turkey' (1997) 15 *Netherlands Quarterly of Human Rights* 161–73.

Reitiker D, 'Strange Bedfellows? The Cross-Fertilization of Human Rights and Arms Control' (2014) 3(2) *Cyprus Human Rights Law Review* 130–59.

Roach A, 'Rules of Engagement' (1988) 14 *Syracuse Journal of International Law and Commerce* 865–78.

Rona G, 'Interesting Times for International Humanitarian Law: Challenges from the "War on Terror"' (2003) 27 *Fletcher Forum of World Affairs* 55–74.

Rooney J, 'Extraterritorial Derogation from the European Convention on Human Rights in the UK' [2016] *European Human Rights Law Review* 656–63.

Rowe P, 'The Obligation of a State under International Law to Protect Members of Its Own Armed Forces during Armed Conflict or Occupation' (2006) 9 *Yearbook of International Humanitarian Law* 3–24.

Rygaert C, 'Clarifying the Extraterritorial Application of the European Convention on Human Rights' (2012) 28 *Utrecht Journal of International and European Law* 57–60.

Sardaro P, 'Jus Non Dicere for Allegations of Serious Violations of Human Rights: Questionable Trends in the Recent Case Law of the Strasbourg Court' [2003] *European Human Rights Law Review* 601–30.

Sari A, 'Jurisdiction and International Responsibility in Peace Support Operations: The Behrami and Saramati Cases' (2008) 8 *Human Rights Law Review* 151–70.

'Untangling Extra-Territorial Jurisdiction from International Responsibility in Jaloud v. Netherlands: Old Problem, New Solutions?' (2014) 53 *Military Law and Law of War Review* 287–318.

Sassoli M, 'The International Legal Framework for Stability Operations: When May International Forces Attack or Detain Someone in Afghanistan?' (2009) 85 *US Naval War College International Law Studies* 431–64.

Sassoli M and Olson L, 'The Relationship between International Humanitarian and Human Rights Law Where It Matters: Admissible Killing and Internment of Fighters in Non-International Armed Conflicts' (2008) 90 *International Review of the Red Cross* 599–628.

Schabas W, 'Problems of International Codification – Were the Atrocities in Cambodia and Kosovo Genocide?' (2001) 35 *New England Law Review* 287–302.

'Retroactive Application of the Genocide Convention' (2010) 4 *University of St Thomas Journal of Law and Public Policy* 36–59.

'Synergy or Fragmentation? International Criminal Law and the European Convention on Human Rights' (2011) 9 *Journal of International Criminal Justice* 609–32.

Schaefer M, 'Al-Skeini and the Elusive Parameters of Extraterritorial Jurisdiction' [2011] *European Human Rights Law Review* 566–81.

Schmitt M, 'Investigating Violations of International Law in Armed Conflict' (2011) 2 *Harvard National Security Journal* 31–84.

Schwelb E, 'Crimes against Humanity' (1946) 23 *British Yearbook of International Law* 178–226.

Scobbie I, 'Principle or Pragmatics? The Relationship between Human Rights Law and the Law of Armed Conflict' (2009) 14 *Journal of Conflict & Security Law* 449–58.

Semmelman J, 'Due Process, International Law, and Jurisdiction over Criminal Defendants Abducted Extraterritorially: The Ker-Frisbie Doctrine Reexamined' (1992) 30 *Columbia Journal of Transnational Law* 513–76.

Shahabuddeen M, 'Does the Principle of Legality Stand in the Way of Progressive Development of Law?' (2004) 2 *Journal of International Criminal Justice* 1007–17.

Shany Y, 'Taking Universality Seriously: A Functional Approach to Extraterritoriality in International Human Rights Law' (2013) 7 *The Law & Ethics of Human Rights* 47–71.

Sheeran S, 'Reconceptualizing States of Emergency under International Human Rights Law: Theory, Legal Doctrine, and Politics' (2012–2013) 34 *Michigan Journal of International Law* 491–558.

Shelton D, 'Normative Hierarchy in International Law' (2006) 100 *American Journal of International Law* 291–323.

Sivakumaran S, 'Re-envisaging the International Law of Internal Armed Conflict' (2011) 22 *European Journal of International Law* 219–64.

Skinner S, 'Deference, Proportionality and the Margin of Appreciation in Lethal Force Case Law under Article 2 ECHR' [2014] *European Human Rights Law Review* 32–8.

Skoutaris N, 'Building Transitional Justice Mechanisms without a Peace Settlement: A Critical Appraisal of Recent Case Law of the Strasbourg Court on the Cyprus Issue' (2010) 35 *European Law Review* 720–33.

Solomon S, 'Targeted Killings and the Soldiers' Right to Life' (2007–2008) 14 *ILSA Journal of International & Comparative Law* 99–120.

Stubbins Bates E, 'Hassan v. The United Kingdom' (2015) 54(1) *International Legal Materials* 83–129.

Talmon S, 'The Responsibility of Outside Powers for Acts of Secessionist Entities' (2009) 58 *International & Comparative Law Quarterly* 493–517.

Tamura E, 'The Isayeva Cases of the European Court of Human Rights: The Application of International Humanitarian Law and Human Rights Law in Non-International Armed Conflicts' (2011) 10 *Chinese Journal of International Law* 129–40.

Taqi I, 'Adjudicating Disappearance Cases in Turkey: An Argument for Adopting the Inter-American Court of Human Rights' Approach' (2000) 24 *Fordham International Law Journal* 940–87.

Tittemore B, 'Guantanamo Bay and the Precautionary Measures of the Inter-American Commission on Human Rights: A Case for International Oversight in the Struggle against Terrorism' (2006) 6 *Human Rights Law Review* 378–402.

Trilsch M and Ruth A, 'Bankovic v Belgium' (2003) 97 *American Journal of International Law* 168–72.

van der Wilt H and Lyngdorf S, 'Procedural Obligations under the European Convention on Human Rights: Useful Guidelines for the Assessment of 'Unwillingness' and 'Inability' in the Context of the Complementarity Principle' (2009) 9 *International Criminal Law Review* 39–76.

Verdirame G, 'Human Rights in Wartime: A Framework for Analysis' [2008] *European Human Rights Law Review* 689–705.

Vranes E, 'The Definition of 'Norm Conflict' in International Law and Legal Theory' (2006) 17 *European Journal of International Law* 395–418.

Wallace S, 'Much Ado About Nothing? The Pilot Judgment Procedure at the European Court of Human Rights' [2011] *European Human Rights Law Review* 71–81.

Watkin K, 'Controlling the Use of Force: A Role for Human Rights Norms in Contemporary Armed Conflict' (2004) 98 *American Journal of International Law* 1–34.

'Stability Operations: A Guiding Framework for "Small Wars" and Other Conflicts of the Twenty-First Century?' (2009) 85 *US Naval War College International Law Studies* 411–30.

Wilde R, 'Legal "Black Hole"? Extraterritorial State Action and International Treaty Law on Civil and Political Rights' (2005a) 26 *Michigan Journal of International Law* 739–806.

'The "Legal Space" or "Espace Juridique" of the European Convention on Human Rights: Is It Relevant to Extraterritorial State Action?' [2005b] *European Human Rights Law Review* 115–24.

Zegveld L, 'The Inter-American Commission on Human Rights and International Humanitarian Law: A Comment on the Tablada Case' (1998) 38 *International Review of the Red Cross* 505–12.

## D. CONTRIBUTIONS TO EDITED BOOKS

Bowring B, 'How Will the European Court of Human Rights Deal with the UK in Iraq? Lessons from Turkey and Russia' in Shiner P and Williams A (eds), *The War in Iraq and International Law* (Hart Publishing 2008).

Buergenthal T, 'To Respect and to Ensure, State Obligations and Permissible Derogations' in Henkin L (ed), *The International Bill of Human Rights: The Covenant on Civil and Political Rights* (Columbia University Press 1981).

Buis E, 'The Implementation of International Humanitarian Law by Human Rights Courts: The Example of the Inter-American Human Rights System' in Quenivet N and Arnold R (eds), *International Humanitarian Law and Human Rights Law: Towards a New Merger in International Law* (Brill 2008).

Cassese A, 'Prohibition of Torture and Inhuman or Degrading Treatment or Punishment' in MacDonald R, Matscher F, and H Petzold (eds), *The European System for the Protection of Human Rights* (Martinus Nijhoff 1993).

Crawford J and Olleson S, 'The Nature and Forms of International Responsibility' in Evans M (ed), *International Law* (3rd edn, Oxford University Press 2010).

Crawford J and Viles T, 'International Law on a Given Day' in Crawford J (ed), *International Law as an Open System* (Cameron May 2002).

Gioia A, 'The Role of the European Court of Human Rights in Monitoring Compliance with Humanitarian Law in Armed Conflict' in Ben-Naftali O (ed), *International Humanitarian Law and International Human Rights Law* (Oxford University Press 2012).

Happold M, 'International Humanitarian Law and Human Rights Law' in White N and Henderson C (eds), *Research Handbook on International Conflict and Security Law* (Edward Elgar Publishing 2013).

Henckaerts J-M, 'Concurrent Application of International Humanitarian Law and Human Rights Law: A Victim Perspective' in Quenivet N and Arnold R (eds), *International Humanitarian Law and Human Rights Law: Towards a New Merger in International Law* (Brill 2008).

Jachec-Neale A, 'The Right to Take Life: Killing and Death in Armed Conflict' in Yorke J (ed), *The Right to Life and the Value of Life: Orientations in Law, Politics and Ethics* (Ashgate 2010).

Krahenmann S, 'Positive Obligations in Human Rights Law during Armed Conflicts' in Kolb R and Gaggioli G (eds), *Research Handbook on Human Rights and Humanitarian Law* (Elgar 2013).

Lawson R, 'Life after Bankovic: On the Extraterritorial Application of the European Convention on Human Rights' in Coomans F and Kamminga M (eds), *Extraterritorial Application of Human Rights Treaties* (Intersentia 2004).

'Really Out of Sight? Issues of Jurisdiction and Control in Situations of Armed Conflict under the ECHR' in Buyse A (ed), *Margins of Conflict: The ECHR and Transitions to and from Armed Conflict* (Intersentia 2011).

McGoldrick D, 'Extraterritorial Application of the International Covenant on Civil and Political Rights' in Coomans F and Kamminga M (eds), *Extraterritorial Application of Human Rights Treaties* (Intersentia 2004).

Milanovic M, 'Extraterritorial Derogations from Human Rights Treaties in Armed Conflict' in Bhuta N (ed), *The Frontiers of Human Rights* (Oxford University Press 2016).

O'Boyle M, 'The European Convention on Human Rights and Extraterritorial Jurisdiction: A Comment on 'Life After Bankovic' in Coomans F and Kamminga M (eds), *Extraterritorial Application of Human Rights Treaties* (Intersentia 2004).

O'Boyle M and Costa JP, 'The ECtHR and IHL' in Rozakis C (ed), *The European Convention on Human Rights: A Living Instrument* (Bruylant Press 2011).

Quenivet N, 'The Right to Life in International Humanitarian Law and Human Rights Law' in Arnold R and Quenivet N (eds), *International Humanitarian Law and Human Rights Law: Towards a New Merger in International Law* (Brill 2008).

Sari A, 'The Status of Foreign Armed Forces Deployed in Post-Conflict Environments: A Search for Basic Principles' in Stahn C, Easterday J and Iverson J (eds), *Jus Post Bellum: Mapping the Normative Foundations* (Oxford University Press 2014).

Singh R, 'Justiciability in the Areas of Foreign Relations and Defence' in Shiner P and Williams A (eds), *The Iraq War and International Law* (Hart Publishing 2008).

Wilde R, 'The Extraterritorial Application of International Human Rights Law on Civil and Political Rights' in Sheeran S and Rodley N (eds), *Routledge Handbook of International Human Rights Law* (Routledge 2013).

## E. REPORTS

Borelli S and Lyngdorf S, *The Impact of the Jurisprudence of the European Court of Human Rights on Domestic Investigations and Prosecutions of Serious Human Rights Violations by State Agents* (DOMAC/7, 2010).

Committee of Ministers, *Item Reference: 1144th Meeting DH (June 2012) – Revised Action Plan / Action Report 2 May 2012* (DH – DD(2012)438, 2012).

Dhani A and Kaiza P, *Police Service Strength, England and Wales, 31 March 2011* (Home Office Statistical Bulletin: 13/11, 2011).

Forbes T, *The Report of the Al Sweady Inquiry* (2014) HC 818-I.

Gage W, *The Baha Mousa Public Inquiry Report* (The Stationery Office 2011).

Gaggioli G, *The Use of Force in Armed Conflicts: Interplay between the Conduct of Hostilities and Law Enforcement Paradigms* (International Committee of the Red Cross 2013).

Gibson P, *The Report of the Detainee Inquiry* (Her Majesty's Stationery Office 2013).

Her Majesty's Inspectorate of Constabulary, *HMIC Royal Military Police Special Investigation Branch Inspection* (Ref: J276389, 2006).

*HMIC Royal Military Police Special Investigation Branch Inspection Re-inspection* (Ref: J284574, 2007).

House of Commons Defence Committee, *UK Armed Forces Personnel and the Legal Framework for Future Operations: Twelfth Report of Session 2013–14* (The Stationery Office 2014).

House of Commons Defence Committee, *Who Guards the Guardians? MOD Support for Former and Serving Personnel* (The Stationery Office 2017).

Inter-American Commission on Human Rights, *Report on Terrorism and Human Rights* (OEA/SerL/V/II116 Doc 5 rev 1 corr, 2002).

International Committee of the Red Cross, *"Incapacitating Chemical Agents" Law Enforcement, Human Rights Law and Policy Perspectives 24–26 April 2012* (Montreux, Switzerland 2012).

Marty D, *Secret Detentions and Illegal Transfers of Detainees involving Council of Europe Member States: Second Report* (Council of Europe Committee on Legal Affairs and Human Rights AS/Jur (2007) 36, 2007).

Rowe P, *Control Over Armed Forces Exercised by The European Court of Human Rights* (Geneva Centre for the Democratic Control of Armed Forces Working Paper No56, 2002).

Smith K and others, *Homicides, Firearm Offences and Intimate Violence 2010/11: Supplementary Volume 2 to Crime in England and Wales 2010/11* (Home Office Statistical Bulletin: 02/12, 2012).

Tugendhat T and Croft L, *The Fog of Law: An Introduction to the Legal Erosion of British Fighting Power* (Policy Exchange 2013).

Turkel J, *The Public Commission to Examine the Maritime Incident of 31 May 2010: Second Report: Israel's Mechanisms for Examining and Investigating Complaints and Claims of Violations of the Laws of Armed Conflict According to International Law* (2013).

United Nations Committee on Crime Prevention Control, *Basic Principles on the Use of Force and Firearms by Law Enforcement Officials* (U.N. Doc. A/CONF.144/28/Rev.1, 7 September 1990).

United Nations Human Rights Council, *Report of the Committee of Independent Experts in International Humanitarian and Human Rights Laws to Monitor and Assess any Domestic, Legal or other Proceedings Undertaken by both the Government of Israel and the Palestinian side, in the light of General Assembly Resolution 64/254, including the Independence, Effectiveness, Genuineness of these Investigations and their Conformity with International Standards* (A/HRC/15/50, 2010).

## F. NEWSPAPER ARTICLES

Lister S, 'Investigation into historic allegations against British troops in Iraq to end following 'scathing' report', *Independent* (London, 10 February 2017).

Mendick R, 'Senior police repeatedly warned bosses about Iraq inquiry witch hunt... but were ignored for years', *The Telegraph* (London, 4 March 2018).

Payne S, 'Unforgiveable armour delay caused death', *The Daily Telegraph* (London, 19 December 2006).

Sabey R, 'Legal witch-hunt of British Army veterans set to be over in MONTHS after it sparked outrage', *The Sun* (London, 14 July 2018).

Shackle S, 'Why we may never know if British troops committed war crimes in Iraq', *Guardian* (London, 7 June 2018).

Soames N, 'Mr Cameron MUST stop these vile witch-hunts against our brave troops: From a former Armed Forces minister who's Winston Churchill's grandson, a blistering call to arms...', *The Daily Mail* (London, 20 January 2016).

## G. ELECTRONIC SOURCES

'Al-Sweady Inquiry' <http://webarchive.nationalarchives.gov.uk/20150115114702/http://www.alsweadyinquiry.org/> accessed 11 September 2018.

Bernard F, 'Deprivation of liberty in armed conflicts: The Strasbourg Court's attempt at reconciling human rights law and international humanitarian law in Hassan v. UK' <https://strasbourgobservers.com/2014/10/02/deprivation-of-liberty-in-armed-conflicts-the-strasbourg-courts-attempt-at-reconciling-human-rights-law-and-international-humanitarian-law-in-hassan-v-uk/> accessed 15 August 2018.

'Hassan v United Kingdom Hearing' (European Court of Human Rights, 11 December 2013) <www.echr.coe.int/Pages/home.aspx?p=hearings&w=2975009_11122013&language=lang&c=&py=2013> accessed 11 September 2018.

'Iraq Body Count' <www.iraqbodycount.org/database> accessed 11 September 2018.

'Iraq death due to kit shortage' (*BBC News*, 31 July 2006) <http://news.bbc.co.uk/1/shared/bsp/hi/pdfs/sgtroberts31_07_06.pdf> accessed 11 September 2018.

'Jaloud v Netherlands Hearing' (European Court of Human Rights, 19 February 2014) <www.echr.coe.int/Pages/home.aspx?p=hearings&w=4770808_19022014&language=lang&c=&py=2014> accessed 11 September 2018.

Pinto de Albuquerque P, 'Is the ECHR facing an existential crisis?' (Mansfield College, Oxford, 28 April 2017) <www.law.ox.ac.uk/sites/files/oxlaw/pinto_opening_presentation_2017.pdf> accessed 15 August 2018.

'Q&A: Baha Mousa inquiry' (*BBC News*, 8 September 2011) <www.bbc.co.uk/news/uk-14698722> accessed 11 September 2018.

Secretary of State for Defence, 'Letter to the Chair of the Joint Committee on Human Rights' (28 February 2017) <www.parliament.uk/documents/joint-committees/human-rights/correspondence/2016-17/170301_SoS_to_Chair_re_Derogation.pdf> accessed 23 August 2018.

'Statement by Paul Robert Kernaghan' (Chilcott Inquiry, 9 June 2010) <www.iraqinquiry.org.uk/media/46162/kernaghan-statement-final.pdf> accessed 11 September 2018.

UK Ministry of Defence, 'Government to protect Armed Forces from persistent legal claims in future overseas operations' (4 October 2016) <www.gov.uk/government/news/government-to-protect-armed-forces-from-persistent-legal-claims-in-future-overseas-operations> accessed 11 September 2018.

# Index

Printed in the United Kingdom by TJ Clays Ltd.